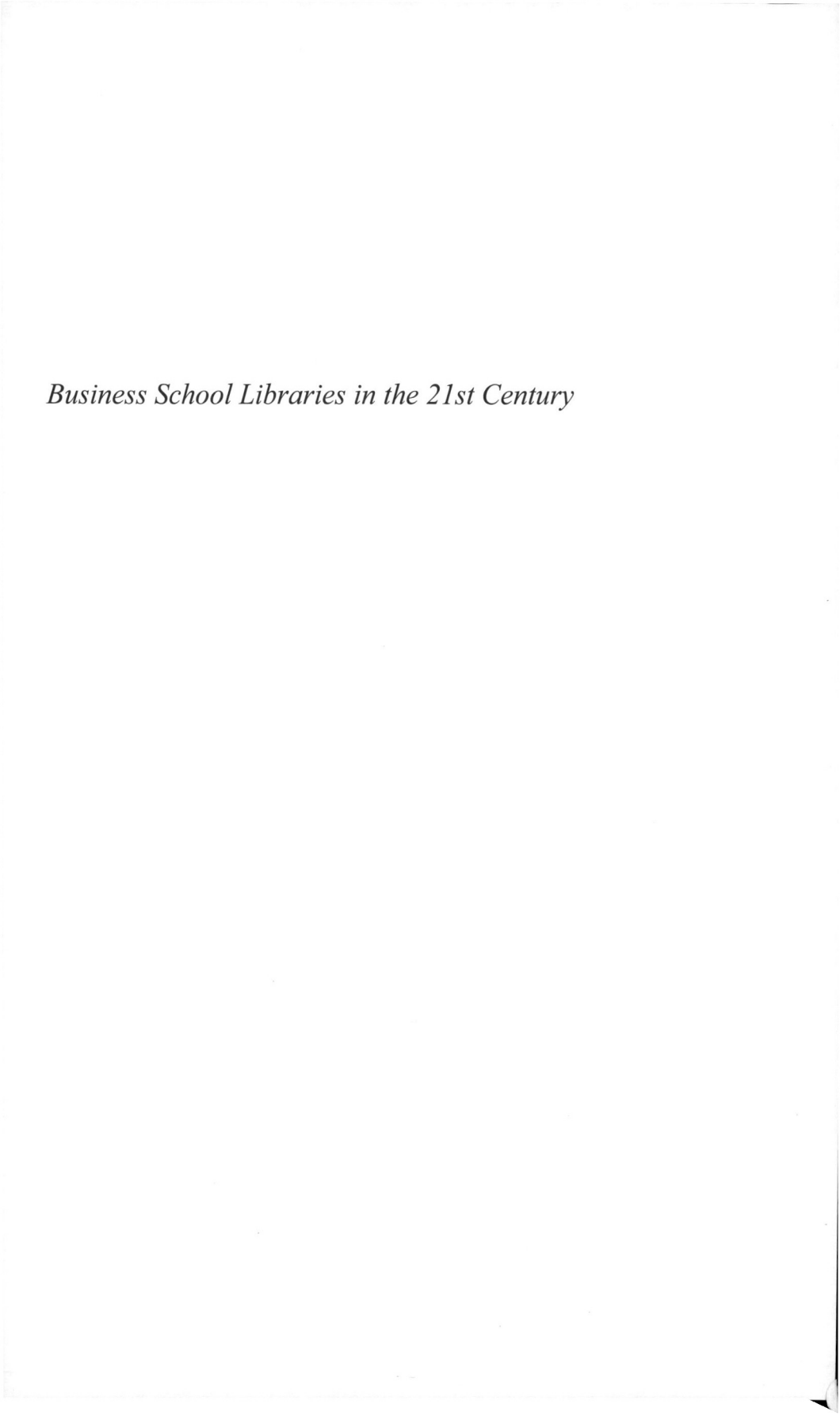

Business School Libraries in the 21st Century

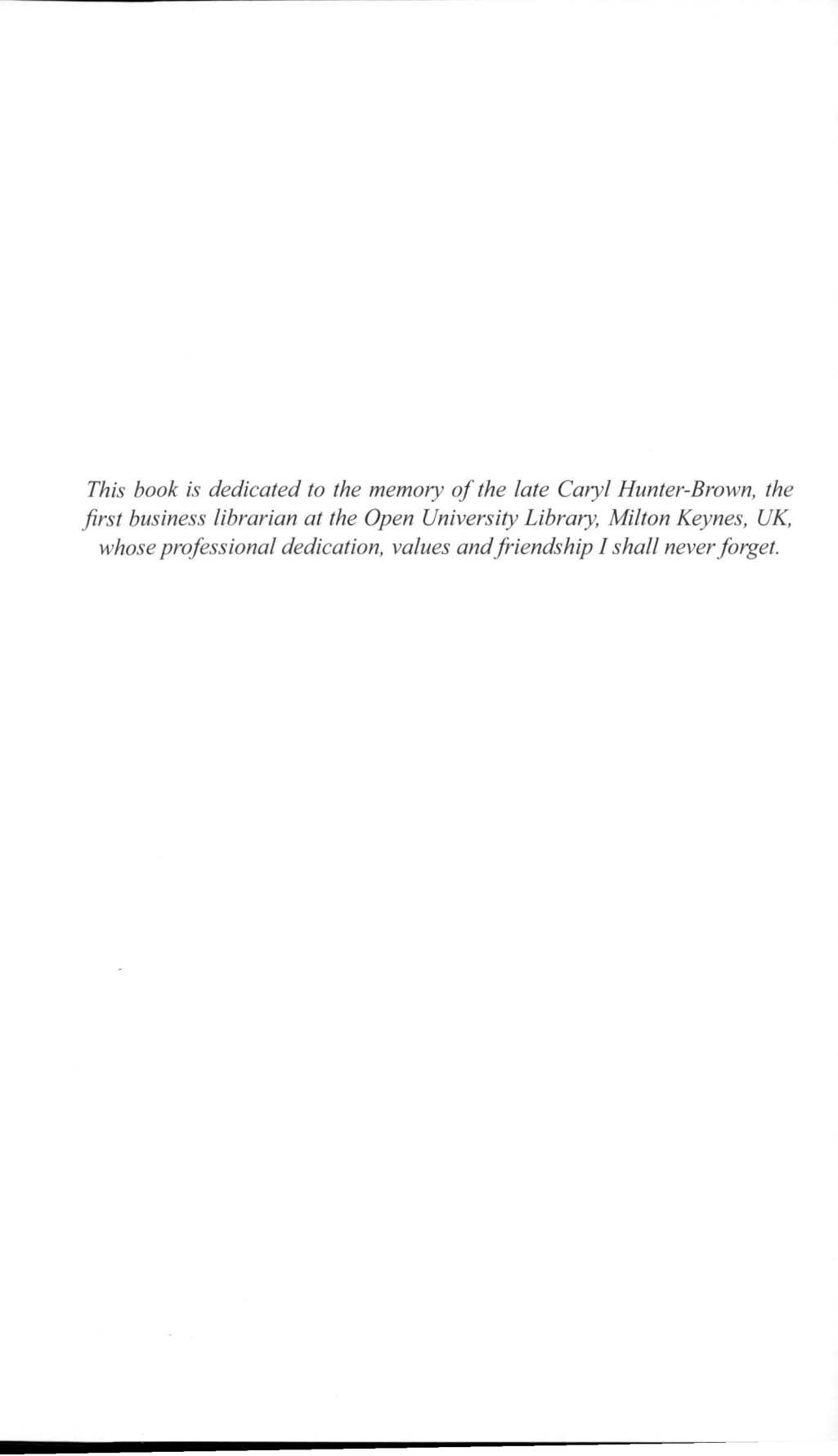

This book is dedicated to the memory of the late Caryl Hunter-Brown, the first business librarian at the Open University Library, Milton Keynes, UK, whose professional dedication, values and friendship I shall never forget.

Business School Libraries in the 21st Century

Edited by

TIM WALES
London Business School, UK

ASHGATE

© Tim Wales and the contributors 2014

All rights reserved. No part of this publication may be reproduced, stored in a retrieval system or transmitted in any form or by any means, electronic, mechanical, photocopying, recording or otherwise without the prior permission of the publisher.

Tim Wales has asserted his right under the Copyright, Designs and Patents Act, 1988, to be identified as the editor of this work.

Published by
Ashgate Publishing Limited
Wey Court East
Union Road
Farnham
Surrey, GU9 7PT
England

Ashgate Publishing Company
110 Cherry Street
Suite 3-1
Burlington, VT 05401-3818
USA

www.ashgate.com

British Library Cataloguing in Publication Data
A catalogue record for this book is available from the British Library

Library of Congress Cataloging-in-Publication Data
LoC data has been applied for

ISBN 9781409465652 (hbk)
ISBN 9781409465669 (ebk – PDF)
ISBN 9781409465676 (ebk – ePUB)

MIX
Paper from responsible sources
FSC
www.fsc.org
FSC® C013985

Printed in the United Kingdom by Henry Ling Limited, at the Dorset Press, Dorchester, DT1 1HD

CONTENTS

List of Figures and Tables		*vii*
List of Contributors		*ix*
Foreword		*xiii*
Preface		*xvii*
Acknowledgements		*xix*
List of Abbreviations		*xxi*
1	**Introduction: Business School Libraries in 2013** Tim Wales	1
2	**Organizational Design Considerations for Delivering Value in the 21st-Century Academic Library** Deb Wallace	11
3	**Change Management in Business Libraries** Thorsten Meyer and Claudia Liebetruth	29
4	**Business School Libraries on the Radar: Not Seen and Not Heard?** Andy Priestner	49
5	**Return on Investment (ROI) from a Business School Library: An Indian Perspective** Dr H. Anil Kumar	65
6	**Technology Challenges for the Business School Library** Jonathan Eaton	85
7	**Open Archives in France: An Overview of the Academic Sector** Agnès Melot and Sophie Forcadell	105

8	**Collaboration in Business Libraries: Careers and Entrepreneurship** *Marcella Barnhart and Cathy Ogur*	121
9	**Revitalizing Library Spaces for a Sustainable Future: A Hong Kong Perspective** *Lai Fong Li*	143
10	**The Physical Library in the Business School of the Future** *Kathleen Long*	159
11	**Conceptualizing the Future of the Business School Library** *Chris Flegg*	175
12	**Business School Libraries' Futures?** *Tim Wales*	193
Index		*213*

LIST OF FIGURES AND TABLES

FIGURES

2.1	Harvard KLS strategy reflection: organizational design framework	17
2.2	Harvard KLS reporting structure/organizational chart, February 2013	28
3.1	Former ZBW organizational structure	31
3.2	The ZBW's change process	34
3.3	Change impact diagram	38
5.1	Perceptions of Indian business school librarians	76
8.1	Geographical distribution of careers and entrepreneurship support survey respondents	125
8.2	Degree programs supported by careers and entrepreneurship survey respondents	126
8.3	Percentage of survey respondents offering wider entrepreneurial research support	132
12.1	Embedded library research team model	199
12.2	Library hub model	201
12.3	Heritage library model	204
12.4	Virtual library model	206

TABLES

1.1	Estimated business school libraries worldwide, 2013	3
1.2	Types of business school library	4
5.1	Top Indian business schools (2010–2011)	73

5.2	Indian business school libraries: percentage changes from previous year's library budgets	74
5.3	Perceptions of Indian business school librarians	75
7.1	Open archives management challenges	110
8.1	Types of instructor for career research and entrepreneurship courses	128
8.2	Promotional methods for career research and entrepreneurship resources/services	129
8.3	Promotional methods used by career services and entrepreneurial programs staff to promote library resources/services	130
8.4	Ratings for library cooperation with career services and entrepreneurial programs	134
9.1	Students' preferences for various library areas	148
12.1	Key challenges affecting business school libraries in the next five years	194
12.2	Opportunities for business school libraries in the next five years	196

LIST OF CONTRIBUTORS

Tim Wales (editor) has been Head of Library at the London Business School, UK, since May 2011. He was previously Associate Director (E-Strategy) at Royal Holloway, University of London, UK, where he was responsible for Library e-resources, systems and open access development. He spent eight years as a business librarian supporting the Open University Business School in Milton Keynes, UK, after a brief spell in the City of London as a researcher for a boutique investment bank. He holds an MSc in Information Science from City University London, UK. His first graduate job was assistant editor for a trade publisher, and he has continued publishing ever since on topics ranging from alumni support and e-libraries to e-learning and veterinary information-seeking behaviour.

Marcella Barnhart is Assistant Director of the Lippincott Library of the University of Pennsylvania's Wharton School, USA, where she oversees public service and outreach efforts to the Wharton community. Prior to working at Penn, Marcella worked for the Thomson Corporation (now Thomson Reuters), managing the customer education and training operation in the Americas for Thomson Scientific. She holds a BA in Political Science from Rice University, an MA in Political Science from the University of Wisconsin, an MS in Library Science from the University of North Carolina-Chapel Hill, and an MBA from Temple University.

Jonathan Eaton is Senior Content and Systems Manager at London Business School Library, UK, where he is responsible for the Library's extensive e-resource portfolio and the technical infrastructure for delivering the customer experience along with the management tools and processes used by the Library team and external collaborators. Professional interests include authentication and usage data analysis. Jonathan was previously at the University of Hertfordshire and has been an editorial board member of the journal *Program* since 2001.

Chris Flegg is the Bodleian Business Librarian with the Bodleian Library, University of Oxford, UK. She started her career in 1973 as a Reference Librarian at the (then) Melbourne State College Library – now part of the University of Melbourne Library.

She moved in 1975 to the Baillieu Library, University of Melbourne, to become the Assistant Information Services Librarian in 1982. She held that post until 1988 when she was invited to manage the Graduate School of Management Library, which was, at that time, a branch library of the newly formed Graduate School of Management at Melbourne University. She remained there until 2009 seeing it through its reincarnation as an independent, but university affiliated, library when the School became The Melbourne Business School at the University of Melbourne. In September 2009 she was appointed as the Bodleian Business Librarian at the Sainsbury Library at the University of Oxford – one of the few 'embedded' libraries of the University, being located at the Saïd Business School.

Sophie Forcadell is the Assistant Library Director at HEC Paris, France. Before joining HEC Paris she worked at CFJ, the top French school in journalism, and also within strategy management at PPR, the French holding company of consumer and luxury brands. Today, she is specifically responsible for project management and supporting change within the HEC Library.

Dr H. Anil Kumar is Librarian and Head, NICMAN, Indian Institute of Management Ahmedabad, India. He has a doctoral degree in Library and Information Science from the MS University of Baroda, India and a Master's and Bachelor's degree in Library and Information Science from Bangalore University. He has accumulated more than two decades of professional experience at renowned academic institutions such as the National Law School of India University, the British Library and the Entrepreneurship Development Institute of India, Nirma University. He is the recipient of the Asian Professional Award (2011) from the Special Libraries Association (SLA), USA and the Best Librarian Award (2008) by Management and Libraries Network (MANLIBNET), India. He is currently the President of Management Libraries Network (MANLIBNET) India and founding member of the International Centre for Technology and Entrepreneurship.

Lai Fong Li is Head of Information, Research and Instructional Services (IRIS), Chinese University of Hong Kong Libraries, Hong Kong, China. She received her MLS degree from the School of Library and Information Science at the University of Toronto and her MSc in Financial Management from the University of London. She has public library and business library experience in Toronto, as well as over 20 years' experience in Hong Kong academic libraries. She was heavily involved in the new library building project at CUHK, and in planning and implementing the Learning and Research Commons. Her professional interests include the development of information literacy competencies and library learning space planning.

Claudia Liebetruth was appointed Head of Organizational and Human Resources Development at the ZBW German National Library of Economics – Leibniz Information Centre for Economics, Germany, in March 2012, having previously worked as an expert in human resources development at the ZBW from 2009.

Claudia began her career at Deutsche Telekom in 2006 as a project member, working in the team responsible for intellectual capital development. In 2008 she joined the Dr Schwab Management Group as a consultant assistant in training and coaching. She joined Tedrive International in 2008 as a personnel development specialist. Claudia holds an MBA in industrial and organizational psychology from the University of Flensburg, Germany.

Kathleen Long is Library Director for the Stanford Graduate School of Business, Stanford University, USA. She has a Master's degree in Library and Information Science from Simmons College in Boston, USA and a Bachelor's degree in History from the University of Massachusetts in Amherst, USA. She has more than 30 years' experience in a variety of corporate libraries and research departments, including Arthur D. Little, Hewlett Packard, and Strategic Decisions Group. Under her direction, the GSB Library was awarded the Special Libraries Association Centers of Excellence Award for Service in 2006. She is the former president of the San Andreas Chapter of the Special Libraries Association, as well as a former chair and current board member of the Academic Business Library Directors organization, and has presented at numerous conferences.

Agnès Melot has been Library Director at HEC Paris, France for the past 25 years. She is involved in two professional associations of Business School Libraries in France and in Europe: l'ACIEGE (the French Business Schools Librarians Group) and EBSLG (European Business Schools Librarians' Group) both of which she has chaired. For many years she has also been teaching a course at INTD (French Librarians School) on the electronic resources market.

Thorsten Meyer is Head of Department, Collection Development and Metadata at the ZBW German National Library of Economics – Leibniz Information Centre for Economics, Germany. He has been at the ZBW since 2004. He is currently also the President of the EBSLG. He is a graduate of Bamberg, Lunds and Humboldt Universities and has published widely in German library and information science publications.

Cathy Ogur is a Business Research Librarian at the Lippincott Library for the Wharton School, University of Pennsylvania, USA. Along with traditional reference and instruction responsibilities, Cathy builds and strengthens relationships with Wharton constituencies such as the MBA Career Management Office and Entrepreneurship, specifically the Small Business Development Center. Previously, She is former Director of Research for Corsearch, a trademark research firm, and has also been a research analyst for Walker Digital, a lab for the development of entrepreneurial ideas that launched Priceline.com. Cathy gained her Bachelor of Arts degree from Bucknell University, USA ,and her Master of Science in Library and Information Science from Drexel University, USA.

Andy Priestner has worked in both the academic and public library sector since 1994. He is currently Information and Library Services Manager at Cambridge University's Judge Business School in the UK. He was Chair of the Business Librarians Association from 2006 to 2010 and is also active in European librarianship. In 2007 he was awarded a teaching excellence award by the University of Oxford. In 2010 he led the 23 Things social media programme for Cambridge University library staff. In 2012 he co-edited and co-wrote *Personalising Library Services in Higher Education* (Ashgate) and penned case studies on internal marketing and teaching for *The Library Marketing Toolkit*, edited by Ned Potter, and *Rethinking Information Literacy*, edited by Jane Secker and Emma Coonan. He blogs regularly about librarianship as Libreaction.

Deb Wallace is currently Executive Director, Knowledge and Library Services at Harvard Business School, USA. With a team of librarians, economists, statisticians, journalists, technologists, and information management professionals housed in Baker Library, Deb oversees a pre-eminent collection of contemporary and historical business information and a range of customized services for Harvard Business School's diverse community. She is responsible for leveraging the world of business information and the School's priority content to enable high performance in the complex teaching, learning and research environment at HBS and further research by scholars from around the world. Deb holds a Bachelor of Science from Moorhead State University (Minnesota, USA), a Masters of Education from the University of Manitoba, Canada, and a PhD from the University of Toronto, Canada.

FOREWORD: THE IMPORTANCE OF BUSINESS SCHOOL LIBRARIES

Before I moved from India to Boston to attend MIT in 1984, I'd never experienced a real winter. The first time I saw snow that autumn, it was magical. But the second time it snowed—and for much of the rest of the winter—I was cold and miserable. MIT had very limited graduate housing, so I was living in an apartment several miles from campus with three other international students. The heat worked only intermittently. Some days the apartment was freezing; other days it was an inferno. The landlord was completely unresponsive. By early December, I was desperate, and I took refuge in MIT's Dewey Library.

Dewey is right next to the Sloan School, and I was already spending most of each day studying there. One evening, dreading going home to my cold apartment, I noticed the library's many couches. Dewey was open 24 hours, so I thought to myself: "Why should I leave?" I bought a sleeping bag and started spending my nights in the library. There were probably rules against this, but the staff didn't seem to mind. In the morning I'd shower and change at the MIT gym. During the second semester the International Students' Office helped me find new housing, but for two full months, I was like the Tom Hanks character in *The Terminal*, except MIT's library was my makeshift home.

That was really the beginning of a long love affair with libraries. Like most people my age, I've watched libraries transform from places organized via card catalogs with open stacks into institutions filled with media of varying form and shape. Because of digitization and electronic delivery, it's become less necessary to physically visit a library to get information—nowadays, the information often arrives via email. But libraries—and especially the experts who staff them—remain the primary resource we look to for the information we need to do our work. Many of us couldn't do our jobs without their everyday assistance.

In fact, even as so much data becomes available remotely via the web, business school libraries are becoming even more important. Today's business leaders face an overwhelming environment with a growing volume of unique data, changing information formats, and expanding channels of communication via social networks.

In this era of overload, libraries are less important as simple repositories of information; instead, they (and the professionals who run them) are playing a larger role by providing students and faculty with the knowledge base and skills to navigate the data glut in order to find or create quality information to make informed decisions.

I know firsthand how crucial this assistance can be. When I was a young faculty member at Harvard Business School, the staff at Baker Library/Bloomberg Center provided invaluable assistance to me at key turning-points in my career. Specifically, they helped me assemble two large datasets that became a very important part of my academic research—the first covered key events at Fortune 100 companies from 1975 to 1995 and the second was a database of the 1,000 most important business leaders of the twentieth century. These data helped fuel two of the most important research projects in my life, and I couldn't have done them without the Baker staff's assistance. When I talk to my Harvard colleagues, many of them share similar stories about how a librarian helped them do research that would otherwise have proven impossible.

At Harvard, as at other institutions, our leadership is actively assessing how libraries at our various schools can most effectively and efficiently serve the needs of our communities. "I think of the Harvard Library as a bit like the University's circulatory system, providing the lifeblood of information to every part of the academic enterprise," Harvard president Drew Faust wrote in early 2012. She went on to note, in providing context for the University's deep look and reorganization of its own library system, "[I]t is indeed because we love the libraries we cannot ignore the challenges they face." Those challenges are in fact a remarkable opportunity: a moment when we can think differently about what a library is—the services it provides, the capabilities and expertise of the people who provide library services, and the types of collections found there and "through" there. The pace of curricular innovation will only continue to increase, and, as it does, librarians will play ever more vital roles to provide a wealth of content, expertise, and corresponding services to enrich research, enhance teaching, and enable student achievement.

For institutions like Harvard that are blessed with collections that go back several centuries, we need to think strategically about where to best position the library's collections, services, and expertise. How do we create the most value from these assets? How do we curate information from our unique collections that provide our community with information that isn't found anywhere else, in addition to providing a modern "information baseline" from industry-standard data and information sources? In these endeavors, partnering with university information technology managers will be a priority.

The professionals who run Baker and other great business school libraries are right to focus less on the physical footprint they enjoy on campuses and instead on the intellectual footprint they have as important players in the lives of our communities. Still, I believe that at business schools that are fortunate enough to enjoy well-designed and inviting physical structures, libraries will continue to play an important role on our campuses and in our communities, in much the same way as rural churches served an important role that went well beyond being a location for worship in small villages around the world. Even as the stacks become less accessible, even as the information becomes available via online portal, and even if chilled graduate students no longer camp out on its sofas, Baker Library and its brethren will remain the center (and in the case of Baker, the physical center) of our academic communities.

I have had many blessings during my long career at Harvard Business School. Access to Baker Library and its patient and committed team of specialists is one for which I will remain eternally grateful.

Nitin Nohria
Dean of Harvard Business School

PREFACE

The idea for this book came on the eve of the quinquennial joint conference of the American Business Library Directors (ABLD), European Business Libraries Group (EBSLG) and Asia-Pacific Business Libraries Group (ABSLG) at Stanford University, USA, in April 2012.

Conferences present a natural and valuable opportunity to take stock of the state of a sector (and the institutions within), identifying common or disparate themes on a national, international or peer group basis. As a head of service myself, I find myself looking for both reassurance that my library is not alone in facing up to particular challenges and for new ideas to handle them. So it seemed a natural consequence of gathering heads of selected business school libraries around the world together to want to capture and codify our current plans, preoccupations and knowledge on some of the big themes affecting us and being discussed in the warm Californian sunshine.

At this point I should point out that, although this book is not officially endorsed by any of the three professional associations mentioned above, it does draw from some of the conference content, representing both the older, established North American and European libraries and the emerging business education markets of the BRIC countries.

Another motivation for me to compile this book is the lack of published monographs devoted to the business school library sector as a whole, other than brief sections in business information manuals or detailed guides to business resources. This is surprising, first, given library and information science publishers' tendency to bring out books rapidly on most subjects and, second, the business school library sector's traditional vitality and innovation in supporting the missions of its business schools.

A final motivation for me is the incentive to take a snapshot of the preoccupations of the sector now, during a process of fundamental change for libraries in the early 21st century.

Tim Wales
St Albans

ACKNOWLEDGEMENTS

It goes without saying that I need to acknowledge the work of the various international contributors to this book without whom it would still be at the 'Gee, wouldn't it be nice if we could do a book?' stage as we stood on the balcony between conference sessions at Stanford. Of these colleagues, I would particularly like to thank Deb Wallace at Harvard for securing the valued preface from her Dean, Nitin Nohria, as well as contributing her own chapter.

Thanks are also due to Dymphna Evans, Sadie Copley-May, Linda Cayford and Lianne Sherlock at Ashgate Publishing for their patience and advice. I should also acknowledge the indirect help of somebody else connected with the San Francisco area of California – Drew Houston – whose Dropbox invention makes the life of an international editor working across countries (and multiple devices) so much more easier than would have been the case even two years ago.

Finally, I would like to thank my wife Elizaveta, my parents and step-parents and the Kasparova family for their love and support.

Tim Wales
St Albans

LIST OF ABBREVIATIONS

AACSB	Association to Advance Collegiate Schools of Business
ABLD	Academic Business Library Directors of North America
ACIEGE	Association des responsables des Centres d'Information des Ecoles de Gestion (France)
ACRL	Association of College and Research Libraries (USA)
ADBU	Association des Directeurs et Personnels de Direction des Bibliothèques Universitaires et de la Documentation (France)
ALC	Americans for Libraries Council (USA)
APBSLG	Asia-Pacific Business School Librarians' Group
API	application programming interface
BEL	business and economics library
BIRD	Base Institutionalle de Recherche de l'Université Dauphine (France)
BLA	Business Librarians Association (UK and Ireland)
BRIC	Brazil, Russia, India and China
BYOD	bring your own device
CCSD	Centre pour la Communication Scientifique Directe (France)
CLEAR	Centre for Learning Enhancement and Research (Hong Kong)
CNRS	Centre National de la Recherche Scientifique (France)
COUNTER	Counting Online Usage of Networked Electronic Resources
COUPERIN	Consortium Universitaire de Publications Numériques (France)
CUHK	The Chinese University of Hong Kong
DLX	Data Link Express
DOI	digital object identifier
DPO	Degree Programmes Office
DRIVER	Digital Repository Infrastructure Vision for European Research
EBSLG	European Business School Librarians' Group
EPIC	Etablissement Public à Caractère Industriel et Commercial (France)
EPST	Etablissement Public à Caractère Scientifique et Technologique (France)
EQUIS	European Quality Improvement System
ERC	European Research Council
ERM	e-resource management
FTL	full time equivalent

FTP	File Transfer Protocol
GOKb	Global Open Knowledgebase (USA)
GSB	Graduate School of Business
GWK	Joint Science Conference
HAL	Hyper Articles en Ligne (France)
HBS	Harvard Business School
HKU	University of Hong Kong
HKUST	Hong Kong University of Science and Technology
HWWA	Hamburg World Economic Archives
ICT	information and communications technology
IFLA	International Federation of Library Associations and Institutions
INRA	Institut National de la Recherche Agronomique (France)
INRIA	Institut National de Recherche en Informatique et en Automatique (France)
IP	Internet Protocol
IPR	intellectual property rights
IT	information technology
JEL	*Journal of Economic Literature* (USA)
JISC	Joint Information Systems Committee (UK)
JURA	Joint University Research Archive (Hong Kong)
KB	knowledge base
KB+	Knowledgebase Plus
KBART	knowledge bases and related tools
KLS	Knowledge and Library Services (USA)
LED	light-emitting diode
LIS	library and information science
LISU	Library and Information Statistics Unit (UK)
LMS	library management system
LUG	Library User Group (Hong Kong)
MBA	Master of Business Administration
MFP	multifunction printer
MOOC	massive open online course
NCES	National Center for Education Statistics (USA)
Nereus	Network of European Regions Using Space Technologies
OAI-PMH	Open Archive Initiative Protocol for Metadata Harvesting
ONIX	online information exchange
OpenAIRE	Open Access Infrastructure Research for Europe
OpenDOAR	Open Directory of Open Access Repositories
OS	operating system
PC	personal computer
PRES	Pôle de Recherche et d'Enseignement Supérieur (France)
REF	Research Excellence Framework (UK)
REF2014	Research Excellence Framework 2014 (UK)
RFO	research faculty office

ROAR	Registry of Open Access Repositories
ROI	return on investment
SAM	subject area manager/school of management
SAS	software as a service
SBDC	small business development center (USA)
SCCM	Systems Center Configuration Manager (Microsoft)
SQL	Structured Query Language
SUSHI	Standardized Usage Statistics Harvesting Initiative
TQA	Thomson Quantitative Analytics
UGC	University Grants Committee (Hong Kong)
UIUC	University of Illinois Urbana-Champaign
ULC	Urban Libraries Council (USA)
UNC	University of North Carolina
URL	uniform resource locator
USP	unique selling point
VLE	virtual learning environment
WBPC	Wharton Business Plan Competition (USA)
WRDS	Wharton Research Data Services (USA)
WSBDC	Wharton Small Business Development Center (USA)
ZBW	German National Library of Economics – Leibniz Information Centre for Economics

CHAPTER 1

INTRODUCTION: BUSINESS SCHOOL LIBRARIES IN 2013

TIM WALES

Why do business school libraries deserve their own book and what makes them a distinctive branch of librarianship in their own right? Any recent literature on business school libraries tends to appear as case-study articles – an inadvertent homage perhaps to the Harvard case method for teaching business and management which underpins business school curricula around the world today. The (North American) sector has its own dedicated journal, the *Journal of Business and Finance Librarianship*, but books dedicated to business school libraries are rare and may appear in disguise. A good recent example is Priestner's and Tilley's 2012 work which evolved from an initial internal discussion within the University of Cambridge around the value of subject librarians and departmental libraries into an articulate defence of the concept of 'boutique libraries' – a category that includes business school libraries and draws on numerous interesting case studies from the sector.

Otherwise, sections on business school librarianship have appeared in the past within business information handbooks or source guides which attempted the seemingly futile task of enumerating the hundreds of 'core' resources in the sector before the Internet intervened. Karp (2002) provides a typical North American example of this kind of work with 106 pages specifying a core list of business resources and then the same amount again considering different types of resources for different subdisciplines. Only the final 50 pages of the book consider the actual business of the business library, focusing on acquisitions, marketing, organization and reference.

Sheehy (1996) provides a rare (but, again, North American) example of a dedicated edited work devoted to the different aspects of managing business collections. Unfortunately, its relevance to the realities of today's business school library has diminished since it was published at the time of the early Internet – this explains why the copy I obtained was withdrawn from the University of Bristol Library's stock in 2010. However, I shall refer to Soules' (1996) chapter, 'Forecasting the Future' later. Going further back still, Oort (1986) devoted an entire thesis to European business school libraries and their services. It still provides a useful summary of the history of management education in Europe and also serves as a fascinating time capsule for the 12 European libraries selected, documenting in detail their history, development and organizational state at that time, especially with regard to their relationships with their parent institutions. Oort then discusses the role of professional groups such as the EBSLG in facilitating cooperation in areas of common interest. Finally, I should also acknowledge one of my illustrious predecessors at the London Business School Library and founding fathers of British business librarianship, K.D.C. Vernon, who also attempted to document the state of the sector back in the 1970s (Vernon, 1975).

CHARACTERISTICS

Having worked as a librarian in several different subject disciplines before heading up a business school library, I believe that the following list of features and traits defines business school librarianship:

- provision and support for specialist financial, commercial databases and numeric datasets
- provision of market and industry information resources
- support for specialist, non-standard institutional user groups (alumni, corporate, entrepreneurs, interns etc.)
- support for the Harvard case-study teaching method
- very responsive support for time-poor, demanding user groups
- closer relationship with the Careers function of the parent institution than other disciplines due to emphasis on graduate employment and graduate starting salaries in business school rankings
- support for the most dynamic part of a university – its business school – which tends to be in the vanguard of institutional thinking, policy and application of technologies.

This last point deserves further consideration. In my experience, the business school librarian has to mirror and reflect the culture of the business school and, in bigger institutions and their libraries, this usually means either challenging the rest of the library to do things differently, better, faster or more cost-effectively or setting up a pilot project to show the way forward and test the concept. There is therefore, an inherent sense of dynamism, creativity and a 'can do' or even entrepreneurial attitude in business school libraries. And, because they are often in the vanguard of library change initiatives, they serve as a bellwether for the rest of the sector.

THE SIZE AND SHAPE OF THE SECTOR

It can be argued that the thousands of tertiary education institutions worldwide that offer business and management education will have some form of library (physical or virtual) or some employee charged with acquiring information resources for learning, teaching or research purposes, even if the word 'library' is not in their job title. For the purposes of this book we are focusing on membership of the relevant regional professional associations as a proxy indicator both of sector size and of quality and engagement. Indeed, the existence of such associations is itself another defining characteristic of a healthy library sector – that is, a group of librarians in a specific sector consider that they have enough in common to benefit from the formation of a professional body.

Table 1.1 shows my estimate of the number of business school libraries worldwide, based on active membership of the main professional associations with some de-duplication performed to allow for certain regional overlaps. It should be noted that a handful of libraries in these groups are national or state libraries with strong business collections or libraries supporting specialist research institutes. Nevertheless, as Thorsten Meyer's and Claudia Liebetruth's chapter on change management in this book testifies, the work and contribution to the sector from such special business libraries is valuable and should not be discounted.

Table 1.1   Estimated business school libraries worldwide, 2013

Region	Numbers of libraries
UK	121
North America	44
Continental Europe	35
Asia-Pacific	16
South America	182
Africa	27
Total	425

Even within this relatively small number there are a number of unique variations specific to the sector that have to be acknowledged and understood at the outset of this book if the chapters that follow are to have some kind of context. These are explained in the next section.

Small in quantity or not, one other justification for treating business school libraries as an important and distinctive sector in its own right is their spending power in a niche publishing marketplace. On the basis of my own estimates of the average information resources budget for a business school library in 2013, I calculate that information spend totals at least $276 million per annum in our library sector alone.

The importance of understanding organizational structure

One thing I learned early in my career when I was Secretary for the British Business School Librarians' Group[1] from the late Leslie Baldwin (former head of Library Services at the Cass Business School at City University London) was that in order to compare, contrast and understand business school libraries effectively, you have to understand how they fit with their parent institutions. Sure enough, close examination reveals a remarkable heterogeneity between libraries in the academic business and management sector in the same country, let alone on an international basis.

Table 1.2 therefore attempts to provide a standard categorization of business school libraries based on their relationship to their parent institution and, if applicable, other libraries within the same institution.

Table 1.2   Types of business school library

Type	Description	Examples	Own integrated library system?	Shared services with parent library?	Reporting line for library head?
Autonomous	Sole library service for the institution	Ashridge, London Business School (UK)	Yes	N/A	Senior functional director
Collection-based	Business and management collections located within a university library space	Stirling (UK)	No	Most functions shared	Member of senior library management team
Federated	Autonomous business library/site as part of a multiple library system	Harvard, Stanford (USA)	Maybe	Some acquisition & systems support or shared specialist service	Senior business school officer
National	National library for a country (single or multidiscipline)	ZBW (Germany)	Yes	No	Senior functional director

---

1   Since renamed the Business Librarians Association (BLA).

| Satellite | Business site library for a parent university library | Manchester Business School (UK) | No | Some acquisition & systems support | Member of senior University Library management team |
| Specialist | Business and management library not affiliated to a business school | Chartered Management Institute (UK) | Yes | N/A | Senior functional director |

Note: Other variations on the above are possible – for example, some German libraries fulfil a regional/state library role as well as a university mission (for example, University of Cologne). Some business library services are effectively solo librarians.

Is it possible to say which model predominates? If we apply the categorization to the libraries of the top 10 business schools featured in the popular Financial Times Global MBA rankings (Financial Times, 2013), then it can be seen that the model merely reflects the nature of the host institution. Harvard, Stanford and Wharton business schools are independent entities as they sit within federal university institutions and so, it follows, are their libraries. London Business School, INSEAD and IESE are autonomous institutions specializing in business education and so have autonomous, independent libraries. In the UK, given the rich history and heritage of universities, the majority of BLA members are 'collection-based' business libraries.

Other determinants

There are other important differentiators which must be taken into account, especially when considering service portfolio, collections and strategy:

- Teaching scope: bachelor versus master's degrees? Some business schools only specialize in master's level course provision and consequently operate at a comparatively smaller scale.
- Parent institution: state or private? The majority of institutions operate in some kind of charitable or state-funded form, but privately owned corporation models do exist in the USA and UK.
- Parent institution: multidiscipline or monodiscipline?
- Business school rankings. The aspirations of the library can be closely connected to the host business school's performance in the *Financial Times*, *Bloomberg Business Week*, Forbes or *Economist* rankings.
- Regional variations. Some types of business school library exist only in certain countries. For example, there is no real direct equivalent of the German ZBW national research institute library in the UK.

THE TYPICAL LIBRARY

Having understood the structural context, is it possible to outline a typical business school library? The Business Librarians Association conducted a membership survey in 2009, and one of the interesting outputs from the results analysis produced by Andy Priestner (one of the contributors to this book), was a picture of the average UK business school library, reproduced below (Business Librarians Association, 2009). The high response rate (81 per cent of 108 member institutions) and the fact that many of the activities and resources have not changed since 2009 (even if the figures may have) make this a handy introductory overview for the UK and, dare I say it, the European sector.

The average UK business school library in 2009:

- forms the business section of an integrated university library
- supports 125 MBAs, 49 MPhils, 176 MScs, 1265 undergraduates, 42 PhD students and 87 academic staff
- has 3.5 FTE library staff
- provides user education/teaching to users via one-to-one training, hands-on workshops and lectures and tutorials that are either standalone or integrated into the curriculum
- offers self-service issue and return
- chiefly supports its users via email, face-to-face and phone communication.
- is using, or investigating, blogs, federated search systems, screen-capture software and RSS feeds
- is increasingly embracing social media such as blogs, Twitter, Facebook and social bookmarking as a core part of the library service
- spends £180,867 per annum on business and management resources, with the majority of this figure being spent on online databases
- is funded centrally with additional top-up funding from the business school
- provides access to 25,344 business and management printed books and 174 printed journals
- subscribes to MyiLibrary, NetLibrary[2] and Dawson for e-book content
- provides access to databases via IP authentication or a proxy server (or both).
- does not provide online access to walk-in users.

What can we conclude from this? First, the typical *British* business school library is still the classic hybrid library, trying to support print and electronic resource provision while trying to stay on top of new developments in social media and technologies, but continuing to offer library training and enquiry to all sections of its community. The extent to which it shapes its own destiny is open to debate – any significant innovation comes from the suppliers of library resources, systems and

---

2   Bought by EBSCO Publishing in 2010 and renamed EBSCO eBook Collections.

equipment from their own perspectives rather than from libraries themselves. The British business school library does not have the financial resources of its richly endowed American counterparts to innovate other than in operational efficiency and the small-scale application of existing technologies tailored to user needs.

ABOUT THIS BOOK

I have deliberately placed two chapters on change management at the start of the book in acknowledgement that change is one of the defining characteristics of 21st-century business school librarianship. Although the chapters concern two completely different types and sizes of institution, they both serve to remind us where we are starting from and look to where we might be heading, describing how the senior managers of Harvard and ZBW decided to get there, albeit both conscious of the perils of 'change fatigue' amongst their staff.

In Chapter 2 Deb Wallace reminds us that even the great libraries have to evolve with the changing priorities of the parent institution, however valued and well resourced they might be. Deb appropriately presents her change management challenges in the style of the traditional Harvard Business School case study – still one of the defining characteristics of business education pedagogy, by the way – and shines a public light on what are usually very private processes, sharing insights and templates that have been developed along the way.

Thorsten Meyer and Claudia Liebetruth (Chapter 3) take us through a European approach to change management at the ZBW with a practical application of change management theory, grounded in employee consultation and a continuous circle of communication and review. In contrast to Harvard, an external consultant was not used as a 'change agent'. It is insightful for the reader to compare the ability of the old ZBW rigid top-down management structure to cope with emerging customer needs and new developments in librarianship – a structure in which the Library Director has to decide everything (and I mean everything) – with the new bottom-up structure based on the most efficient processes and staff interactions with devolved decision-making built in from the outset.

In Chapter 4, picking up on the second major emerging characteristic of 21st-century business librarianship, Andy Priestner, drawing on his personal experiences at Judge, tackles the communication issue head-on with typical honesty and challenges us to consider whether we should even be calling our services and spaces 'libraries' with all the negative connotations and baggage that go with the title, even in a supposedly modern business school context. He rightly reminds of the dangers of the 'echo-chamber' effect (of which this book could be a guilty example) – talking eloquently inside the profession of our problems and solutions without having the same conversations with the key senior decision-makers who ultimately shape our future. He also describes the inevitable territorial battles between his library and other professional departments as technology blurs boundaries.

Anil Kumar (Chapter 5) provides us with some unique primary research into Indian business school library perceptions of return on investment (ROI), as well as a detailed summary of relevant research into this slippery topic, before setting out his own proposal on the topic. His chapter also reminds us of the different national influences on the sector, with the Indian government attempting a top-down reform of the business education sector, even to the extent of drawing up a list of mandatory business resources for business school libraries (akin to the UK law libraries sector).

In Chapter 6 my colleague at the London Business School Library, Jonathan Eaton, reminds us of the realities and hard edges of content delivery for our libraries, specifically the unique technological challenges still faced by business school librarians who must attempt to procure and set up increasingly flexible access to commercial and complex financial products to meet the demands of pressurized faculty and doctoral students – products that were never designed with the academic marketplace and university IT environments in mind. All this has to be achieved alongside providing the necessary support for other core academic library technologies (for example, library management systems, link resolvers, discovery systems, electronic resource management systems and so forth) in face of the demand for Google-like simplicity and content that is device-agnostic. Jonathan illustrates the importance of trying to capture comparable usage data from this plethora of local and cloud-based systems and rightly emphasizes the necessity for business school librarians of the future to acquire new sets of skills to handle the data delivered by our technology.

Agnès Melot and Sophie Forcadell from HEC Paris continue the technology theme in Chapter 7, this time on a national basis, with our first reference in this book to a cross-institutional library project, the Open Archive in France. As well as highlighting the importance of institutional repositories in promoting French business school research (and the management role played by librarians), the chapter's case studies also underline the value placed on the discipline archive, Social Sciences Research Network, by the business school faculty and the consequent need for interoperability between these different national, institutional and sector systems if full-text submission rates are to increase further. Thankfully, in France at least, the state is fully supportive of the open access movement with a plan already in place, as Agnès and Sophie explain.

As business schools place an even greater emphasis on careers support than other subject groups due to the weighting accorded to average graduate starting salaries in international business school rankings, Marcella Barnhart and Cathy Ogur (Chapter 8) present a growth area for business school libraries – career and entrepreneurship support – and summarize the results of some primary research they have conducted on current practices. Their chapter also illustrates a future role for business school libraries with their alumni.

The final section of the book focuses on space, identity and, ultimately, on our future(s) as the traditional need for library space to accommodate collections disappears, thereby breaking the link between the concept of a library bound up with a physical presence and the services it provides.

Lai Fong Li, in Chapter 9, reminds us that business schools (or departments of management) are not always served by separate, dedicated library entities (or professional library staff), especially in institutions with large numbers of undergraduates. In library terms they are represented by but one subset of resources within a larger collection set. Nevertheless, as evidenced in Hong Kong (and elsewhere), a business school faculty and its students can still benefit from significant capital investment in library facilities by the parent university, adopting the latest thinking in learning space design.

Kathleen Long (Chapter 10) provides us, first, with a terminological toolbox to understand the evolution of library space, reclaiming Nitecki's (2011) concepts of the library as accumulator, service provider and facilitator. She then draws on some very interesting examples of space experimentation within the sector based on the concepts of 'co-location' or 'embedding', bringing to my mind the 'disaggregation' of the librarian from the library in the same way as journal aggregators disaggregated the journal article from the journal issue in the 1990s. She also offers us a unique insight into the development of her own library space to support collaboration and community as part of the new Stanford Graduate School of Business facility.

Chris Flegg (Chapter 11) provides a suitably reflective account of our emerging service identities with which to conclude the book. I particularly like her use of the phrase 'collections arms race' to describe the futility of trying to collect and catalogue everything in a digital world and the ensuing logic of moving to a demand-driven acquisition model but, in so doing, destroying the unique selling point (USP) of the traditional collections-based (business or otherwise) library. Thankfully, all is not lost, as Chris provides us with pointers to the new, broader internal and external roles that librarians can play once they emerge, blinking in the sunlight, from their collection bunkers.

Finally, I return at the end of the book to share the results of an international survey of business school library heads I conducted in 2012 to identify the hopes and fears of my peer group for the near and distant future. I include a case study from my own institution that coincidentally emerged and fitted the future-facing theme of the chapter as I was writing it, requiring me to actively seek answers to the pertinent question: 'What should the business school library of the 21st century look like?'

REFERENCES

Business Librarians Association, 2009. *Benchmarking Survey: Results and Analysis*. Business Librarians Association.

Financial Times, 2013. Global MBA Ranking 2013 [online]. At: http://rankings.ft.com/businessschoolrankings/global-mba-ranking-2013 (accessed 20 April 2013).

Karp, R., 2002. *The Basic Business Library: Core Resources*, 4th edn. Westport, CT: Greenwood Press.

Nitecki, D., 2011. Space Assessment as a Venue for Defining the Academic Library. *Library Quarterly*, 81(1), 27–59.

Oort, B.B., 1986. An Evaluation of the Organisation of Some European Business School Libraries, and the Services They Supply. PhD thesis, Loughborough University.

Priestner, A. and Tilley, E.A., 2012. *Personalising Library Services in Higher Education: A Boutique Approach*. Farnham: Ashgate Publishing.

Sheehy, C.A., 1996. *Managing Business Collections in Libraries*. Westport, CT: Greenwood Press.

Soules, A., 1996. Forecasting the Future. In: C.A. Sheehy (ed.), *Managing Business Collections in Libraries*. Westport, CT: Greenwood Press. 1996, 217–57.

Vernon, K.D.C., 1975. *Use of Management and Business Literature: Information Sources for Research and Development*. London: Butterworths.

CHAPTER 2

ORGANIZATIONAL DESIGN CONSIDERATIONS FOR DELIVERING VALUE IN THE 21ST-CENTURY ACADEMIC LIBRARY

DEB WALLACE

"It was an unusually warm summer day in Boston when HBS announced the Baker Library's new Executive Director ..."

Harvard Business School (HBS) cases typically begin with a standard "story" opener. The protagonist is introduced, contemplating his or her leadership challenge. There is usually mention of the weather or a current event—something to set the stage, often in an informal, if not chatty, tone. Facts about the organization, the industry context, the cast of characters or interesting geographic features follow next—all the salient points woven together to fuel the learning objectives sprinkled with a red herring or two that cause the students to pause and sharpen their analytical skills. The facts are presented, the dilemma restated, and the baton passed to the reader for reflection in preparation for a class the next morning. What is your assessment of the challenge? How would you handle the situation? What parallels do you see from other cases? What is your advice to the protagonist? Supplementary information is found at the end—exhibits that quantify the narrative's key messages include additional data that may or may not help the reader make an informed decision. Of course, the real value of the case study is the discussion with 90 students awaiting the infamous cold call, the opportunity to open the case and lay out the facts in a way that leads to a compelling resolution.

Many HBS cases also have an accompanying teaching note—a resource for the case discussion leader on how to make the most of the learning opportunity. This is not a step-by-step teaching manual but an overview of key points, how to position the material to maximize the learning outcome, and often the back-story to the case development. This chapter strives to combine these two learning resources—case components of our organizational design challenge and reflections to stimulate your thinking and spark your imagination about your own organization.

We have been heralding the transition to the 21st-century academic research library for probably close to a quarter of a century already. But, for the most part, the focus has been on the changing nature of information, the born-digital and analog-to-digital content within our collections and scattered across countless repositories. A great deal of thought has gone into how to find information and then serve it up in a format required by a user's choice of device. We have also spent a lot of time talking about remaining relevant in the wake of Google, which, for many students and researchers, provides in record time more information than they could possibly use to complete an assignment. "Who still needs a library when the world of information is at our fingertips?" is a question that has prompted the re-evaluation of library services at all levels—the redefinition of the underlying value of libraries. While schools of library and information science have morphed into i-schools in the USA, and new curricula have been introduced to teach the competencies required by professionals in the digital library world, little has been written about the organizational structure needed to deliver the new value proposition promised by this 21st-century academic library as outlined by Tim Wales in the Introduction to this book. Even if you subscribe to tried and true adages (got example, "It takes a village"—African proverb) or company slogans (for example, "Our Product is Steel, Our Strength is People"—ArcelorMittal Dofasco Steel Company), without unrelenting attention to the right combination of people and the right organizational structures to enable them to flourish, the best strategy or most compelling vision will have little traction and even the most accomplished leaders will fail. Cloud computing, mobile apps, and "tweeting" aside, in the end, even in the 21st century, it is all about people.

A NOTE FROM OUR SPONSORS: THE ORGANIZATIONAL CONTEXT

As an early entrant in the business management education field, Harvard Business School (HBS) was considered a "delicate experiment" when established in 1908. It offered its first Master of Business Administration (MBA) degree to a graduating class of eight students in 1911. Since its inception HBS has pioneered participant-centered learning through the case method, established a library with extensive historical and contemporary collections, launched an international publishing arm, built a 40-acre residential campus, and continues today to develop the discipline of business management through faculty research, curriculum reform, and alumni engagement.

Nitin Nohria became HBS's tenth dean in July 2010. Since then, he has challenged the faculty and staff to "not sit on our laurels" and outlined five initiatives to chart the School's course into the 21st century. Beginning with innovation in the MBA program, the Dean's priorities also include continued commitment to intellectual ambition, expanding HBS's international strategy, creating an inclusive community in which everyone can thrive, and proactively integrating with Harvard University, a prominent theme of the current President.

An initial gift of $1,000 established a small collection to support the new MBA degree program and faculty research, but it was Dean Gay's (1908–1919) vision of a business library that could parallel the Harvard Law and Medical Schools' libraries combined with Dean Donham's (1919–1942) interest in business history that fueled aggressive collecting efforts. In 1927 a new campus was dedicated, and Baker Library became the permanent home of the business management collections. Between 2003 and 2005 Baker Library underwent a major renovation that also added faculty offices, seminar rooms, and student spaces to create the new Baker Library/Bloomberg Center.

From constituting only a single superintendent of the School's Reading Room in 1910, the staff has increased not only in number but in types of professional, and now includes librarians, researchers, archivists, conservators, journalists, analysts, information architects, search engineers, taxonomists, and administrators supplemented by interns, contractors, and consultants. Similarly, Baker's services have expanded from traditional collecting and research support to include information product development, online publishing, enterprise information management, research data management, and course development. The provision of new, enterprise-wide information management services prompted the renaming of the group to Knowledge and Library Services (KLS) in 2008. However, "Baker" remains the popular brand name.

Today, with nearly 50,000 physical visits to the reading rooms, 500,000 hits on its public website, 3.5 million hits on its online publication *Working Knowledge* about faculty research, and continued growth in contemporary and historical collections, KLS, like HBS, sits at an inflection point with the opportunity to build on its strong foundation and leverage its resources in support of the School's mission at the start of a new century.

CHANGE AS THE ONLY CONSTANT

We are at the beginning of this journey. It is a work in progress. How it all plays out is yet to be realized. Less a journal or series of diary entries and more a collection of lessons learned from an appreciative inquiry perspective by a reflective practitioner, I wish I could say that when I assumed the role of executive director I had a clear vision of how to build the organization I thought we needed to deliver the repositioned value proposition. But that is not the case. I had insights and personal opinions from being a member of the senior management team for six years. But, more importantly, I had a group of incredibly generous people who were willing to join me on this journey: angel investors in the form of senior HBS administrators who removed barriers; entrepreneurial managers willing to form a new leadership team and take risks; and highly dedicated, customer-centric staff who volunteered to engage in the strategy reflection process in addition to their already heavy workload.

Even being dealt a winning hand did not mean that our work was without challenge—we were about to ask the staff, already showing signs of "change fatigue," to fasten their seatbelts once again.

For nearly 20 years, Baker Library's executive directors have continued to lead change initiatives. Information technology was implemented in the mid- to late 1990s. Core collections transitioned from print to electronic resources; catalogs and discovery tools went online; and the library staff became proficient online researchers and web-based information product developers. The Information/Digital Age was well underway, and the new millennium brought a concerted effort to function more like a professional services firm than a traditional academic research library. A proactive, user-centric staff mindset helped shape new services with value-added components to increase faculty productivity and research output as well as student achievement across the degree and executive education programs. Traditional reference was replaced with research services, and student learning was supported through collaboration on course development using curated information to achieve high-order learning objectives. Enduring goals and strategic shifts to achieve a planned future state were identified. A range of new tools and processes was introduced, including a balanced scorecard, project management office, and measurements and metrics in the form of dashboards and customer reports. New groups and repositioned groups were established, including the Knowledge and Information Asset Management Department and the Life Cycle Management Team. Throughout, Baker maintained support from the Dean's Office and senior faculty who functioned in various advisory and governance roles. But, for the most part, the executive directors were trusted to make good decisions. Funding also remained reasonably consistent, notwithstanding reductions in the 2008 economic downturn.

THE PERFECT STORM

The convergence of forceful weather patterns to create a "perfect storm" typically denotes a disaster, but the phrase is morphing in meaning to describe a more positive outcome from multiple drivers converging to create a significant change. KLS's perfect storm was created by a combination of internal and external forces—at the school and university levels, the implementation of the new Dean's aggressive innovation agenda and the Harvard President's mandate to create a unified Harvard Library structure and, at the library level, a new executive director, five open staff positions with an additional three voluntary retirements, and a significant collecting opportunity that would require new staff expertise and a technology infrastructure to ingest electronic records in multiple formats.

An internal appointment to the library's executive director position signaled the Dean's endorsement of KLS's direction, that our strategic shifts and enduring goals were guiding us in the right direction. As the former managing director of

Baker Library Services, my faculty relationships, knowledge of research agendas and curriculum directions, and relationships with public service managers across Harvard's libraries were valuable assets for leading the group. As a first step, I suggested that we should not throw the baby out with the bathwater—that we remain on the course my predecessor had established in implementing many 21st-century-focused components. But, given there were new variables in play, we needed to take stock of the current opportunities by reflecting on our strategy.

While a proponent of the participant–observer research methodology, in which the researcher is also an active participant in the activity being studied and individual and group reflection is a key component, I am also a fan of engaging outside help to guide strategy development with an objective, "disinterested" eye. To that end, we engaged a principal from HOW Management, a boutique change management firm in Boston, who had worked with us on a previous, smaller group redesign, knew our business and could hit the ground running. He crafted a strategy reflection process that helped us assess our current state, identify both pain points and opportunities, and create a new mission, vision, and set of priorities. The goal was to increase relevancy to our community with compelling services that strengthened the Baker brand promise. Key to the approach was broad, meaningful staff engagement, transparency through extensive communication, and accountability for deliverables and milestones.

Worth a chapter of its own, our "Strategy Reflection" produced the desired outcome—a set of priorities that would help us focus our resources in order to realize our vision. Two of the eight priorities spoke to the type of organization—the structure and culture—that we needed in place in order to be successful:

- Create an adaptable organization that empowers us to succeed in achieving our priorities.
- Create a collaborative culture that fosters trust, recognizes performance, values innovation and enhances our capabilities.

First on the list when we transitioned from strategy reflection to implementation was a new organizational design, putting the structural elements in place so that people with the right capabilities could come together to get the work done, to deliver what we had promised to our customers and community.

ORGANIZATIONAL DESIGN: NO TABLETS COMING FORTH FROM THE MOUNT

On this journey, one of the hardest messages for me, as a leader, to get across to my team is that I do not have all the answers. This shift in culture has not happened overnight. A significant factor is the hierarchical nature of academia coupled with the class system of faculty and staff, with librarians at Harvard belonging to the latter category. Another factor is a history of strong leaders with top-down change management approaches. Although efforts were made to engage the staff, the driving force typically came from the corner office.

When I became executive director, I did what many new leaders do: I spent the first 90 days talking to key stakeholders about what they thought was going well and what needed attention—asking their advice on shaping our agenda. A clear message from the library's senior management team was that there was a need for clarity and transparency from my office. I tried to address this common challenge throughout our Strategy Reflection with a collaborative communication framework that clearly laid out: the context—what is driving our actions; the governance—how decisions would be made and who would be responsible for what; and the process—the key steps and milestones that would document our progress against plan. Nowhere were these elements needed more than in the development of our new organization. Our "Organizational Design Framework" (see Figure 2.1) is one of the working documents that we developed at the outset of the design process to provide context. The change drivers provide the backdrop, the design inputs outline the multiple components in play within our environment that a new organizational structure would need to address, and the design principles are factors that should guide decisions.

We spent a lot of time talking about all these factors—an important investment on the team's part in order to address transparency and increase engagement. Our consultant helped us understand that organizational design is much more than creating a chart and moving the boxes around. Outputs of our organizational design work included:

- *reporting structure*—the traditional organizational chart
- *group work structures* describing, for each group within KLS: focus and responsibilities; primary audience(s); examples of work; general management elements concerning workforce planning, professional development, budgeting, and the reporting structure.
- *job designs* supplementing the broader, standard KLS job description with additional information about how current priorities impact on an individual's job, including ongoing work and assigned projects
- *integrating mechanisms*—roles that work across the organizational design structure, ensuring coordination for cross-functional teams or roles that may have multiple reporting lines: for example, the Customer Experience Program, services/infrastructure groups and the leadership structure.
- *performance measures* describing: what success looks like for each of the priorities; the budget; and individuals' goals to be included in the annual performance process.

Design change drivers
1. New Executive Director
2. Updated mission, vision and priorities from Strategy Reflection
3. Widespread ambiguity—need to restore organizational stability and fill open positions.
Design inputs
1. **Leadership change.** New Executive Director's capabilities and faculty/senior administrators' perspectives on opportunities and priorities.
2. **Dean's priorities implemented.** Directions realized and resources expended on 5 Is (innovation, integration, intellectual ambition, inclusion, and internationalization).
3. **KLS staff demographics.** "Graying" of knowledge and library services; need for succession planning.
4. **Harvard Library transition.** Move to shared services model, new governance and management structure, and probable VERIP (Voluntary Early Retirement Incentive Program).
5. **Changing nature of digital scholarship.** Emphasis on digital content and tools; positioning KLS as leading key projects related to digital scholarship and obtaining unique data sources
6. **Faculty research approaches.** Faculty needs to manage information more effectively, especially in terms of its research and publishing (increase in volume of information and types of format available in, collaboration with other faculties, increase in number and ease of use of tools to manage the research process, range of research outputs, focus on translational research to business management practitioners).
7. **Curriculum and learning environment.** Changes to support MBA (first- and second-year curriculum), doctoral, and executive education, including greater global integration.
8. **Heavy reliance on technology.** Recognition of KLS's reliance on technology to deliver on its priorities and to create value at the school through its distinctive capabilities.
9. **HBS landscape/collaborative culture.** Input from customers and partners on concerns about their ability to understand KLS's distinctive capabilities; unclear relationships, responsibilities, and dependencies, especially on shared capabilities/distributed responsibilities.
10. **Re-inventing/positioning library services in the broader academic setting.** Universal discussion of a library's value and impact on the academy—research, teaching, and learning.
Design principles
1. Develop greater agility as an organization; address territorial silos.
2. Support innovation; create culture of risk-taking and experimentation.
3. Develop span of control that optimizes priorities and effectiveness (ED and entire organization); engage middle management and program/services expertise; create clear lines of responsibility and ultimate accountability.
4. Leverage internal capabilities.
5. Foster leadership from within; implement career path and management development; develop inclusive management style to foster internal and

	external collaboration.
6.	Create an easily understood design, given the complex environment internal and external to KLS and HBS, while at the same time recognizing some level of ambiguity in the near and medium term.
7.	Allocate resources to meet changes in demand
8.	Focus on service delivery and infrastructure development.

Figure 2.1   Harvard KLS strategy reflection – organizational design framework

As with the strategy reflection process, we created a project plan for the organizational design, including: a ramp-up period during which we created a formal plan; a review of customer needs; an initial group design in which we identified three large-scale options; a period of exploration and discussion to identify a proposed structure along with the change decisions, resource needs, and communication plan; a round of presentations to finalize the proposed structure with the Dean's Office and HBS Human Resources; and a roll-out/implementation plan that communicated decisions, explained the structure's components, and addressed teams' and individuals' concerns.

OVER-ARCHING PRINCIPLE: STAFF ENGAGEMENT AND COMMUNICATION

Before moving into some of the specifics of the organizational design outcomes, I would like to highlight a guiding principle we followed throughout our strategy reflection process and paid particular attention to throughout our organizational design work. Rewind to "For nearly 20 years, Baker Library's executive directors have continued to lead change initiatives" and the fact that staff were experiencing *change fatigue*. Add voluntary and involuntary workforce reductions during the 2008 economic downturn, an announcement in January 2011 from the Harvard Library Executive Director at an open meeting for library staff about the library transition that the new structure would be based on a reduced workforce, and a Voluntary Early Retirement Incentive Program offering in April 2011. Then stir in the fact that KLS's scores on the Harvard-wide semi-annual survey of employee engagement were among the lowest at HBS. And, *voilà*, you have a recipe for a staffing disaster!

If you recognize that people are your most important resource, then you have to remember that their concerns are your number-one priority. With any level of change comes a high degree of uncertainty and even the *mention* of an organizational design review creates a high degree of anxiety. While you are working behind closed doors at the upper management levels, the entire organization is wondering: "What about me? Where will I land? What group will I belong to? Where will I sit? Who will I report to? How will my job change? Does anyone know what I am really capable of doing? Will I be passed over yet again? What are my options? Here we go again—how bumpy will the ride be this time?"

To address the anxiety factor which, as you know, is an incredible disruptor and resource drain with staff diverting their time to speculation, false assumptions, and rumor-mongering, we built in a crescendo of staff engagement and communication throughout our design process. Groups reviewed their own work function descriptions and recommended modifications; interested individuals joined conversations about proposed new group structures and offered suggestions on roles and responsibilities; updates on progress against plan were given in department meetings, general staff meetings, and via the "Broadsheet," KLS's weekly newsletter; and various staff who might morph into new roles were asked to consider options then draft job designs, recommending how new responsibilities should be shaped. There was no organizational design delivered from behind closed doors. We adopted an "all hands on deck" scenario in which engagement was heavily embraced by both managers and staff.

ORGANIZATIONAL DESIGN OUTPUTS

To be honest, I think the least interesting component of the organizational design is the standard "org chart". Other than showing reporting lines, it tells little about the organizational structure itself. However, because I know that it is the bedrock of organizational design, it is included at the end of this chapter (Figure 2.2). The group work structures and job designs provide much more insight about how our work actually gets done. These are living documents that, to my mind, should always be marked "draft," but the staff is not comfortable with that degree of ambiguity. It was clear in our priority development conversations that accountability is a key staff concern and to be accountable, you need to know exactly what you are accountable for! The "recognizes performance" in the priority is meant to cover both recognizing people for exceptional performance and addressing lack of performance.

The group work structure provides the framework for describing each group's primary responsibilities. We started with a free-form document intended to capture "first thoughts" about how the group perceived its primary responsibilities, the audiences they interact with, the approach they take or need to consider for providing their services, and a list of questions and/or outstanding issues that would need clarification. Next, the groups distilled the information into a chart that collected key points, building to the "big picture" of the organizational design from each group's perspective and in their words.

HBS uses standard job descriptions for categories of jobs that are aligned with Harvard's various job families (for example, IT, Communications, Library and so on).

Our job designs outline specifics about individual responsibilities and approaches to completing work. For example, two staff may have the same job description (say, business analyst), but different job designs based on the nature of their work. For this project, we completed forms only for new or revised positions, or positions that were unclear and needed further explanation. As with the group work structures, they were developed from a free-form list of components and then modified to fit into our standard form.

Integrating mechanisms

New to this organizational design work was the concept of an *integrating mechanism*—a coordinating construct in the form of an individual or a group with responsibilities for providing a cross-functional, cross-KLS perspective in order to synchronize, synthesize, and/or leverage capabilities across multiple components. To begin, we identified three integrating mechanisms:

- services group and infrastructure group within the organizational design
- Customer Experience Program
- leadership structure.

Services and infrastructure groups
These two components are loosely represented on our organizational chart by groups clustered to the left and right with overlap in Special Collections (see Figure 2.2) *Working Knowledge*, Contemporary Research Services, Curriculum and Learning Services, Information Management, and Special Collections' public services team form the Services Group—the departments that directly provide services to customers. The collection development and processing teams in the Special Collections, Information Products & Innovation, Digital Content Program & IT, Business Operations, and Administration & Communications groups form the Infrastructure Group—the group responsible for our organizational capabilities, tools, resources, approaches, and policies that enable the provision of services.

KLS provides a wide range of services to our various customer groups. Rather than organizing by customer (for example, faculty, students, executive education participants, alumni, administrative departments), we have chosen to organize around type of service delivered (for example, knowledge dissemination/publishing, research, curriculum and learning, and information management), the rationale being that due to the complex nature of most of our services, we need to focus on the practice as it is applied to the customer. However, given our commitment to customer-centric service, we are in a bit of a catch-22. Maybe we should be organized by the customer groups? To address this, we have created a Customer Experience Program to work across the Services Group to ensure consistency in our service delivery and look for ways of leveraging engagements through customer relationship management, customer reporting, and services metrics.

The flipside is the Infrastructure Group – the human and material resources, tools, processes, and technology needed by the Services Group to deliver their products and services. The Infrastructure Group provides the enabling components that KLS's customer-facing teams need to do their work, but also works closely with individual groups to provide customized solutions to meet their specific needs (for example, Information Management Services needs a meta-data management tool, Curriculum and Learning Services need information products for student research, Special Collections needs data extraction tools).

Customer Experience Program
We have a long tradition of customer-centric service delivery. We have tried many times to implement a customer relationship management system and have kept statistics on our customer transactions beyond circulation and reading room entrances—the typical Association of Research Libraries' laundry list of statistics. We have tried various approaches to creating liaison roles tied to key customer groups: practice area leads representing customer needs to service providers; pairing faculty with a librarian as an "Easy Button"; and establishing a project management office. All approaches have yielded some results, but not to the level we expected. Given the importance of high-quality customer service to the Baker brand, we decided to create a management position devoted to the program and to situate that position within the Services Group, not within the Executive or Business Offices where responsibility lay in the past. The Job Design for the Manager—Customer Experience Program clearly laid out areas of responsibility and deliverables. For example:

- **Knows our customers**. Develops and manages mechanisms for collecting faculty project profiles, project approach information, and statistics/metrics related to the service provided.
- **Keeps us organized**. Manages project pipelines and stewards consistent project management process across customer service areas. Manages opportunity clearinghouse process as needed to support service groups' resource allocation and a balanced resource capacity for project commitments. Acts as liaison for cross-KLS projects.
- **Knows what we know and share our knowledge**. Gathers statistics for internal quarterly reports, quarterly budget reviews and reforecasts. Maintains KLS services dashboard. Assembles and produces customer reports to KLS constituents.

Leadership structure
In an effort to flatten the organization, we moved responsibility for professional development and budgets from the Executive Office to each of the divisions within KLS. Strategy management also became a shared responsibility, with each priority having an "owner" and a volunteer team of staff who shaped the priority statement, outlined the goals to achieve it, and managed progress against plan through tracking

the status of deliverables. We also repositioned the former senior management team (executive director, managing directors, and directors) that used to meet on a weekly basis with a multifaceted leadership structure that provided management oversight, linked "big picture" strategy management with priority-related projects and ongoing work, and created a forum to engage individual and group contributions to KLS leadership decision-making. This series of focused working meetings ensure that the "right" people are in the room to move the agenda forward include:

- Leadership Exchange—opportunity to share information, solve problems, and position opportunities across KLS groups
- Customer Experience—mechanism for customer relationship management and to ensure a consistent customer experience across our priority audiences
- Organizational Capabilities—addresses infrastructure needs across KLS groups.
- Strategy Management—ensures that the work needed to achieve our priorities is on track.

Generally speaking, the expected outcomes of these leadership meetings are to:

- track progress—outline project status, create a shared understanding of where KLS stands with respect to strategic priorities and what needs to be accomplished going forward
- make decisions/solve problems—provide a venue for putting our collective wisdom to work, creating shared solutions
- share information—bring everyone up-to-date with current information.

There is no question that this leadership structure is much more complex than our previous senior management meetings. It is also the first time that we have pulled together all the various leadership and management components into one document. Frankly, it is a bit overwhelming, but it provides a physical reminder of how much we all interact in managing our resources, making decisions and ensuring that we are moving forward against our promised priorities. We are still getting used to the rhythm of the components as well as experimenting with communicating between meetings (for example, some meetings take place only once a month) and keeping staff informed of meeting content and outcomes. I confess to keeping my leadership structure chart handy so that I know what is being discussed when. But we are seeing the benefits of the focused agendas and voluntary attendance. We are able to use some meetings as working meetings, some to share information, and others to resolve specific challenges. Not all directors need to be at all meetings. There is no longer a standard two-plus hours a week for scheduled management meetings.

Performance Measures

In *The Progress Principle* (2011) HBS Professor Teresa Amabile writes about the importance of knowing how our work makes a difference, knowing where we are with our work—how it is progressing toward completion. We have always had a very comprehensive performance management approach both for individuals (HBS Human Resources Program) and our projects (roadmaps, project management tools) and we continue to track performance at the organizational, group, and individual levels.

New with our current work are roadmaps for each priority (we used to have roadmaps for each practice area) where we track progress against the goals on a quarterly basis. We are experimenting with having the volunteer group that developed the priority (wording of the statement, goals and tasks to achieve, and deliverables) continue to monitor its progress. It is a way of keeping the group engaged: they came together because of their interest in the particular priority and now they are responsible for ensuring that we continue to move toward its achievement.

Truth be told, the real performance measure for the organization is our budget. The budgeting process, which extends over almost five months, begins with stating our three-year goals, discussing what we need to meet the needs of our partners and customers (for example, IT, Operations/Facilities, Executive Education Program, and so forth), prioritizing IT resources for large administrative projects school-wide or at the department level, and presenting the business case for our operating budget and any special project-funding requests in two rounds—the last with the Dean who makes final decisions. In addition, we have quarterly reforecasting and the opportunity to request additional funds "out of cycle" when opportunities arise.

As you can imagine, this is no small task! My first budget preparation came just on the heels of completing our Strategy Reflection, so we were well situated with newly defined priorities and a vision. We clearly aligned with the school's inflection point, the Dean's "5 Is" (innovation, intellectual ambition, internationalization, inclusion, integration), and the Harvard Library transition. But we had to "sell" the idea of Baker 2.0 – creating the next generation academic research library. We are getting there. For the most part, the Dean and his executive team understand the challenges of living in this rapidly evolving digital world. They, too, are drowning in information, frustrated with trying to keep up with the latest technology, yet excited about the possibilities that new channels of knowledge dissemination bring. To help frame the investments we need, we developed a list of 13 strategic shifts (a Baker's Dozen, no less), showing how key library elements are moving from their traditional format to the 21st-century equivalent.

BUT THIS IS *NOT* AN IT PROJECT!

One of the key things we are still wrestling with (and, by the way, it just happens to be a key critical success factor for libraries of any type trying to add value in the Digital Age), is how we create the technology infrastructure we need to not only do our current work, but also enable our strategic shifts, particularly in how we manage our collections, provide discovery tools, and preserve priority content into the future. While people are the most important asset a library has and organizational culture trumps anything you try to do, our extraordinary reliance on computer and information technology cannot be emphasized enough.

Previous Baker Library executive directors have been thought-leaders in the information and knowledge management industries; I am not. And while not close to being classified a Luddite, I struggle with outlining a collaborative framework in which information technology groups and libraries have a truly symbiotic relationship.

At the time of writing, HBS is without a chief information officer. Knowledge and Library Services, Marketing and Communications and the Information Technology Group are struggling to define the "three legged stool" which brings the distinctive capabilities and areas of responsibility for information and content management, brand and communication standards, and the information technology infrastructure together to meet our shared customers' business requirements. There is no question that HBS's demand for a state-of-the-art research, teaching, and learning technology environment outstrips the possible supply of our IT Group's resources. At the same time, as part of the Harvard Library's distributed model, KLS relies on Harvard University Information Technology for the provision of many traditional library-related systems (for example, library management system, discovery tools, interlibrary loan systems, and so on) as well as platforms and tools that move us into the Digital Age (for example, web archiving, open access publishing platforms, research data repositories, and so on).

Without clearly defining the collaboration framework between the library and information technology group, we limp along trying to position the technology infrastructure, standards and practices that we need to ensure long-term access and preservation of the school's priority content. (Note: KLS is responsible for standards for content and repositories across HBS, not just those within Baker Library collections.) We used to have an information technology manager who was responsible for our hardware/software inventory, acted as liaison to the HBS IT group and reported directly to the Executive Director. But that position became vacant when the incumbent accepted an early retirement package. As a first step, we established a new department with a director-level position to create a Digital Content Program, the foundation of Baker 2.0. We added responsibility for KLS's technology infrastructure to this new role, given our heavy reliance on IT now and for the foreseeable future.

We are in the early phase of defining the program (work functions), team members (job design), and strategy. But, as we head into my second budget preparation, we have a much clearer picture of what we need to accomplish our strategic shifts. And although it took me a year to figure out, we realize that we cannot move forward on all of the Baker's Dozen. To succeed, we have to have a narrower focus, remember our SMART goal training, and be realistic about what is achievable. Picking that "sweet spot" was iterative, involved the whole leadership team, and is now taking shape in our FY14 budget planning process.

PREPPING FOR THE COLD CALL

For any of you who have participated in or observed a cold call, you will know that the opportunity to "open" the case takes a lot of preparation. Can you artfully bring together all the salient points of the protagonist's leadership challenge? Can you clarify a complex financial component when you are challenged with balancing your own checkbook? Will you pick up on a cultural norm that any "global" leader should be sensitive to? Or will you eloquently expand on an element with great confidence only to learn that it was one of the case's red herrings?

If I were opening the Baker Library 2.0 organizational design case, here are the points I would highlight as either contributing to success or providing springboards into further discussion:

- Early and persistent engagement of the Chief Financial Officer, the Chief Human Resources Officer, and the Associate Dean for Administration (my boss): this built the case for resourcing strategic shifts through a thorough understanding of the library's value proposition.
- Investment in a strategy reflection process that fed into the budget development cycle: this enabled a clear and articulate a vision aligned with the school's priorities and areas of investment to get there.
- Grounded thinking and change management approaches in HBS faculty's work: the resulting findings and recommendations were used to guide our processes.
- Positioning of people's work as a team sport. with library leadership positions as player/coaches working alongside their team members: this flattened the organization, broadened areas of responsibility, and focused on building a collaborative culture based on accountability and trust.
- Development of a "stake in the sand" approach to design to address ambiguity whether in a job design, work structure, or background document, iterated through drafts where the people who needed the clarity took the lead in developing final versions.

- Encouragement of broad engagement and transparent communication that resulted in greater buy-in and employee satisfaction.
- Miserable failure in utilizing information management and communication tools: the Department ShareSite (operational repository/information bank) is a mess and has definitely failed to provide a best-practice example of basics!

LESSONS LEARNED AND CRITICAL SUCCESS FACTORS

I am a strong proponent of appreciative inquiry—looking at what is working and building from a position of strength, and thinking of lessons learned as elements that were successful, not failures to avoid the next time. It is the old SWOT analysis without the "W" or "T". I am also a devote of William Glasser, an educator from the 1970s who tirelessly promoted creating schools without failure, setting up learning environments so that students *could* succeed. To that end, I tend to approach a new challenge or opportunity by first looking at the "critical success factors": what do we need to have in place in order to succeed? It is the careful preparation of soil before planting, the creation of a solid foundation before building. In short, whether in a leadership or individual contributor role, as you reposition your value proposition or how you are going to deliver on your brand promise, you might consider how the following statements play out either for you personally or your organization.

- It is all about people—how they think about their work and value their contribution. On top of that, culture trumps everything.
- Strategy (including mission, vision, and other types of statements) is important, but without the capabilities to deliver its components, performance will always fall short. A strategy without the individual and organizational capabilities behind it brings to mind the emperor's new clothes.
- Organizational design is more than filling in boxes on a chart.
- We build the road as we travel. We are a learning organization that is not risk-averse, systematically reflects on our approaches, is agile enough to make mid-course modifications, and holds people accountable for performance.
- Do not make a mad dash to implement someone else's best practice. Have a thorough understanding of the context and change drivers, and be explicit about what is needed to be successful within that particular environment.
- Think about the difference between leadership and management. Be a leader.
- And, like Thoreau, strive to *simply simplify*.

WHAT IF

… you tried something different. You recognized the contributions from your long tradition of high-quality service, identified your core capabilities, zeroed in on your priority customers' pain points, identified some low hanging fruit as well as longer-term aspirations, and acted like a start-up? You did your industry analysis, wrote the business case, secured some seed money from an angel investor, prototyped a new product and/or service offering, and took your idea to market.

How but by studying great leaders and organizations might you have the opportunity to truly rethink the academic library of the future? Surrounded by people studying effective organizations, you have the opportunity to be a test-bed of experimentation, an engine of innovation, and a reflective practitioner. From what I have seen in academic business libraries around the world there is an untapped treasure trove of expertise and ideas already shaping an extraordinary array of change—strategic shifts that can position business information services well into this century, if not the next.

My hope at the end of this chapter is that you take away some ideas that can help you design and manage or actively participate in your organizational design. I did not intend to write a step-by-step technical guide. Rather, this is just one example of many where an organization invested time in thoroughly considering its options and strategically planned an approach. In our case, choices were made on the basis of our value proposition—an explicit statement of what the library provides to our community—and a thorough understanding of our broader environmental/organizational landscape—the drivers and influencing factors at play. We made what we considered to be informed decisions about how to bring the right people with the right capabilities together in the right way in order to deliver the most value to our community. As an *adaptable organization*, we will continue to assess these decisions and adjust accordingly. Stay tuned; the story continues.

REFERENCE

Amabile, T. and Kramer S., 2011. *The Progress Principle: Using Small Wins to Ignite Joy, Engagement, and Creativity at Work*. Boston, MA: Harvard Business Review Press.

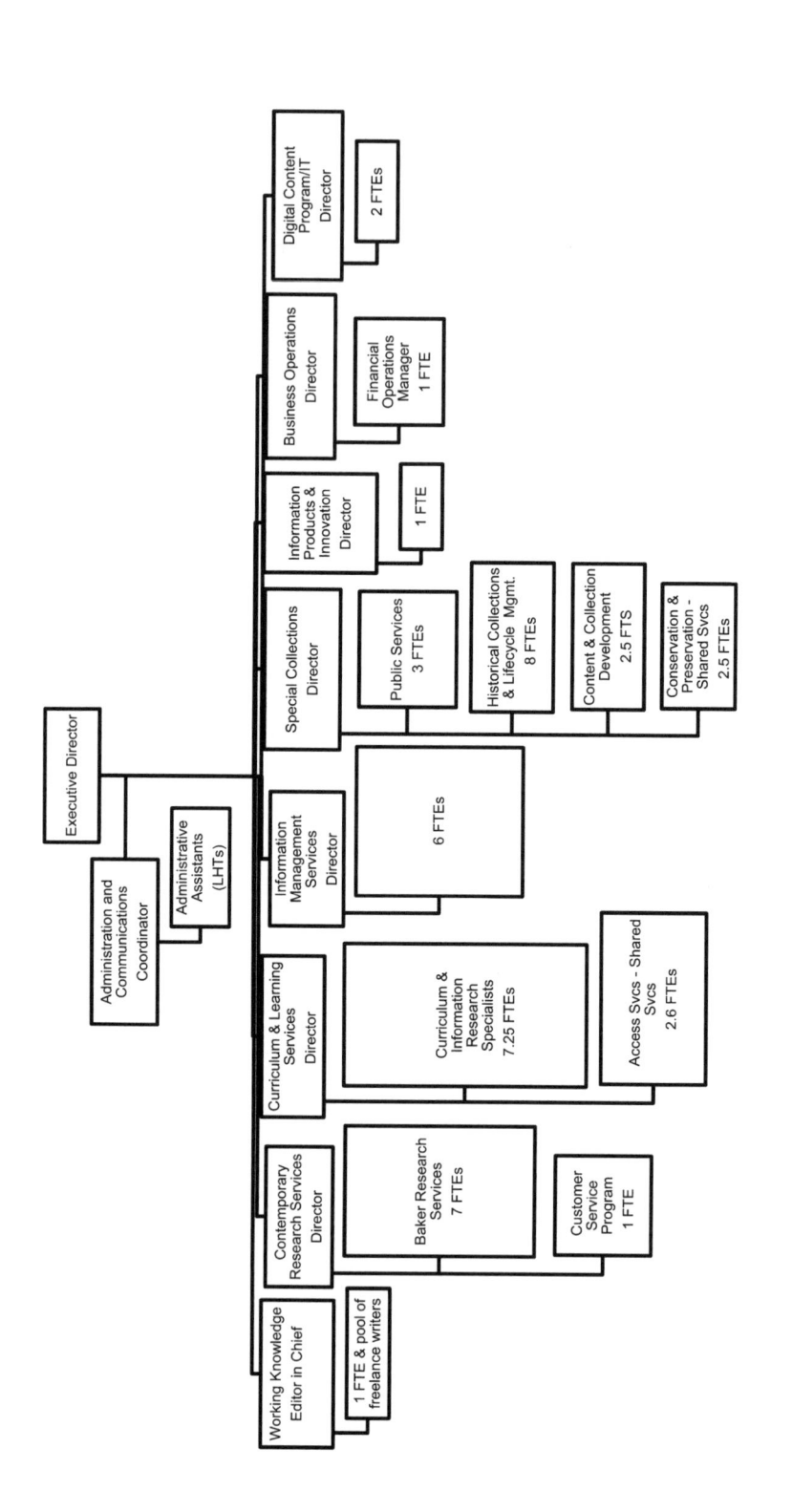

Figure 2.2 Harvard KLS reporting structure/organizational chart, February 2013

CHAPTER 3

CHANGE MANAGEMENT IN BUSINESS LIBRARIES
THORSTEN MEYER AND CLAUDIA LIEBETRUTH

WHY DO WE NEED CHANGE MANAGEMENT?

Life is all about change; it is universal and we cannot avoid it. We encounter change in every stage of our lives: starting at school or later at university; getting our first job; then changing workplaces later on or moving to another city. All these changes demand quite an effort on our part to adjust and adapt to new ways of life and new challenges. You may have to change your levels of self-awareness in order to take on a new role in life, become accustomed to a new environment, develop new skills or build up a new social network. We either welcome these changes or resist them, and sometimes it is a bit of both. There are also lots of little changes that we may not really notice, such as getting a new mobile phone and having to learn a new interface. Business, too, is all about change, especially in our society where broad access to information and the speed of technological innovation accelerate business activities faster than ever. This affects our day-to-day work in general and the way in which libraries work in particular. Now that information can be accessed quickly and from almost anywhere, expectations of libraries have changed – they are no longer just about the archiving of knowledge and distribution of books. They have to turn into information centres and adapt to new technologies in order to meet customer needs. Information centres now have to compete with the likes of Google (which currently comes closest of all to meeting these changed customer needs) in order to survive. Furthermore, business libraries (as a special type of library – for example, because of (partly) private funding), have to deal with budget constraints and general fiscal environments which can hinder service delivery.

Even though humans adapt to changes in their day-to-day life sometimes without noticing it, changes at work can be more difficult to deal with. One reason may be that these changes are often imposed on staff without giving them the opportunity to shape or lead them. Another reason is that work is 'earning for a living' so that any change can evoke fears of job insecurity. Change at work can appear in many different forms – for example, the introduction of a new technology that leads to new and more efficient processes with a consequent reduction in the staffing levels required to support such processes. Changes in processes often demand changes in working routines or the development of new skills, sometimes in a completely new discipline. Another example is a restructuring process of a library. Reorganization represents a great threat to the majority of staff as most of them anticipate the worst-case scenario: there will be no job left for them at the end of the process. And ending up with new duties and responsibilities within the same library is sometimes perceived as worse than being downsized!

In this chapter we would like to give advice to managers handling change in order to facilitate its acceptance by staff. As change is now prevalent in our society, change management is a critical success factor for a library. We will describe the role of change management by explaining how we used it as a backbone for our restructuring process in our own library. We finish the chapter by presenting our lessons learned when applying change management techniques so that other library staff can be successfully prepared and escorted through the change process.

STARTING POINT

To give a better understanding of the restructuring process we would like to start by describing briefly our organization and the reasons why we had to start the process.

The German National Library of Economics – Leibniz Information Centre for Economics (ZBW) is the world's largest specialist library for economics and business studies. It was founded in 1919 and has been a member of the Leibniz Association since 1966. The ZBW is a foundation under public law, financed by the federal and state governments, and invests more than €2.5 million per year into the acquisition of current titles in economics and business studies, both print and online.

With its 270 employees the ZBW is the primary archival centre in Germany for economic literature published worldwide. In addition, the information centre offers various services and products supporting researchers and students in their work and studies, such as research or storage tools. These products and services are developed by applied research in the fields of web science, semantics and knowledge discovery. Furthermore, the ZBW is the institutional library of the Kiel Institute for the World Economy and affiliated to the Christian-Albrechts University of Kiel.

The reasons for our restructuring in 2010 were manifold. The organizational structure (see Figure 3.1) existing at that time had been designed to meet the needs of the merger with the Library and Documentary Department of the Hamburg World Economic Archives (HWWA) in 2007. Even though a new structure had been created, some compromises had been made with regard to the existing structure: for example, the Editorial Department (which is responsible for publishing the magazines *Wirtschaftsdienst* and *Intereconomics*) was not well integrated into the new organization – because the department's function is not a traditional library activity it did not seem to fit into the former organization. Another example was the

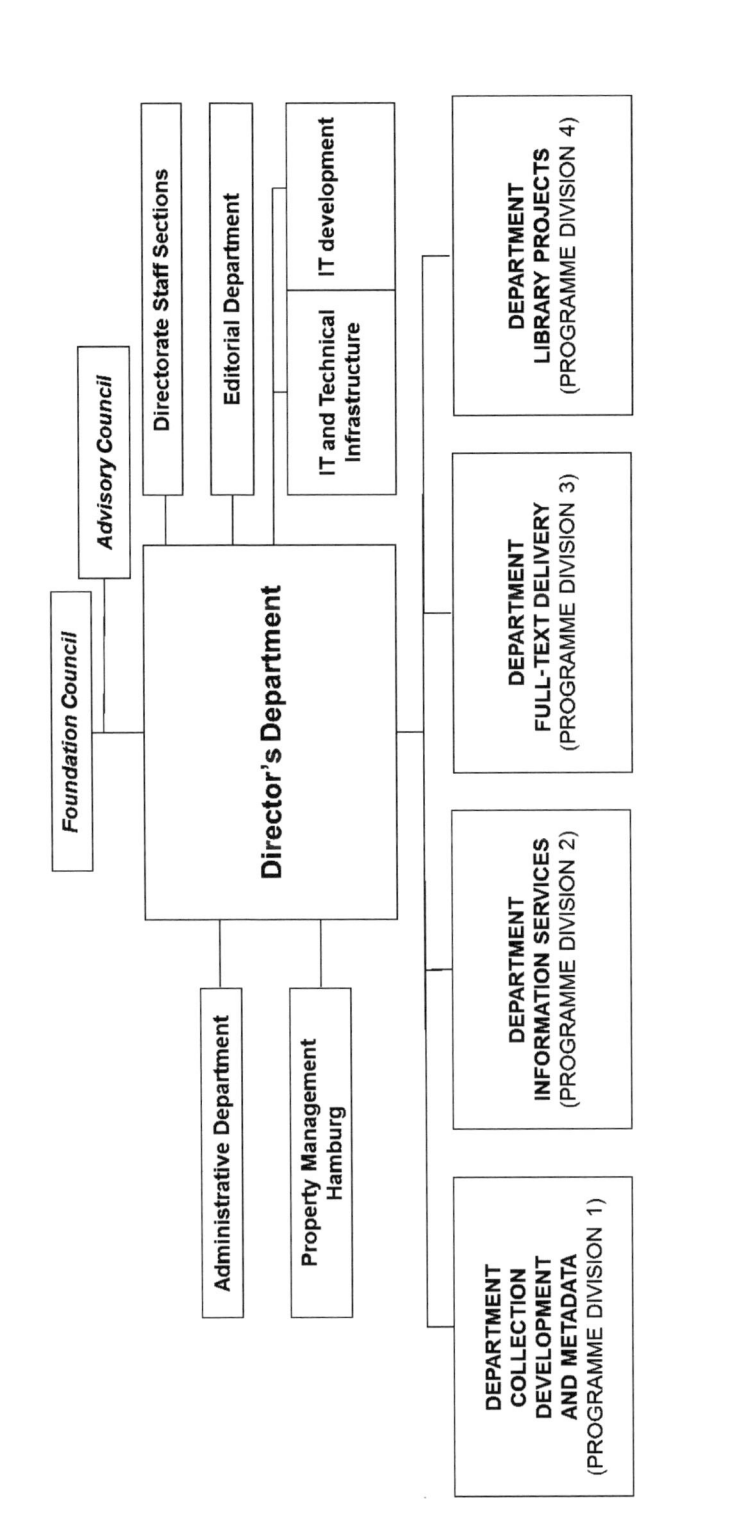

Figure 3.1 Former ZBW organizational structure

Library Projects Department (Programme Division 4) which was formed because its then relatively new activities did not fit easily within the old structure.

The hierarchical organizational structure was based on the model of a library in which the director had to decide upon everything – from strategic decisions and budget-related issues to micro-administrative decisions like the approval of staff annual leave requests. The structure was mostly oriented around the functional workflows of a traditional library. Customers' needs had not really been the focus of our operations.

During the last few years of its existence, the structure became increasingly inappropriate. Workflows and processes were very inflexible as a result of the way in which activities had been distributed across organizational units, making it almost impossible to integrate new tasks and services. A silo mentality had also developed during this time. One consequence of this was the development of services within different organizational units, independent of each other and with no proper interconnection. In the end, this broad portfolio was not managed at a common strategic level, and it was confusing for the customers.

Furthermore, the hierarchical structure led to a lack of organizational flexibility. First, since all decisions had to be made by the director, the decision-making process naturally became rather lengthy. Second, the director was so involved in administrative tasks that his ability to work at a strategic or political level was really quite limited.

The development process of the ZBW's new strategy in 2009 already showed that the existing structures did not fit into the overall vision and objectives. However, the organization was unable to undertake the necessary changes directly as a change of management took place at that time and the evaluation operated by the Leibniz Association lay ahead. At this point, we need to provide some background information:

> *Leibniz institutions are funded jointly by the Federation and the* Länder. *At the Joint Science Conference (GWK) the Federation and the* Länder *agreed that they would evaluate the institutions regularly – at the latest every seven years – to ascertain whether they still fulfilled the prerequisites of supraregional importance and national scientific interest in order to continue receiving joint funding. ... The Joint Science Conference (GWK) has delegated responsibility for conducting the evaluation procedure to the Senate of the Leibniz Association. The latter draws on the recommendations of the Senate Evaluation Committee (SAE) which is also composed of external members: members of the Senate, academics not employed by Leibniz institutions, representatives of the Federation and the* Länder. *(Leibniz Association, 2013)*

Most importantly, the results form the basis for the official decision on our funding for a further seven years. The focus of the evaluation is to assess whether an institution still meets the requirements of the Leibniz Association in regard to content, structure and overall strategy. Special focus is set on the quality of output, such as research, services and infrastructure. The positive effect of these audits is that every member has to constantly review its strategic objectives and processes (which is not very common in the German public sector). This external scrutiny can provide guidance and can also be used as a driver for change within the organization.

Within the ZBW, the upcoming evaluation supported the strategy development process in 2009, both as a catalyst for the process itself and by aligning institutional objectives to the requirements of the Leibniz Association. The successful evaluation in 2010 gave us the green light to implement our strategic objectives since the evaluation committee acknowledged the problems we were encountering and believed that our intended solutions were on the right track. This also made it easier for us to explain to staff why we had to change, and we were able to convey our confidence that our vision was approved and was deemed promising.

The aims of our restructuring process were:

- to create efficient workflows
- to implement applied research into our institution
- to create a clear product portfolio based on the customer's needs.

It became rather obvious that the necessary structural changes would have a huge impact on the staff as well as changing work environments or processes. We were convinced that the changes could not be implemented without the commitment of the employees. To ensure a successful process we applied a change management framework. Change management describes a structured process whereby an organization moves from an existing state into a new state. In this context we understand change management as '… a systematic approach to dealing with change, both from the perspective of an organization and on the individual level' (Song, 2009, p. 7).

PROJECT PHASES

To illustrate the key elements of our change process we would like to envision the process in three phases as illustrated by Figure 3.2.

Phase 1: Preparing for the change

The first step of a change process is to understand and define the change initiative: how much change management is necessary for the project?

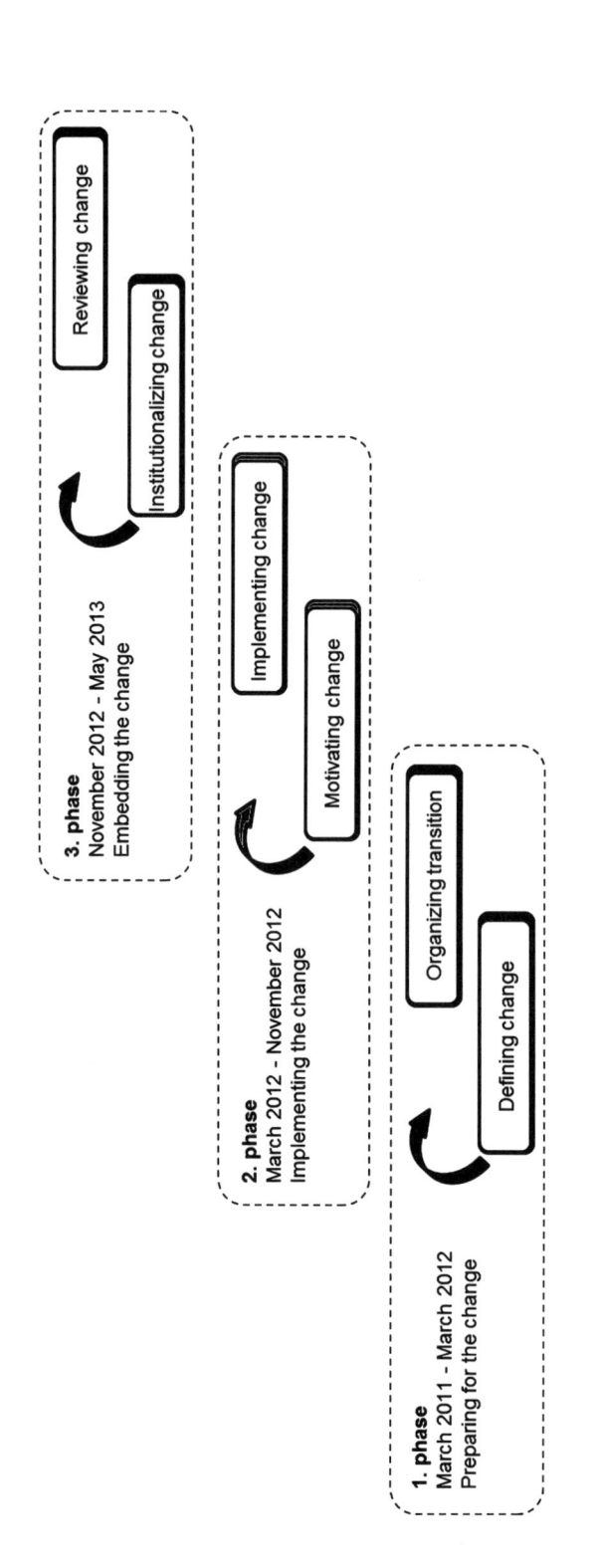

Figure 3.2 The ZBW's change process

To understand the characteristics of the change, the following questions should be answered:

- What is the scope of the change?
- What is being changed – processes, systems, job roles and so on?
- How radical is the change?
- Does the change require the adoption of, for example, completely new processes or skills or are only minor adjustments necessary?

To answer the first questions and to get a deeper understanding of the organization we applied Marvin Weisbord's six-boxes model (Weisbord, 1976). This involves examining the existing structure in order to ascertain what the ideal structure should be for each of the following six dimensions:

- purpose
- structure
- relationships
- rewards and incentives
- leadership
- supporting mechanisms.

Weisbord's six dimensions consider formal and informal structures. The model helps to both identify the interdependencies and bring together the formal structures (which also meet the institution's aims and obligations) with the informal structures that develop through interactions of staff members outside the formal workflows.[1]

Some goals had already been identified from the inefficiencies in the former structure. The *purpose* of our restructuring process was to design a new organizational structure that better supported the delivery of our strategic objectives – in particular, to better integrate our customers' perspectives and their needs into our day-to-day workflows. In addition, we wanted to design internally transparent decision-making structures with flatter hierarchies. However, it is important to agree precisely not only the purposes of the process, but also those purposes that might be important to some people but will not be addressed during the restructuring process. A restructuring process cannot solve every problem arising within an institution. Part of the change management approach is to properly timeline and organize the communication of what constitutes the purposes of the change project and what issues will not be addressed by this effort.

A restructuring process is performed on an organization's *structure*. Therefore, it is necessary to scrutinize the existing structure to find its desiderata. To develop our own optimal structure we first defined those workflows that were not working

---

[1] Cf. Mintzberg (1979) as one example for the concept of informal structure.

well. The explicit consideration of existing formal and informal structures helps to identify both problematic and well-functioning aspects. These should be taken into account in the later stages of the process.

When looking at the *relationships* between existing organizational units, we identified the well-functioning aspects as well as those interactions which we expected to have greater potential for improving coordination, division of labour and communication. In addition, we singled out conflicts that disrupted the interaction of organizational units. This was a starting-point for designing the new formal organizational structure. We merged into one department, for example, all activities related to stock preservation – digital and print – previously located in different organizational units. Examining relationships and interactions also allowed us to draw conclusions about the existing informal structures. As a result, we identified well-functioning workflows which had not previously been reflected in the formal structure. We were then able to consider these workflows when redesigning the structure. That led to a new composition of programme divisions consisting of departments in which staff had already worked very well together.

The dimension of *rewards and incentives* helps strengthen the acceptance of a formal structure for the institution. When we looked at our former structure there was no formal incentive system for those who accepted greater responsibility and management activities. As the structure was very hierarchical there had been no need for management training. Our aim to decentralize management decision-making meant that we needed more managers, so we had to think of ways of rewarding those colleagues who were willing to take on more responsibility. Our solution was to develop a benefit system for those employees who took on management duties within the new organization. The benefit system defines monetary rewards for three explicitly defined management levels: programme division managers, department managers and group managers. Furthermore, change management was crucial again as we identified what training staff would need in order to work in the new structure. Addressing and dealing with these aspects led to increased staff motivation and acceptance of the new structure.

Coming from a strongly hierarchical culture, it was not difficult to identify which managing levels were formally fixed in our system in terms of the *leadership* dimension. As the former structure was outdated, an informal structure was developed in order to fill in the gaps. Thus, some staff members took on managerial functions even though they had not been formally appointed to take them. As a result, decision-making processes developed in parallel to the officially installed structures. These competencies had to be acknowledged in order to encourage staff members' willingness to change. On the one hand, the informal decision structures had to be made formal, if applicable. On the other hand, not all the informal decision-taking was helpful, and some had to be replaced by more efficient formal decision-making processes. To achieve these aims we identified the different levels of management required, including a new team management level. The purpose was to empower all organizational units to do their work and to make decisions that would help them work efficiently. To this end, we clearly defined the responsibilities of each management level. These comprise the approval of holidays as well as the framework in which a broader organizational unit is able to organize and develop its groups and teams strategically. We defined the roles and responsibilities of the different management levels very clearly and made them transparent to all staff.

Supporting mechanisms seem to be quite small and unimportant at first glance. Nevertheless, they are crucial for ensuring an efficient and accepted organizational structure. Mechanisms include meeting structures and processes to facilitate decisions and discussions, as well as supportive measures for control such as budget-monitoring assistance. Analysing these mechanisms is very helpful, even if it turns out that it is not appropriate to establish statutory meeting structures for all organizational units. Indeed, in one unit, efficient collaboration was best supported by deliberately not establishing *any* statutory meeting structures.

In addition to the six dimensions outlined above, the question of who in the organization is being affected by the change (and how) has to be answered. In order to understand this further, we first created a kind of map to illustrate the impact of the change on certain employee groups (see Figure 3.3). After that, we could then identify the changes for each staff member.

Figure 3.3 is, of course, a rough draft, but it may give a good overview on the changes that took place within the organization. For example, it became rather obvious that the anticipated changes would be more radical for the staff working in the more traditional parts of the library ('Collection Development & Metadata' and 'Customer Services & Collection Care' in Figure 3.3). In these programme divisions the structural changes were quite extensive, encompassing new team structures and management levels. As a result, some processes had to be readjusted to the new structure and job roles changed. The general mood in these programme divisions was quite tense, since the employees feared losing responsibilities or tasks – some people even feared that they would lose their jobs even though the day-to-day work itself was not changing at all.

Other units of the organization were only slightly affected, so these employee groups were rather unfazed by the upcoming changes. Knowing which departments would be affected by the restructuring and how was an important basis for planning individual measures that would best fit the employees' needs.

But how can people be convinced of the necessity to change? Change in an organization seldom comes naturally, and people rarely embrace change, especially when it is imposed on them. Instinctively, people adopt habits; they like stability and security. Forcing them off into the unknown might trigger fear of the disadvantages

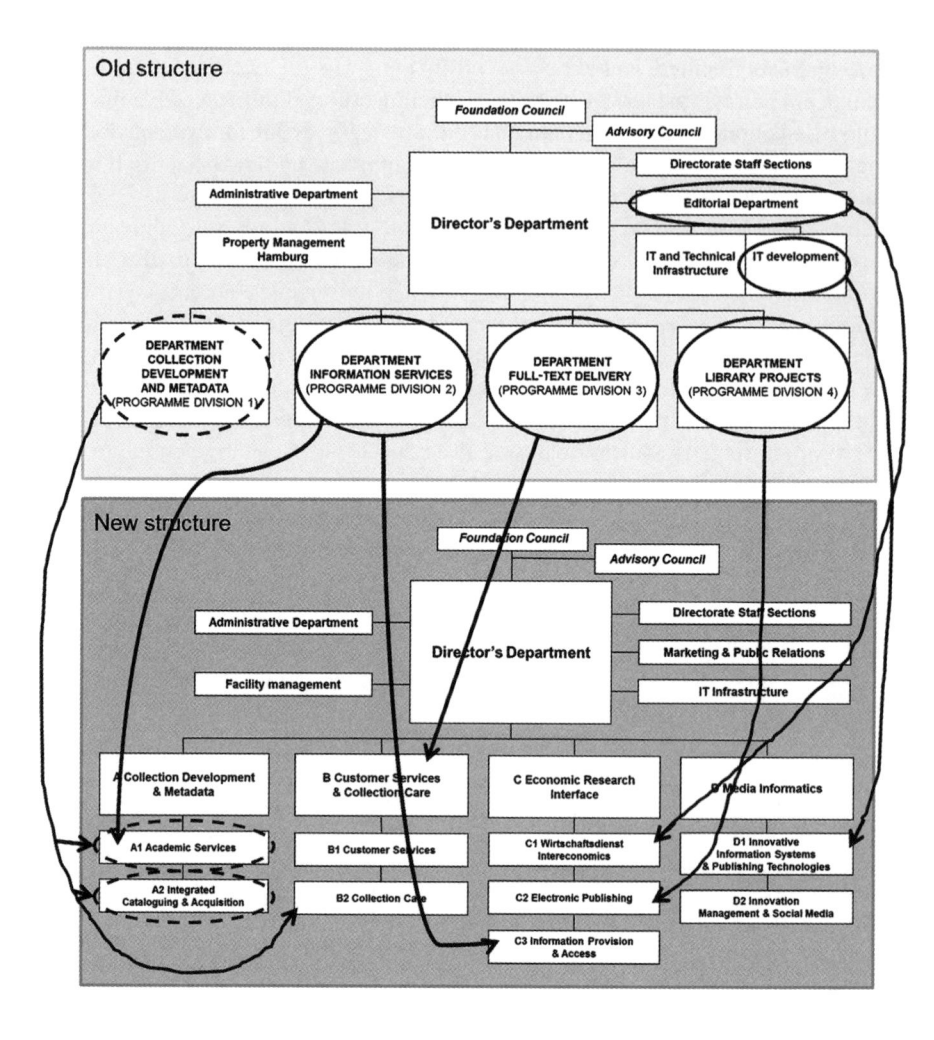

38 BUSINESS SCHOOL LIBRARIES IN THE 21ST CENTURY

Figure 3.3 Change impact diagram

believed to be a result of the change and fear of losing the advantages provided by the status quo. Beckhard and Harris (1987) have developed a change equation that explains how this fear or resistance to change can be overcome:

$D \times V \times F > R$

D = Dissatisfaction with how things are now
Make people feel dissatisfied with the current situation and thereby create the need or the motivation to alter something. The way to get there is to explain why it is undesirable to conduct business in the same way or what is going to happen if we do not change. What are the disadvantages of doing nothing?

As we have already stated earlier in this chapter, we had a strong case for change from the Leibniz evaluation exercise we had gone through. We presented our main challenges and our ways of solving them and, on this basis, the evaluators attested that the ZBW had a promising future and should continue to be funded. Thus, our line of argument was that we had to keep the promises made during the evaluation and that we would not pass the next evaluation if we did not deliver on them.

V = Vision of what is possible
Give a clear vision of what the organization will look like after the change is made. Having destabilized the current situation, a direction to aim for has to be given. This picture of the future state comprises the advantages gained by the change in answering the question: 'How do we remove current disadvantages by making the change?' Everyone affected by the change should be given a clear view of their place in the new organization.

> *A great change vision is something that is easy for people to understand. It can be written usually in a half page, communicated in 60 seconds, is both intellectually solid but has emotional appeal, and it's something that can be understood by the broad range of people that are ultimately going to have to change ... (Kotter, 2011)*

Our change vision had to meet our strategic goals. Our goal is to generate value-added services in a world where information can be found easily and for free via the Internet. To reach this goal, we focus all our activities on the customers' needs. This is our ultimate principle. The change vision was, and is, to be a competent partner to our customers, accompanying them throughout their whole research process. Furthermore, we strive to position the ZBW as a leading national and international highly interconnected infrastructure institution. Amongst our traditional library services, we also provide services for research in economics and business studies (for example, EconStor, EconBiz).

F = First, concrete steps that can be taken towards the vision
In order to outline the major milestones that are intended to be reached, it is crucial to demonstrate the 'practicality of the change'. This is important for keeping people motivated. It is not enough to raise dissatisfaction with the status quo and to give a vision of the future state. The way to get there has to be shown as well. Even though not every step to reach the objectives is known right at the beginning one should be aware of the key elements and communicate them. The plan should comprise the

objectives, measures and a schedule. It should say who is going to be involved and how, and it should offer a communication plan.

We outlined the different phases of the change process to the employees in a roadshow and explained what activities were planned in what timeframe. We introduced the work groups we established to solve specific topics by explaining the background, the objectives, who was going to work in these groups and when we expected the results. In addition, we described when and how the employees would participate in the process and how we were going to keep them informed.

R = Resistance to change
Often, this is described as 'costs of change', meaning what is needed in order make the change happen In this context, costs depict insecurity about the development of one's own situation, fear of losing power or status and so on. To answer this, it is also necessary to know what experiences the organization has already had with other change projects and to identify how much change is concurrently taking place. These two aspects can exert a very negative influence on the current change initiative: if earlier change initiatives failed, then the reasons for that failure need to be analysed and strategies developed to overcome similar obstacles in future. Most important is to address such topics directly in communication with the employees and explain how past mistakes will be avoided in future.

In our case, the organization had already had several experiences with change processes in the past, which we had to be aware of. On the one hand, there had been other reorganization projects that had been planned and announced but ultimately came to nothing. On the other hand, the ZBW had undergone a huge change in 2007 when it merged with the HWWA. Many employees were also well aware that public-sector organizations are not immune to closure. Even though there had been no job losses previously, the fear of redundancy lived on. Another experience from this previous merger was that employee participation in the process was allowed, but most of the outcomes from it were never realized.

These previous experiences were the main reason why we wanted to put more effort into helping the staff during the restructuring process by being as transparent as possible. When we informed the staff about the restructuring plans, the reaction was one of reluctance because of what had happened in the past. Some of the employees were not against it but felt that it was unnecessary as nothing would change anyway. So one important aspect of our communication at that time was first admitting that errors were made in the past and then informing the staff how we wanted to tackle these issues. Furthermore, in past restructuring processes there had been no clearly defined responsibilities for certain aspects of the change process: those who planned the change could step away from their responsibility by not supporting the change in the end.

To set up a clear process and create ownership, we assigned a change manager who developed a project plan outlining the next steps to be taken. The project plan included a timeline with milestones describing the objectives and the expected outcomes of each phase of the project. Later, it included a communication strategy and a strategy for employee participation. The change manager was supported by an external expert supporting the change management process, especially by preparing and moderating the workshops with the staff and by advising managers when they were having to make decisions during the process.

Diverse channels of communication should be used in order to reach as many employees as possible. Direct communication is, of course, the most effective, as this allows people who to directly voice their opinions or concerns. Direct communication can be created by roadshows, workshops, team meetings and so on, but it does have disadvantages, too: not everyone feels comfortable voicing his or her opinion in public or asking what might be perceived as 'silly questions'; not every leader communicates in the same way, so people may receive a differing amount and quality of information. To counterbalance this tendency, other, more formal, communication channels also have to be set up. These may be newsletters, a specific space on the intranet or a feedback mechanism, amongst others.

We agreed on a mixture of different communication channels: presentations from the ZBW Director; workshops for those departments facing the greatest organizational changes; discussion panels and an intranet page containing all information on the change effort. At that point our major aim was to gain readiness for change by communicating the change story ('Why do we have to change? What is going to happen if we do not change? What are we aiming for?') and explaining what steps we were about to take. One important aspect was to show how the employees could participate in the process within the different phases. This was especially important at the very beginning, since we were initially only able to inform about the outcomes produced by several work groups. Later on we were able to allow direct employee participation during workshops where we offered to discuss the new structure. We addressed colleagues directly, gave opportunities to discuss and comment openly or anonymously.

Whenever possible, employees' participation in the change process should be allowed so their commitment to it can be increased. Of course, it is not always possible to involve every person in every decision, but one should at least try to involve them in decisions directly affecting their section.

We believe the following questions need to be answered:

- Who has to be involved?
- In which way do people/groups get involved?
- What is the objective of getting people/groups involved?

- When/at what stage of the process do you involve people/groups
  - during analysis
  - in the decision-making process
  - while developing the implementation plan
  - during implementation
  - during evaluation?

With regard to our own process, we were able to minimize resistance to change by working out a first draft of a new structure within a small group and then subsequently developing the draft further with more and more people. With the gradual introduction of more people, acceptance of the aims of the process and the new structure itself became more profound. At the same time, this approach has delivered an efficient procedure for developing a new structure. The discussion on all levels was more effective when there was an initial "Aunt Sally" draft of the structure as discussions focused on developing this draft further. Before asking for feedback on the drafts we always made clear, at the beginning of each workshop or meeting, which parts of the draft could still be discussed and which aspects we did not want to change. This approach was essential to avoid dissatisfaction from employees, since they were discussing only those topics which they were able to influence.

Another important factor in minimizing resistance to change is to think about what should be preserved. As Jim Collins (1995) says, 'Change is good – but first, know what should never change'. This will help give direction and to a certain extent maintain organizational stability and is psychologically important if employees are to be opened up for change. As stated earlier, making people feel uncomfortable with the current situation is important to get them moving, but the process can grind to a halt if direction and continuity are not provided as well. In communicating the vision one should always include what is going to stay as it is.

So the formula $D \times V \times F > R$ states that if one is able to

- raise dissatisfaction with the current situation,
- create a clear vision of the future state and
- develop a plausible plan to reach the scope or vision,

it is possible to outweigh the costs of the change for the people and thus minimize resistance to change.

Of course, the factors described above cannot be quantified to get a mathematical result. But the formula helps to determine which factors are crucial to get people engaged. It can be used:

- as a tool for analysis at the beginning of the change process or
- to identify the key elements of a change story or
- to plan how specific stakeholders can be convinced of the change initiative.

One of the first tasks of the project was to identify the key colleagues who should be involved in the organizational review stage – this helped immensely in establishing a common sense of why and how the change should work. We included the heads of departments and groups in the review. These leaders have been crucial for the whole process as they were in charge of the change and supported it throughout.

The first phase was a good pilot exercise for establishing how successful we had been in keeping the change equation $D \times V \times F > R$ in balance. We use the word 'pilot' here because the leaders represented the staff as well. They have different work histories in the ZBW, different views on where the institution should be going and different personalities. When doing the organizational review we built the basis for a common understanding and agreement on what had to be done. We identified the negative aspects that were dissatisfying to one or more groups (D). We thought of what the organization would look like when the process would be finished (V). By doing the organizational diagnosis, we took the first concrete steps towards this vision (F). In the end, we all had the same understanding of the needs, steps and purpose of the restructuring process. All the leaders acted as multipliers, promoting the restructuring amongst staff. With this method, any resistance to a new organizational structure could never grow too strong.

We set up working groups to find solutions for those crucial workflows and interactions between organizational units which had been identified as unsatisfactory. One working group defined the management responsibilities of each management level and another working group discussed the management bodies, such as the management board or board of department heads, as well as the necessity of statutory meeting structures.

We finished this process with a central meeting in which we informed all employees about the final draft of the organizational structure at department level, the results of the working groups and other crucial decisions. This central meeting was followed by workshops for every unit of the ZBW within the existing structure: the aim was to gain a common understanding of the new structure and to explain how the structural changes would impact on employees individually. Another objective was to ask colleagues what needed to be done and prepared in advance as a prerequisite for working efficiently in the new structure. In some cases, the leaders had individual meetings with those employees most affected in order to explain in more detail how their role was going to change and to offer help in dealing with it. If an employee had to change departments, the managers involved had to prepare the transfer together and both held individual meetings with the employee.

When the preparatory phase on the restructuring level resulted in a formal structure proposal, the change initiative gained momentum. The main purpose now was to discuss the new structure with all staff and to gain acceptance for the change.

Phase 2: Implementing the change

From a change management perspective, the key element of this phase was to motivate staff to implement the change whereas the main objective of the project management phase of the process was to fine-tune the formal organization structure and enable staff to work within the new structure. In retrospect, these two phases worked very well together. We conducted workshops in several new departments to give emotional and practical support. The workshops' aims were: to dedicate time to discuss the change; to give staff the opportunity to give feedback to management; to improve the change's credibility and acceptance among staff; and to begin the metamorphosis into the new organizational structure.

A general format for the workshops was developed to start with. This included group work and capturing the feelings of staff about the new structures before and after the workshops. As both the departments and the groups of staff differ, we then needed to differentiate the workshops' outlines without losing the overall purpose. This was just as applicable when a whole existing department was switching 'as is' to another department or programme division. For example, our bookbindery was merely moved from one programme division to another to bring together all preservation activities. Within the bookbindery, nothing had to be restructured. For the "Information Services" area, it seemed suitable to do the workshops in the new departments straight away as their previous existing informal structure was confirmed by the new structure. Thus, we were able to let staff participate in the fine-tuning of the department's workflows. This level of participation was not possible in the old structure.

Some organizational units did not change in terms of their composition of people and tasks, but changed completely in terms of their internal structure. Our Cataloguing and Acquisition Department, for example, existed as an organizational unit in the old structure as well. However, it had no internal substructure even though, with more than 60 employees, it was the largest department. In the new structure this unit became a department with an internal structure comprising five groups. The aim was to make the department both more efficient and manageable. The first workshop for this department had already been held during the preparation phase in order to involve staff as much as possible in the early stages of the process in the hope of to increasing credibility and acceptance of the new structure. The subsequent feedback and discussions were of great assistance to the managers in structuring the department more efficiently, and they were able to apply some of the informal structures that already existed. Furthermore, most of the processes, like getting a book from order to shelf had already been mapped out to a very detailed level and proved so efficient that the processes did not need to be changed at all.

The results of the workshops helped us give individual practical support to a group or individual – for example, by defining participation structures. Another result was the agreement on milestones between departmental managers and their staff. The workshops were also intended to establish a common understanding of the role and purpose of the organizational unit itself. The agreements between management and staff on milestones were a crucial aspect of the whole phase. Although it was mostly homework for management, the milestones had to be realistic to be achievable and also had to meet the needs of staff. In retrospect, it was very helpful to have a fixed day as a starting date for the new structure. Many agreements on milestones consisted of two parts – what had to be accomplished before this date (15 March 2012) and which milestones had to be accomplished at a specific time afterwards. This not only helped managers gain quick wins, but also helped staff see that all of their needs were being recognized and dealt with at some point in time. However, our experience was that the milestones after 15 March 2012 should have been dated within a certain timeframe not exceeding 3–6 months. Discussing the milestones leads to a compromise between management ('I need a realistic timeframe') and staff ('Why can't this aspect be resolved tomorrow?'), enhancing the understanding not only between them, but also of the process of change in general.

Having agreed these milestones, the management had to incorporate them into their plans in order to accomplish them in time, and staff had to refer to them in order to monitor the change process and so reinforce their own willingness to change. In retrospect, it is crucial to document and communicate the accomplishments as well as delays. It may be that delays surface aspects that have not previously been considered but are crucial to the whole process. We have documented the agreements and reported on the process regularly in every department.

When the workshops and meetings were finished and milestones agreed, we presented the new structures and the aims of the organizational units as a whole to all staff members. On the start date for the new structure we communicated the new organizational chart, indicating every staff member so that everybody could see where they and their colleagues fitted into the new structure.

Phase 3: Embedding the change

Even though the change initiative might be implemented successfully, it is not a given that the change will last. It is all too easy for people to fall back into familiar habits instead of applying new work procedures. In order to guarantee long-term effects, measures have to be planned to embed and thus stabilize the change.

At the ZBW, although we have worked in the new structure since 15 March 2012, that was not the end of the restructuring process. On the one hand, management posts had to be staffed, milestones had to be accomplished and structures had to spring to life. On the other hand, most of the staff had to get to grips with new structures, maybe realizing that much of the day-to-day-work was the same. This third phase of a change process is where everything has to find its place. We held further workshops to help staff and management form teams and define tasks. There were even new responsibilities for managers in existing posts, necessitating the organization of training sessions for new managers. Once all the management posts had been filled, we developed and announced a system of incentives for unit heads to further strengthen their position within the institution and to reward their acceptance of greater responsibility. In addition, we started a process to establish a rewards system[2] for all staff members who carried out excellent work in addition to their normal duties. This will be applied in autumn 2013.

After a period of operating the new structure, the monitoring phase should be completed with a review to identify those aspects of the structure where the theories and plans did not work in practice and would therefore require alteration. This could be done by conducting workshops in departments which faced the greatest change as well by identifying those inefficiencies within the new structure that need to be optimized. In our case, a staff unit will now become a department within our programme division of media informatics as we want to bundle our research activities in this programme division. Even though we have already had to adjust some parts of the new organizational structure, these adjustments nevertheless confirm the success of our change project, proving that our structure is sufficiently flexible to react to new needs and developments even from outside the ZBW.

LESSONS LEARNED

Change affects staff more than management can imagine. Normally, managers have more detailed information on what is going on in the institution. Even though there are communication strategies to keep all staff members up-to-date, it is difficult to achieve complete information-sharing and facilitate a common understanding of this information. Therefore, change management is very much centred on communication and involvement of staff so that they accept the change.

As already pointed out, change affects staff in different ways, depending on the content of change and the extent to which staff are involved with it. This means that change

---

2 To date, this system is still in discussion between the directorate and staff council. Furthermore, it is undergoing a legal check. The aim of the agreement is to establish a transparent and accepted routine to reward innovative ideas as well as excellent work in all areas of the ZBW.

management is never going to be an 'out-of-the-box' concept that can be applied to all situations wherever change is involved. Furthermore, in our own restructuring process we tried to define standard structures for workshops, communication strategies and so on, but learned very quickly that these common structures had to be altered to incorporate the specific needs of organizational units and to reflect the personal characters of the staff members involved. Ultimately, our lesson learned was to define common structures and purposes of workshops and communication measures in mutual agreement with key leaders. Whenever alterations to workshop formats and communication methods had to be made, this was solely due to the different personalities and situations in the departments involved. Alterations were made to generate credibility and to involve staff as efficiently as possible. As is ever the case: 'The exception proves the rule.'

The main recommendation arising from our own reorganization process is to take your time. The more change is involved the more time is needed for staff to become accustomed to it. This investment in time pays off handsomely in terms of acceptance and efficiency. Nevertheless, it is crucial to communicate and then stick to specific dates like starting and finishing points of phases. When planning changes like a restructuring process, be aware that this process cannot be repeated. Furthermore, because so many measures imply change for staff members, it is crucial to be alert to change fatigue amongst staff. Change fatigue will lead to a lack of acceptance of, and less willingness to participate in, future change projects. A well-planned change management project, in combination with management awareness of change and its impact on staff, helps a library develop further to best meet its customers' and funders' needs and requirements. It will also ensure that library employees are sufficiently well motivated to accept change and come to terms with it within a new structure.

REFERENCES

Beckhard, R. and Harris, R.T., 1987. *Organizational Transitions: Managing Complex Change.* Reading, MA: Addison-Wesley.

Collins, J.C., 1995. Change is Good—But First, Know What Should Never Change [online]. At: http://money.cnn.com/magazines/fortune/fortune_archive/1995/05/29/203150/index.htm (accessed 21 March 2013).

Kotter, J., 2011. How to Create a Powerful Vision for Change [online]. At: http://www.forbes.com/sites/johnkotter/2011/06/07/how-to-create-a-powerful-vision-for-change/ (accessed 21 March 2013).

Leibniz Association, 2013. The Evaluation Procedure Conducted by the Senate of the Leibniz Association [online]. At: http://www.leibniz-gemeinschaft.de/en/about-us/evaluation/the-evaluation-procedure-conducted-by-the-senate-of-the-leibniz-association/ (accessed 21 March 2013).

Mintzberg, H., 1979. *The Structuring of Organizations: A Synthesis of the Research*. Englewood Cliffs, NJ: Prentice-Hall.

Song, X., 2009. Why Do Change Management Strategies Fail? Illustrations with Case Studies. *Journal of Cambridge Studies*, 4(1), 6–15.

Weisbord, M.R., 1976. Organizational Diagnosis: Six Places to Look for Trouble with or without a Theory. *Group & Organization Studies*, 1(4), 430–47.

CHAPTER 4

BUSINESS SCHOOL LIBRARIES ON THE RADAR: NOT SEEN AND NOT HEARD?

ANDY PRIESTNER

> *'Unless we give our funding bodies better and more compelling reasons to support libraries, they will be forced by economic reality to stop doing so.'*

So wrote Rick Anderson in a bleak but realistic article in the *Journal of Academic Librarianship* (2011, p. 90). His call was subsequently taken up by the ACRL Research Planning and Review Committee, who penned the '2012 Top Ten Trends in Academic Libraries' article in *College & Research Libraries News* and designated effective communication as one of the top priorities for academic librarians today, stating: 'Librarians must be able to convert the general feelings of goodwill towards the library to effective communication to all stakeholders that clearly articulates its value to the academic community' (2012, pp. 311–12). It is a stance with which few of us business school librarians could or would disagree; however, achieving this in practice is far from easy.

Despite the fact that we all work in business schools with lecturers who are experienced management educators – and, therefore (one would hope), effective management practitioners with a good grasp of effective communication techniques – our institutions rarely, if ever, operate as beacons of communication best practice. Why communication within business schools is so poor, possibly poorer than in other academic library sectors, could easily take up a chapter on its own and would no doubt refer to the doubtful strategy of putting research-focused academics in charge of an organization that has to make clear business decisions and, more importantly, a profit. What is pertinent and relevant for us to consider here is what this endemic ineffective communication means for us business librarians, especially given our position near the bottom of the business school 'food chain'. It is a situation which makes our task of effective communication upwards and across our institutions very challenging indeed. To my knowledge, very few business librarians, in the UK at least, have either a voice or influence at a strategic level in their organizations; some do not even find there is room for their presence at management or research committees, and in fact a great many of us spend time simply trying to make sure our existence is appreciated or, in some cases, remembered at all.

There are a number of interrelated reasons why we struggle to be heard. Perhaps paramount amongst these is the age-old problem of outdated and traditional perceptions of what librarians actually do – those in charge still struggle to see our library services as anything more than a room containing books. And this view persists despite the swathes of electronic resources we now consistently and expertly deliver, the engaging teaching we offer in the classroom, and successful forays into new media which, had they been championed by our colleagues in marketing or IT, would have been welcomed with open arms. Another possible reason is the fact that, more often than not, business school libraries are regarded as things that 'tick along very nicely thank you' and therefore do not require much attention. They are rarely complained about, they are not regarded as problem departments and they are ignored as a result. This perception derives in part from a considerable underestimation of the complexities of modern library services. Collection development, for example, continues to be a minefield of uncertainty as we juggle print and electronic delivery and all manner of new technology options for accessing content. Similarly, the multitudinous implications of the open access movement, which has seen us librarians in the thick of the action, are woefully misunderstood.

Underestimation of complexity aside, there is the equally galling problem of polite disinterest. I am reminded of a time when, halfway through a term, I met a faculty member in the corridor, who told me he was not enjoying teaching the current cohort on a course for which he was the programme director. When I concurred that they had not been an easy group this year, it took him some time to understand that I shared his opinion because I had direct experience of them as I, despite being the librarian, taught them regularly too (in fact I remember checking and, by that point in the term, I had more teaching hours under my belt with them than him!). When this same academic disinterest leads to the library being forgotten when relevant projects in which we should be involved (or, given our professional skills, should lead), are discussed, it becomes damaging as well as galling – and not just to the library but to the school as a whole. How many projects can you think of for which we librarians could have usefully – and cheaply – contributed our expertise, only for other departments, or consultants, to be drafted in instead? A number, I would wager.

New policies or decisions which impinge upon, or apparently disregard, the services we provide are also a result of this apathetic disengagement. Common examples include:

- promises of database access to 'friends of the business school' which could put us in breach of contract if actioned because database suppliers would class them as commercial users;
- last-minute decisions to offer new courses without any consideration of budget for appropriate books or data;
- the always painful discovery that an academic has been negotiating access to data for which we already pay an annual subscription.

All these examples are far too familiar, but can we do anything to stop them occurring? Can we get on the radar of our business school so that we are remembered, involved or, better still, understood? Experience and a healthy dose of realism would suggest that the latter is unlikely, but surely it would be a grave mistake to just accept the status quo and not try harder to be heard?

In recent years the global economic recession has prompted swingeing cuts at most higher education establishments, and libraries have been very much in the firing line, perhaps partly because we're considered to be soft targets – 'nice to have', rather than essential, unlike other business school activities. But how much does each of us actually do to counter or seek to address such an assertion within our institutions? Are we ready to level strong contrary arguments and fight our corner when required? As with the time spent battling for recognition and understanding, are such attempts to prove our value equally fruitless?

In this chapter I will seek to argue that although we may think we currently communicate enough within our respective business schools and that our excellent services speak for themselves, we actually live in an age in which there is no room for this sort of complacency and we must make better use of the many and varied communication channels open to us.

PRE-EMPTIVE ACTION

At the heart of the problem is a dangerous tendency amongst academic librarians to sit back and wait to be asked for information about our services: a tendency to wait until statistics on loans, enquiries and database use or a weekly breakdown of typical staff activities are directly requested; to wait until a new and innovative service is noticed rather than promoting it extensively; to wait until someone else identifies that a project or approach we currently undertake is perhaps not the best use of staff time. Business schools are becoming more and more accountable. These days, the bean-counters are very much in charge – very few deans or directors have no accounting or operations management background – and they only want to know facts and figures, not how you, or others, feel about the service or how you 'think' it is doing. At the very least I would advise that we need to be collecting the following key statistics:

- footfall to the physical library
- visitors to the library's electronic presence (whether it is a website, portal or blog)
- usage of databases
- cost of database subscriptions relative to use and each other
- loans and percentage use of printed collection

- usage of e-books – downloads and views
- the number of enquiries received and fulfilled by staff in person, by email, or instant chat.

However, it is not enough just to collate this data and wait to be asked for it. It is far better to ensure that the people who need to know this stuff are informed, at least once a year, of these top-level statistics, *before* they ask for them: a pre-emptive strike, if you like. I am convinced of the value of this pre-emptive approach because of my own painful experiences at Oxford University's Saïd Business School and Templeton College (which was responsible for management library provision prior to the institution of Saïd), where the services we were operating were regularly subject to the whim of senior management decisions, taken on the basis of false assumptions, because academics just did not have this sort of data at their fingertips. When academics scrutinized our services we had plenty of qualitative information to share but not nearly enough quantitative data, and, quite naturally, they were far more interested in the latter.

Here at Cambridge I currently present this vital quantitative data in the form of an annual report and think very carefully about its audience. I use images throughout the report to sell my service. In fact, I think of it more as an in-house marketing brochure rather than a flat management document. I see it as key that I do not just use this platform to drily report our activities. I explain why, for example, we have decided to install a proxy server – in order to offer users seamless access to databases – not just the bald fact that we have installed one: this way my decisions are better understood and appreciated. Although my reports tend to be rather long – running to 10–12 pages – I include a one-page executive summary at the start, containing all the key statistics to ensure that the important top-level messages will be read. Although I see my annual report/statistics bulletin as a significant tool, I do not regard it as a panacea. I back the report up with: verbal summaries in staff–student or library committees, again presented in digestible and eyecatching form; other reports on projects our service has undertaken; or student survey results, which help justify the time and energies expended on strategic service choices. Beyond this, I am always on the look-out to hold forth about my service whenever and wherever the opportunity presents itself, detailing its value, its purpose and its direction, with a view to overturning traditional misconceptions and challenging narrow thinking.

Although I think that the collation of facts and statistics is essential, this is not to say that qualitative comments on service are redundant. I keep, and regularly delve into, a praise folder that I regularly quote from and liberally sprinkle across the many reports I write. However, what I have come to understand about this type of evidence of service value is that it will only be admitted as ancillary information to back up an argument or approach, and will never succeed in supporting it on its own.

BEWARE 'TAKING YOUR FOOT OFF THE GAS'

A few years ago I was told by my manager at Judge – the Director of Operations, who reports directly to our Dean – that we had all got the message about the service I was offering and that perhaps I did not need to continue to fight the library corner in quite the same enthusiastic, and full-on, vein. Although I was pleased that my message was being regarded as clear and 'out there', I chose to disregard his advice, which was effectively to 'tone it down', because I just do not think we, as librarians, can afford to do this. As I have already outlined, we are always going to be high up on the list of soft targets in the event of funding cuts, and our profession and our activities are always going to be largely misunderstood. It is my view that as soon as we 'take our foot off the gas' and stop communicating our service offering, then the old stereotypical thinking and the familiar misconceptions about libraries and librarians, which are ever-present and merely lying dormant, will quickly reassert themselves. In workplace meetings there are always going to be colleagues present for whom the penny has not yet dropped. And, for those who already have a decent grasp of the library's role, there is absolutely no harm in reinforcing the message. Another reason why I chose to ignore the advice of my line manager is that business schools generally have a high staff turnover, and this means that there is always someone new to educate and inform.

IS YOUR ELEVATOR PITCH READY?

Of course, sometimes it is difficult for librarians to get into important meetings and to get quality time with deans and other key faculty staff; this is one of the main reasons why we should always be ready to share our vision for our service with them on the off-chance that we meet them in a corridor, while getting coffee, or in an elevator. For all of these situations, it's a very sensible idea to have an off-the-cuff elevator pitch ready, with which we can sell the library and ourselves. The pitch should not be too rehearsed or too structured and, most importantly, should feel natural to say.

So what would my own elevator pitch sound like? Well I would probably furnish the listener with some interesting information such as the percentage increase of visitors to our information and library website coupled with the interesting fact that physical footfall to our information centre is also on the rise – proving that we are getting the technology right but that the physical library still has its place. I might also talk about how we have now bought pretty much as many e-books as are currently available in business and management and that we would like more of them, but publishers are not prepared to release the textbook titles we need for fear of losing print revenues – proving that we are often constrained by problems and complexities that prevent us from going as far as we would like. Another likely topic might be an instance of technical progress, such as our instant chat enquiry service and its popularity with students – proving both our innovative approach and interest in better meeting student needs. Another tack might be to talk about a recent teaching session that went well – an important reminder of our activities beyond the library walls. It is simply a case of identifying aspects of a library's service that might engage, interest or perhaps even surprise the listener.

CHAMPIONS AND RELATIONSHIP-BUILDING

Of course, one of the most effective means of getting the message across about the value of our services is to have others present it, rather than ourselves. A faculty member's words in defence of our service and offerings naturally carry more weight than our own. So how do we win these champions? Occasionally there are academic staff who are already self-avowed library champions, but these are few and far between and sometimes they can have a negative impact if they are supporters of a more traditional library model than the one currently being offered. More often than not, we have to win champions afresh by offering them genuinely excellent support that surpasses their expectations. In my experience this is not as hard as it sounds as expectations are usually much, much lower than they should be. The difficult part is actually establishing that they need the help in the first place. It is not always helpful to generalize – something I will explore later in this chapter – but, generally speaking, academics are busy and often shy and private people, self-starters, who are used to researching independently. There are, however, several ways of connecting with their needs: a personal one-to-one induction for new academic starters, explaining that we are always there to help them with their teaching and research; direct marketing to academics and researchers (a leaflet or email detailing all the time-saving things we can do for them); suggested attendance at a faculty group subject meeting to sell our wares; or simply personably passing the time of the day with them whenever our paths cross. Of course, the hope is that a particularly productive encounter with a member of academic staff will lead to recommendations and others will surely follow.

Chris Powis, Head of Library and Learning Services at the UK's University of Northampton, regularly gives a fascinatingly insightful interactive presentation to librarians in which he asks his audience to identify the characteristics of professors, faculty and teaching staff. Hearty responses always come thick and fast as words like 'difficult', 'annoying', 'uninterested' are shouted out, which Chris duly scribes on a flipchart. Less negative responses are also suggested, such as 'time-poor' and 'overworked'. Chris then deftly turns the tables as he asks the audience what they would say of us librarians. As well as 'helpful', 'weird' and 'quiet', some of the same words used to describe faculty staff often come up, such as 'difficult' and 'annoying'. Chris's summation of this name-calling exercise is that we are all too eager to accept our preconceptions of our work colleagues and assign stereotypical labels that prevent us from connecting before we have even tried. In reality, while there may be some commonalities between academic staff and librarians, within our groupings we are all very different people, and we should not assume that academics are difficult, uninterested or too busy to talk to us. The opportunity is there to discard the labels, connect unconditionally and build a working relationship. Whether we are willing to admit it or not, most of us do not engage or connect with academics half as much as we should or could, myself included, and yet the rewards if we do are obvious. And, do not forget, they are rewarded too, with a support hotline straight into the library service. Everybody wins.

While academics are obvious candidates as library supporters, administrative staff such as programme heads and managers are perhaps less so, but given their close and regular contact with faculty and involvement in course design we would be missing a trick if we didn't also reach out to these colleagues and show them what the library can do for them. They present another opportunity for the library to be remembered and involved.

SHOW, DON'T TELL

One of my favourite mottos is 'Show, don't tell', and I am convinced that it can be gainfully applied to the library environment in respect of our approach to communication. When describing their services, librarians have traditionally been very good at packaging their offering in terms of total book stock, number of database subscriptions and opening hours (although, as I have stated, this is as far as quantitative data-gathering usually goes) rather than unpacking these components to explain how our service can actually help our users and what the specific end-result will be for those who do choose to utilize us. Instead of spending time generically promoting the 'broad and exciting range of resources we offer', we should be stopping and thinking about what our users can do with the tools we offer and selling the end-result – for example, 'improving your research' or 'working more productively'. As well as selling the result rather than the tool, we should – as far as we are able – also show it in action: using Feedly to gather blogposts of relevance to their subject area or a database-alerting function which matches their research query. In other words, we should be ready to practically demonstrate both our value and the value of our products. This way, we can far more directly engender engagement and appreciation of what it is that we, and our resources, can do for them. It sounds simple, but it is all too easy to retreat back to those broad-brush generic descriptions which mean that users have to work far too hard to understand how they could usefully employ our services. It prompts some, of course, to give up before they have started.

WHAT'S IN A NAME?

The debate over the names we use to describe ourselves and our physical spaces has raged for some 20 years now. In the 1990s there was a definite shift away from 'libraries' to 'learning resource centres', and we spent the next 10 years reassuring our users that, despite our strange new monikers, we were indeed still the library and could help them. The opening scene of the first episode of the excellently observed Australian comedy series *The Librarians* depicts a flashy learning resource centre, a title that is proclaimed in expensively engraved glass on the exterior of the building. The picture then scans across the glass to a sheet of A4 paper clumsily taped to the window, with the word 'Library' scrawled in felt-tip (*The Librarians*, 2007). The 2000s saw most of us embrace the term 'library' again, although personally I was quite happy to buck the trend and rename our physical space at Judge – which had never been called anything other than a 'library' – the 'Information Centre', while concurrently adopting the umbrella name 'Information and Library Services' for our overall offering. I made this decision because whatever way you look at it, the word 'library' still comes with heaps and heaps of unhelpful baggage. Anyone who is still clinging to the romantic notion that the word 'library' can be reclaimed to mean more than just books, only needs to open a newspaper or turn on the television to find that society at large still thinks that all we librarians do is stamp, shelve and shush. Unfortunately, the views of business school faculty and staff are not so very different from society at large and if we call ourselves 'library', whatever we do and say, our stakeholders are going to think books first and all the other stuff we do second (if at all) and make judgements and decisions accordingly.

Did the name-change here help? For one thing, it highlighted just how disarmingly conventional people's perceptions of the library were. After it was announced, several teaching staff felt the need to approach me and tell me, almost tearfully, that they loved books. I replied, 'I do too. You should see my home, bookshelf in every room, even the toilet.' They just could not see that their passion for books was completely irrelevant and their misapprehension precisely the reason why I instituted the change: I am operating with a £350,000 per annum information resources budget, of which 88 per cent is spent on electronic resources, and yet a large percentage of faculty still thought we were about books. Some of our more 'switched-on' staff were pleased to hear that we were now a more professional and corporate-sounding information centre; however, I received comments from several administrative colleagues along the lines of 'if were honest with ourselves we were not really about information and that this was simply a branding exercise'! Staggering but true, and a very clear indication of how much of a mountain we all still have to climb. Retitling a library service can therefore serve as a reminder of our true purpose and activities.

ESCAPING THE ECHO CHAMBER

Over the past three years, here in the UK, there has been much talk about how librarians are operating within an 'echo chamber'. Chief exponent of this idea, Ned Potter, an academic liaison librarian at the University of York, UK, has been arguing that librarians are mounting a good defence of their worth and value but that these ideas are being shared in, and bounced around, a closed space – or echo chamber – of like-minded individuals (Potter, 2010). He argues that this preaching to the converted, however well-meaning, is not furthering understanding of our profession as it stands today at all and that we should be engaging instead in advocacy beyond librarianship. He makes a great point – a point which is directly relevant to our communication problems within our business schools. ABLD, EBSLG and APBSLG are excellent for sharing expertise and innovation, but they are also echo chambers and we should be careful not to complacently assume that because we have a collective understanding of what librarians and librarianship stand for today, this is a matter somehow understood, by osmosis perhaps, by key figures in our institutions. Ned also makes the point that we should not be directing our advocacy energies towards our already devoted patrons, but instead to those who do not currently make use of our service. When I first started work as the head librarian at Judge, I was told by my new team that everyone loved the library and that were really very few problems for me to solve. I felt differently. For one thing, the physical library seemed strangely quiet to me, with only about a third of the desks occupied at any one time; for another, there were far fewer requests for database assistance than I had been used to at the equivalent business school library in Oxford. As time went by, I discovered that there was indeed a contented core of library patrons, but these were rather traditional book-focused users. Little or no energy was being put in to reach the swathes of extant non-library users at the business school – those people who were uncomfortable with, or disinterested in, using a library. Over time, we have slowly but surely reached them, with both footfall to our physical library and visitors to our electronic platform having more than doubled over the past five years. Of those users, academic staff are now very prominent, and database enquiries have rocketed. Although we now offer a service that is undeniably being used by members of the business school who have no natural predisposition to visit a library, I am certain there are many more potential library users out there.

UNBEATABLE COMPETITION?

In their support of non-business subjects, librarians have all but accepted that Google Scholar and so-called discovery platforms have won the day and are the way forward for libraries. However, in business we have many non-journal databases that do not easily translate to, or work on, such platforms and can only ever be effectively searched via the interfaces designed by database suppliers. For this reason, we business librarians must continue to offer a way into these databases that is sufficiently engaging, quick and seamless to draw in our staff and students. Of course, now more than ever before, we are facing intense competition for our users' attention from 'all-singing and dancing' websites or apps, with their slick and eyecatching look and feel, and the reality of today's consumers who have a startlingly short concentration span, are trained to scan rather than read and are drawn to colour and sparkle like oversized magpies. So what, if anything, can we do about it?

In essence, we must stop doing all those things that come naturally to librarians: detail, comprehensive descriptions, asides, wordy explanations and more detail. Yes, our highly detailed approach means that the engaged user we imagine when we write support materials will have absolutely all the information they need about the product or service we are describing, but the problem is that these users are almost entirely mythical. And the grim reality is that our content is not being read by nearly enough of our users. So what is the alternative? For one thing, we need to learn to write more journalistically. Not necessarily in soundbites, but certainly in punchier sentences rather than heavy paragraphs. We also need to use high-quality images that sell the same message as, and reinforce, our text. In addition, as I mentioned earlier, we need to explain the result of using the tool or database in question, rather than expounding the dry facts. Here at Judge we redesigned our website, actually a WordPress blog, using these tenets and have held intra-team training sessions and workshops to improve both our written attempts to engage and skills at sourcing appropriate imagery. The result is our very popular website which received 93,000 visitors last academic year, one of the most visited of all of the pages on our business school's website. Another crucial aspect of this success was communication with the site's users in focus groups to explore usability, layout and content expectations. The outcome was a site that was not built *for* our users, but *with* our users. This has ensured that it communicates with them effectively.

MISUSE OF EMAIL

No chapter on communication would be complete without mention of what I believe to be the most misused communication channel of our times: email. Although it is clearly our primary information channel, easily beating face-to-face communication in terms of frequency, that does not excuse using the facility to send out untargeted, wordy and dull emails, because '[i]n pursuit of "inbox zero" today's stakeholders will guiltlessly delete generic emails from library staff regardless of their content' (Potter, 2012, p. 162). Faculty in particular admit to deleting without compunction. For this reason, we need to stop spending so much time crafting a lengthy explanation and exhortations to use our products and services and instead send pithy, jargon-free emails, which grab attention and are digested, even if realistically they are only skim-read. We should also stop relying on email almost exclusively. We need to mix up our communication channels, so our message is received through different mediums. This way, we communicate on a variety of platforms and interface with the user on their preferred medium rather than expecting them to sift for our content on a platform on which they are already completely overwhelmed with content.

I recently crafted an exercise which I employed at the Danish Research Librarians 2013 winter conference to demonstrate that, even when emails are read, very little information is retained. The exercise involved a very detailed librarian-penned email written for students and intended to introduce a library service at a fictitious university. The email was distributed to three volunteers from the audience, each of whom would have different amounts of time to read the email – 10 seconds, 20 seconds, and 45 seconds respectively – thereby representing different attention spans. After their time was up the volunteers were asked to answer questions about what they had retained from the email. The highest score was 1.5 points out of a possible 6, achieved by the volunteer who had spent the longest time reading. The other scores were '1' and '0'. Before the conference, I carried out the exercise with my own team, and exactly the same scores were recorded. In both instances the volunteers were actively seeking to digest and retain data, and yet less than a third of the message content was remembered, even by the person who had time to read the whole email. If so little is retained when librarians – trained to gather and synthesize information – read emails, just how much of our content is actually reaching non-librarian audiences?

EMBRACING NEW MEDIA

Perhaps the most obvious new communication channel that deserves our attention is Twitter, especially insofar as academics might employ it, to disseminate their research, establish their expertise as they comment on world business affairs, find individuals researching similar topics and potentially build a dynamic professional network that would otherwise have been hidden from view. Because of channels like Twitter and the abundance of available productivity and cloud storage tools, now when I recruit new members to my team I actively seek candidates who have a keen interest in new and social media and place this awareness above the many more traditional components in my selection criteria. My reasoning is straightforward – an ambition to have my service exploit all the varied and different information avenues and channels available to us, with a view to better reaching the whole business school community. By choosing to build presences on these platforms and establishing ourselves as social media gurus and new technology experts into the bargain, we have taken a new and, to some, surprising position within our institution. Some faculty have questioned why we are now engaged in Twitter, Prezi and blogging workshops, but, more often than not, these have been the same faculty who think that all librarians do is maintain a printed book collection, so it has not caused me to lose much sleep or question this new direction. Others have applauded the way we have 'filled an information gap' within our institution and have understood that we are information professionals as well as librarians and therefore well placed to advise on presenting and sharing information. What is more, my team have very much enjoyed the variety and fun involved in exploring and maintaining these new mediums and have all risen to the challenge beautifully. However, there has been a rather large fly in the ointment, or rather two flies: the reaction of our IT and marketing departments.

COLLABORATION OVER COMBAT

If I am completely honest, my first reaction to the news that IT and marketing were bewildered and upset by our repositioning as social and new media gurus was one of anger and frustration. I reflected that, unlike us, neither of those departments had had the wit or the foresight to investigate these new opportunities. Furthermore, we were, as several academics had asserted, only filling a gap with our teaching and advice in these new areas. What I had underestimated, however, was just how challenged these groups felt by both our confidence and our expertise. Part of it was, quite naturally, the familiar confusion around why we were not shelving books instead and a definite feeling that we were encroaching on their territory, coupled perhaps with a wish that we would behave more like our film and television counterparts. I was called to account for myself, and our new sessions on social media, by my boss, who informed me that our actions had upset a few people. On discussion with the IT manager, common ground was found, but only after a full and frank discussion about the modern-day convergence between IT and library functions, especially in terms of the web and new media, and the stark fact (which was difficult for him to swallow) that technology is no longer the sole preserve of IT guys, but available and usable by all in this BYOD (bring your own device) era. Whether they like it or not, we do not need IT to install Twitter or Prezi accounts and we are better placed to show people how they work because, unlike them, we've always presented and shared information. Information is our game. While all the above may be true, the mistake I had made was to try to proceed in isolation, without considering how these other departments, specifically IT in this instance, might react. Not only did they fail to anticipate our expertise or interest in these areas, which they saw as their protected territories, but my approach to delivery had given them nowhere to go. No involvement. No way in. I realized I needed to change tack and have since fought my natural instincts to 'plough my own furrow' and sought a collaborative approach instead. This has involved simple things like suggesting to IT that they co-teach with us or provide content input to sessions. The interesting thing is that this open invitation to collaborate is very much appreciated despite the fact that, in practice, it is rarely taken up; but simply because it is offered, conflict is averted. We librarians need all the allies we can get, and identifying crossovers of approach or remit with departments like IT and marketing (whom I recently appeased by bringing our website back to the business school fold) and using them to build relationships and communicate effectively is a great way of forging shared understanding, even if the effort involved in that collaboration is often, if not always, going to be more one-sided than we would like.

BEYOND THE LIBRARY WALLS

Perhaps one of the most important messages we can communicate to our academic staff, which should probably come before all those aspects I have covered above, is the importance of our visibility beyond the library walls. Being seen to be operating outside of the physical library emphasizes that we are not defined by our book stock alone. Classroom teaching is perhaps the most potent indication of our information credentials and, what is more, our talents in this area have the potential to easily surpass faculty and student expectations. It is my contention that librarians should teach and train constantly and, more importantly, well. Teaching that is not going to make the grade is worse than no teaching at all as it will take away from an offering that is already considered of dubious value by most users. Our status as librarians can in fact help us in this regard as the expectation is that we will not be able to teach and will probably be insufferably boring as well! When we prove, conversely, that we know what we are talking about, and are engaging too, then we are on to a real winner. There is not sufficient room here for a treatise on effective teaching or whether librarians should secure library qualifications (personally, I consider this unnecessary), but the bottom line is that we should interact as well as inform, sell the benefits rather than the tools, and prove that what we are telling them works, practically, with a hands-on demonstration if possible.

We should also make ourselves available beyond the library walls in common areas where we can communicate freely with users whether we are manning an information point, attending a social function or attending a staff coffee event. The point is that in these circumstances you are interacting without any of the traditional trappings, and this will encourage connection and communication, especially if you give of your personality too. Another key extra-library activity should be a willingness to go out to faculty and staff offices to solve problems off-territory as roving support, rather like IT. All too often amongst my own team, I observe meetings arranged to take place in the information centre rather than in the open-plan offices elsewhere in the building where we can be seen to be helping other departments and are available to answer other questions while we are there. It should chiefly be about convenience for the person we are helping, but it also can be about visibility.

VALUE AND IMPACT

While I firmly believe that we should communicate our value to our stakeholders, I have grave concerns about taking this too far and aligning everything we do with quantifiable impact (for example, on student assignment marks), especially as this could easily lead to budgets being tied to such measurable impact (such as the cancellation of databases that have not been deemed to be as useful as others for a particular assignment). Is student or faculty success accurately measurable? Should all we do be synthesized into a score or grade of our relative value? As a business librarian with 18 years' experience under my belt I would argue that a lot of what we do is not measurable and does not necessarily directly impact on student grade point averages. It is an approach that takes no account of our pastoral role as frontline support for disorientated users, of our role as social and new media gurus, introducing valuable productivity, networking and online identity tools and resources, or of our position as information skills educators, especially when the latter often rubs off on the students we advise in an ad hoc, unrecorded way rather than via formalized information literacy teaching.

Sage recently commissioned a project from Loughborough University's Library and Information Statistics Unit (LISU, 2012) which drew on research from the USA, Scandinavia and the UK. In summary, the project showed that librarians are very actively gathering evidence but that, as Stephen Barr (2012) noted on the Guardian Higher Education Network blog 'much of it is evidence of activity rather than evidence of value and impact'. I suspect that much the same is true of the business librarians sector, but maybe if all we end up communicating is that we cannot make a direct correlation, then perhaps that is no bad thing?

COMMUNICATING OUR ALIGNMENT

A factor that has been identified as common to UK academic library services which have suffered severe staffing cuts in recent years is the failure, in numerous cases, to communicate how their activities aligned with the mission and goals of the organization they existed within – the cutting of many library posts at London Business School and Bangor University being obvious examples and something of a watershed moment for UK academic libraries (Priestner and Tilley, 2010). On the face of it, their failure to consider wider organizational objectives sounds remarkably shortsighted and foolish, but the reality is that it's something we could all pay more attention to. This is not just about the fact that we should be seeking joint goals. It is doing this, yes, but, just as importantly, *communicating* that we are doing this, so that senior management definitively know that we and our service are both appropriately aligned and actively listening.

STAYING ON THE RADAR

In conclusion, then, although there is no question that it takes a great deal of effort for us librarians to ensure that our service gets on – and, more importantly, stays on – the institutional radar, there are in fact many, many means and ways open to us to make this happen. Admittedly, some of the approaches I have outlined are not very traditional – regular teaching, embracing new and social media, selling results rather than products, being permanently ready to pitch, ditching generic overly detailed emails, comprehensive statistics collation, operating beyond the library walls, writing more journalistically – and may put some of us outside of our comfort zones, but the alternative could well prove even more uncomfortable. And, yes, some approaches will work better in other countries and organizational cultures than others, but something that I am sure holds true, regardless of where we work, is that there is an urgent need for us all to communicate with our academic staff far more than we currently do if business school libraries are to survive in the 21st century.

REFERENCES

ACRL Research Planning and Review Committee, 2012. Top Ten Trends in Academic Libraries: A Review of the Trends and Issues Affecting Academic Libraries in Higher Education. *College & Research Libraries News*, 73(6), 311–20.

Anderson. R., 2011. The Crisis in Research Librarianship. *Journal of Academic Librarianship*, 37(4), 289–90.

Barr, S., 2012. How Should Academic Libraries Communicate their Own Value? The Guardian Higher Education Network [online]. At: http://www.guardian.co.uk/higher-education-network/blog/2012/aug/20/academic-libraries-value-research-teaching (accessed 20 November 2012).

The Librarians, 2007. ABC Television.

Library Information Science Unit (LISU), 2012. How Can Libraries Demonstrate their Value? Working Together: Evolving Value for Academic Libraries [online]. At: http://libraryvalue.wordpress.com/report/ (accessed 20 November 2012).

Potter, N., 2010. Moving Beyond the Echo Chamber. *Library & Information Update*, 9(7), 23.

Potter, N., 2012. *The Library Marketing Toolkit.* London: Facet.

Priestner, A. and Tilley, E., 2010. Boutique Libraries at Your Service. *Library & Information Update*, 9(6), 36–9.

CHAPTER 5

RETURN ON INVESTMENT (ROI) FROM A BUSINESS SCHOOL LIBRARY: AN INDIAN PERSPECTIVE

DR H. ANIL KUMAR

INTRODUCTION

Libraries and the library profession are currently experiencing one of the most difficult periods in modern history. In the financial-crisis-impacted USA, UK and European Union, libraries are facing multiple challenges, including budget constraints, restricted funds and reducing grants, not to mention the increasing cost of books and periodicals. Perhaps unsurprisingly, this pressure on libraries, whether academic or public, is continuing to increase (Aabo, 2009). The intensity of the challenges posed to libraries seems to have grown with the proliferation of search engines like Google and social media platforms like Facebook that deliver quick results irrespective of the location of the user. Libraries have been looking at this digital landscape with awe and devising plans to work with and against these developments. Interestingly, studies since the financial crisis reveal that community libraries have witnessed increased use in terms of walk-ins and have also functioned as job 'search and seek' facilitation centres. The increase in the use of community/public libraries during the financial crisis contrasts with the general feeling that there is a trend towards a decrease of reading habits among students. It is also a pity that during these times when libraries were most required, government was reluctant to fund them (Eakin and Pomerantz, 2009).

During the same period in emerging economies such as India, we have seen large investments and a surge in the number of educational institutions being established by public and private organizations (Sarnikar, 2010). This overall increase is evident across the education landscape in India, ranging from primary education to higher education institutions. Plans are also afoot to develop the vocational education scene in India, with large investments in skill development programmes. The government is attempting to address issues of access, admissions, delivery, teacher training, and research and evaluation processes across various education sectors. It is against this background that we see improvements in both the quantity and quality of Indian education. This phenomenon has had implications for the library sector. New libraries are being established along with new institutions, and the infrastructure and financial resources of existing libraries are being enhanced. It is therefore rare to hear about challenges like budget cuts, withdrawal of funds and so on from any major Indian library.

These developments do not imply that all is well with libraries in India, but broadly reflect the fact that the financial crisis has not affected their budgets or operations. However, this certainly does not indicate any lack of challenge for Indian libraries, compared to those faced by their counterparts globally, in making their value explicit. Business schools are not only being judged by the placements that their students secure, but more so by the salaries offered. It is not uncommon for a student who rarely visited the library or consulted scholarly papers and used a single textbook for an entire course to end up with dream salary in a great company. It is also not a rare occurrence for students to get good grades with limited class notes and no extra reading at all. Such instances reflect the poor standing of libraries and their non-existent role in the education process.

However, we are now witnessing a trend to improve the quality of business education in India. One of the main factors responsible for this positive trend is the active regulatory role of the government. The recent unfavourable response by the market, in terms of a drop in applications and unemployability of graduates, is also forcing business schools to introspect and offer quality programmes. Attempts are being made to increase the number of teachers, adopt new teaching methods, focus on learning opportunities and emphasize research. Active regulation in India, though leaving much to be desired, has been encouraging with respect to mandating institutions to subscribe to library resources. Recently, the Indian regulatory body of technical education, in a circular, clearly mandated subscription to e-resources like EBSCO and ABI Inform by business schools. A focus on research is becoming very important at business schools that desire qualitative growth, and this will hopefully result in the development of good libraries.

In this context of review and introspection, business schools are rethinking their existing investments, making it is all the more important for libraries to make their value more explicit. Even the harshest of critics will agree that using libraries does help – and definitely over the long term.[1] This is even truer in academic settings where education is the core activity for all stakeholders involved. In fact, a survey among US and Canadian students, conducted by Cain and Reynolds (2006), found that the library was one of the main facilities rated extremely highly in students' choice of institution. The same authors found that the library was not only important in the selection or rejection of the institution, but also scored highly on the satisfaction rating by the students once they joined the institutions and experienced the library's services. It is in this context that this chapter focuses on return on investment (ROI) for a management or business library.

---

1   See Stone, Pattern and Ramsden (2012) for recent statistical evidence.

RETURNS FROM LIBRARIES

It is now being realized that it is necessary to measure the value delivered by libraries and express that value in concrete terms. It follows, then, that we need to understand library outcomes, impact and returns. Library outcomes are broad indications of the desired objectives that a library aspires to achieve. To simplify these terms of outcomes, impact and returns, let us presume that the desired outcome of a public library is to improve information literacy among its community members. The impact of the library can be said to be the change in information literacy level among the community members who use the library. Thus, one of the returns of this library could be measured as the number of people who have enhanced their information literacy level through library use. Extending this concept is the term 'ROI' in which returns correspond to the investment made. White states that:

> [ROI] is simply defined as a ratio of resources (usually financial) gained or lost in a process/investment/result to the total amount of resources provided. A positive ROI indicates that more benefit than cost has been generated by the process/investment/result; a negative ROI indicates less benefit was generated than the resource provided. (White, 2007, p. 6)

Since other studies (for example, OCLC, 2003) also indicate returns in the form of tangible and intangible benefits, it may be appropriate to delve into the concepts of 'tangible', 'intangible', 'direct' and 'indirect' in the context of benefits and costs:

- Tangible benefits or costs are those that are explicit and can be easily identified and measured whereas intangible benefits or costs are those that are implicit and cannot be easily identified or measured. In the context of an academic library, tangible benefits would include number of downloads of papers, user walk-ins and so on, while tangible costs would include the library's budget, staff salaries and so on.
- Intangible benefits of libraries would include the library's contribution to the academic ambience of a business school and its contribution to users' positive perceptions of the quality of the institution, amongst other things, and the intangible costs could include the value of the faculty's time in developing library policies.
- Direct benefits are those benefits that are derived directly – for instance, an increase in the ranking of a business school based on the large collection of its library.
- Indirect benefits of a library are those that are not direct outcomes. For instance, a library provides services to faculty of other business schools and consequently benefits the students of those schools. While this does not directly benefit the host business school, it may be a desired benefit, if the larger objective of the host business school is to improve quality of management education in the country.

- Direct costs are costs that are directly invested in a library such as library budget, library staff salaries and so on.
- Indirect costs are costs incurred indirectly for the functioning of a library such as salaries of accounts staff of the host institution, who handle library bills, salaries of computer professionals who maintain the institute network and the like.

Measuring ROI is a complex process because identifying intangible benefits is not simple and straightforward and the timeframe to actually experience the benefits from using libraries is quite long. Yet, although measuring value in terms of intangible benefits may be difficult, it is not impossible. This is precisely why it is important to develop a framework to measure libraries' ROI while exploring various methods to determine the ROI.

PUBLIC LIBRARY ROI STUDIES

The valuation or evaluation studies of libraries has generally included simple surveys conducted to collect data on a variety of issues like satisfaction, perception, quality and relevance of various library services. Data are generally collected from users, staff and management through questionnaires, and, in some cases, interviews are conducted. These time-tested methods provide only a limited indication of the value of libraries, but do offer useful insights for internal management and policy-making. In fact, it is worth noting that these methods of collecting data for studies relating to reviewing the value of libraries have been found useful (OCLC, 2003, 2005, 2010).

One of the earliest studies in this area was heralded by the National Center for Education Statistics (NCES) that has provided data on staffing, collection size, operating expenditures, programmes presented, circulation and so on for public libraries in the USA since 1989. The NCES Public Library Peer Comparison Tool is used to assess services that are provided in terms of satisfaction, usage and efficiency.

ROI studies have been undertaken for various types of libraries, including public libraries, school libraries, special libraries and academic libraries. Some of the studies that have been popularly quoted, especially in the US public-library sector, were conducted by the Americans for Libraries Council (ALC), the Urban Libraries Council (ULC) and the states of Colorado and Florida (Imholz and Arns, 2007a, 2007b; ULC 2007; Steffen et al., 2009; McClure et al., 2001). These studies look at the ROI of public libraries and give a favourable verdict. For example, the report by the ULC (2007) states that the public libraries are essential for cities and that they provide economic value to the community through, amongst other things, literacy programmes, preparation of technology workers and resources for small businesses.

All the studies cited above note the variety of methods that have previously been used in ROI studies. Imholz and Arns observe that '... public library valuation researchers have sought and adopted valuation methods from the field of economics ... The studies reviewed clearly demonstrate the field's growing sophistication, showing advancement from simple questionnaires to complex surveys' (2007a, p. 32). In the same authors' summary of reviews of existing methods, they highlight: (1) cost–benefit analysis; (2) contingent valuation; and (3) secondary economic impact analysis. These can be described as follows:

1. *Cost benefit analysis* is the cost of running a service as compared to the benefit provided by the service. Most of the studies using this method looked at the direct benefits, while listing the indirect benefits.
2. In *contingent valuation* methodology, a value is assigned to each service based on the users' perception of the value. The users' perceptions can be captured through a survey to find out how much the users would be willing to pay for such a service and, on the basis of these perceptions, a value is assigned to the service.
3. *Secondary economic impact analysis* considers the knock-on benefits to the external community from the existence of libraries, such as library staff living and spending locally, and the existence of other businesses – for example, book vendors, binding, printing, computers – dependent on, or benefited by, libraries. Though not direct, these factors are considered important, as they have an economic impact in the library's immediate environment.

In their study, Imholz and Arns (2007b, p. 26) propose a new method called 'Social Return on Investment' (SROI), which they define as '... a measurement approach developed by expanding traditional cost/benefit analysis to include the economic value of cultural, social, and environmental impacts'. The main argument in favour of this method is the fact that the social impact of libraries, especially public libraries, cannot be ignored. This approach is extended by the balanced scorecard and the triple bottom line methods when calculating ROI: the balanced scorecard looks at SROI issues by including the social costs and returns; in the triple bottom line approach, the idea is to include ecological (environmental) and social factors, in addition to the finances, when calculating the organization's bottom line.

ROI IN ACADEMIC LIBRARY SETTINGS

The studies on ROI clearly indicate not only a worldwide interest and concern, but also the continuing evolution of various ROI methods and techniques. While it may look easier to evaluate the performance of a public library than that of an academic library, one must agree that calculating the value of libraries is itself complex and difficult. Among all the ROI studies, the ones that focused on public libraries dominated, constituting about 80 per cent (Aabo, 2009). However, in the case of public-library ROI studies too, it can be said that methods were evolving and it would take time for a mature universal model to be developed.

In the academic libraries sector, it may be interesting to understand the various approaches and methods adopted in the studies undertaken. Studies on ROI have predominantly been supported by library associations, and one of the noteworthy studies on academic libraries was by the Association of College and Research Libraries (ACRL, 2010). One of the core objectives of this report was to focus on library value that is demonstrated mainly to external audiences, and it does not emphasize measures of perception of quality and satisfaction with library services. The ACRL report (2010), with a mandate to address the concerns of institutional leaders, lays out 10 parameters for measuring library value:

1. *Student enrolment*: strongest profile of students joining the institution or, in other words, the best of the students choosing to join the institute;
2. *Student retention and graduation*: the number of students initially joining the institution, who stay on and graduate;
3. *Student success*: success of students in terms of ability to perform well in internships, placements secured or entry to reputed institutions for further education;
4. *Student achievement*: success in terms of academic performance and grades;
5. *Student learning*: the library's direct and connected role in student learning;
6. *Student experience*: the library's role in the students' experiences in the future;
7. *Faculty research productivity*: quality and quantity of faculty research publications and the library's contribution;
8. *Faculty grants*: the library's role in the success of grants being awarded to faculty;
9. *Faculty teaching*: the library's role in the teaching success or effectiveness of faculty;
10. *Institutional reputation*: the library's role in the overall reputation of the institution.

The report also suggests various initiatives to document the role of the library in delivering value in these 10 areas and recommends a host of activities around these 10 areas to increase value. It is interesting to note that of the 10 areas, six are related to students and include the library value, from before students decide to join an institution, to the point at which they actually experience the library. For the faculty, the report looks at research productivity, grants that can be obtained, teaching and the role of the library in these areas. The last area listed in the report is institutional reputation and the role a library plays in this area.

The ROI research carried out by Grzeschik (2010), based on the work of Luther (2008), which reviewed the University of Illinois at Urbana-Champaign, USA, focused on the Berlin School of Library and Information Science and the University

Library of the Humboldt University, Berlin, Germany. Luther's (2008) study of ROI can be considered the first study in an academic library setting. It was based on the work of Strouse (2003) who developed a ROI model for corporate and government libraries. Strouse's (2003) model was based on the concept of the outcome or contribution of corporate and government libraries to their parent institutions, in terms of the time and cost saved by its users and also the income generated by using the library resources. Extending this to academic settings, Luther (2008) mainly looked at the success rate of grants awarded to faculty and its relation to the contribution of the library in the process. Grzeschik (2010) developed a similar model wherein the citations used in proposing grants by the faculty were included as a contribution by the library, and this was compared to the number of grants that were awarded with citations from the library and the average grant amount awarded. Luther's (2008) study reflected a healthy ROI of $4.38 for every $ spent at the University of Illinois at Urbana-Champaign (UIUC) library. Grzeschik (2010) and Kaufman (2008) report the utility of the UIUC model in calculating the ROI in academic library settings.

Mays, Tenopir and Kaufman (2010) present a report of important ongoing studies on ROI in academic libraries. The White Paper by Tenopir et al. (2010) was a result of the second phase of an Elsevier-sponsored study on ROI in academic libraries, and the study results showed the returns ranging from 0.64 to 15.54 for every $ invested in the library. The study included eight institutions across eight countries and, among them, six institutions provided more than 1:1 returns. The study also revealed that in addition to generating grants, the library also furthered administrative goals such as 'attracting and retaining productive faculty, fostering innovative research, facilitating interdisciplinary collaboration, and raising the university's prestige' (Tenopir et al., 2010, p. 3).

The paper by Sidorko (2010) also indicated that faculty use of library resources to raise grants may have its own limitations, with variance due to the academic and research environment in the country of operation, the mission and nature of parent institution, difficulty in getting reliable data and so on.

In research conducted by Fonseca (2010), the ROI of an academic library is calculated by first considering circulation, interlibrary loan, computer accessibility and reference desk services offered by the library. The model then proposes to calculate the savings accrued to the users based on the cost of these services if they had been offered at a fee based on the cost of accessing these services. In simple terms, the ROI was:

> ... [the] ratio of value to cost. For example, if it were determined that the library's making accessible books in the sciences saved the library's clientele $300,000 annually, and the library spent $100,000 for those books, the ROI

ratio for that service would be 3:1, which could be better expressed as a return of $3 for every $1 invested. (Fonseca, 2010. p. 89)

On similar lines is Cornell University's value calculation. This included: circulation, interlibrary loan, laptops borrowed, Cornell content distributed through their e-commons system, in-depth consultations and research assistance by the library (Cornell University, 2013).

Chadwell (2011) researched into the value of academic library consortia and how it could be conveyed to all stakeholders, including students and faculty. The approach taken by Jackson and Hahn (2011) differed in the sense that it drew on methods from psychology of religion to derive the value of the place offered by academic libraries in their traditional form.

Brown (2011) undertook an interesting study by adopting three methods of value survey, calculator and contingent valuation to develop a value indicator in an academic library. Neal (2011) criticized the approach of looking at ROI from a perspective of investment on collection and returns from grants and argues in favour of exploring ROI from the impact value perspective in addition to financial value, and he urged librarians to go beyond existing studies that have left much to be desired so far as the value of an academic library is concerned.

THE INDIAN BUSINESS SCHOOL LIBRARY PERSPECTIVE

The area of ROI has been, directly and indirectly, dealt with in many studies, of which some have been quoted in the earlier section. ROI has been looked at from the purely financial perspective of returns to investment and has also been dealt with in terms of impact of libraries through the value generated. There is no doubt that, regardless of whether or not one is open to the idea of calculating ROI, it is pertinent to prove the worth and value of libraries. It is in this direction that I have attempted to explore ROI from a business library perspective in an Indian context. For this purpose, a brief survey was conducted among librarians from the top 10 business schools of India (see Table 5.1).

A request, along with a simple two-page questionnaire (in two sections), was sent to the librarians of these 12 business schools.[2] The first section of the questionnaire requested data on library budget for from 2008–09 to 2011–12. The objective of this section was to understand the financial position of libraries over a four-year period and also to look at the effects of the financial crisis, if there were any, on the budgets of Indian libraries.

---

2   No questionnaire needed to be sent to the author's business school; hence 12 questionnaires were sent out but 13 responses are recorded in Table 5.1.

Table 5.1   Top Indian business schools (2010–2011)

| | Rankings Publication 2010–2011 ||||||
| | *Business India* || *Business Today* || *Outlook* ||
Business Schools	2010	2011	2010	2011	2010	2011
Faculty of Management Studies (FMS)	11	11	10	10	5	5
Indian Institute of Foreign Trade (IIFT)	13	13	7	7	9	9
Indian Institute of Management Ahmedabad (IIMA)	1	1	3	3	1	1
Indian Institute of Management Bangalore (IIMB)	2	2	1	1	2	2
Indian Institute of Management Calcutta (IIMC)	3	4	2	2	3	3
Indian Institute of Management Indore (IIMI)	15	15	4	4	8	8
Indian Institute of Management Kozhikode (IIMK)	16	16	6	6	7	7
Indian Institute of Management Lucknow (IIML)	6	6	5	5	NI*	NI
Indian School of Business (ISB)	4	3	8	8	NI	NI
Management Development Institute (MDI)	7	8	22	27	6	6
S.P. Jain Institute of Management & Research (SPJIMR)	8	7	14	15	10	10
XLRI Jamshedpur	5	5	11	10	4	4
IIM Shillong	NI	NI	9	9	NI	NI

Note: The leading sources of business school rankings in India are *Business India*, *Business Today* and *Outlook* magazines. The rankings of the latest two years – that is, 2011 and 2010 – were studied. The top 25 schools were selected from each of these rankings. From these top 25, every business school that ranked among the top 10 of any of these rankings were taken as the sample for this study. The master list as shown in Table 5.1 included 13 business schools.
* NI = not included.

The second part of the questionnaire attempted to understand: the perceptions of business school librarians on the most important benefits of the library; the important challenges that could be foreseen for the library in the future; whether the library's ROI could be measured and how; and whether libraries will still be relevant in the future. The rating for benefits and challenges was sought on a Likert scale of 1 to 10 where 1 was most important and 10 was least important.

From the questionnaires sent, responses were received from eight institutions. There were nine respondents in total (including my own institution), and this constituted a response rate of almost 70 per cent. The budgets from each library were compiled, and the percentage change from the previous year's budget is shown in Table 5.2.

Table 5.2 clearly shows that all institutions, except one, witnessed an increase in budget allocation over a four-year (2008–11) period, with the year 2008 being considered as the base year. From Table 5.2 it is also evident that there were three instances of a decrease in budget allocation as compared to the previous year's budget. However, it was found through informal sources that in the two instances where the decrease was substantial (over 20 per cent) the reasons were attributed to change of leadership in the library and could be termed as instability of leadership at the top in the library.

Table 5.2   Indian business school libraries: percentage changes from previous year's library budgets

Business school	2009	2010	2011	Average % change
IIMA	11	19	11	14
IIMB	11	8	32	17
IIMC	−7	37	29	20
IIMI	49	33	−33	16
IIMK	7.5	5	5	6
IIML	16	6	11	11
ISB	0	6	−21	−5
MDI	12	6	16	11
IIMS	24	7	7	13
Average	**14**	**14**	**6**	**11**

It can also be seen from the data collected that where there was an increase in budget, all except one business school had an increase of more than 10 per cent over their previous year's budget. It can be inferred that the library budgets of top Indian business schools have been increasing over the past four years. If these libraries are considered together, the total average increase in budget over a four-year period was more than 11 per cent. This might imply that the financial crisis of the Western world does not seem to have affected library spending in Indian business schools.

Table 5.3 shows that the main benefit from a library perspective is seen as increasing the research output of the business school. The data also indicate that there is comparatively less variation in responses so far as the perception that libraries help students in their placements was concerned. It may be worth noting that the responses pointed to an intangible benefit of the library – that is, the library adds value to the academic culture of the business school. In terms of information sought on future challenges for the library, responses were quite varied. Among these, it is interesting to note that faculty and student underuse were considered important, as was the issue of reduced staff and availability of good staff from the market. As seen in the library budgets section, the issue of budget reduction did not seem to worry Indian business school librarians. In terms of challenges, management cooperation was rated as least challenging. The variation in the responses of librarians on future challenges is worth noting.

Table 5.3   Perceptions of Indian business school librarians

	Value of Library?	Mean	SD	CoV
1	Increase in the research output of business school	1.50	0.53	33.88
2	Students perform better in the exams	2.88	1.20	43.27
3	Helps students in their placements	3.75	1.12	30.49
4	Helps faculty more than students	3.63	2.13	61.78
5	Helps students more than faculty	4.38	2.57	62.54
6	Helps faculty and students equally	3.25	2.45	81.65
7	Adds value to the overall academic culture of the institution	1.63	1.00	60.00
Future Challenges				
8	Reduced library budget	5.00	2.68	56.14
9	Management cooperation	4.50	2.45	56.53
10	Faculty underuse	3.63	2.00	60.00
11	Student underuse	2.75	1.74	68.09
12	Reduced library staff	2.75	1.86	66.81
13	Difficulty in recruiting good staff from the job market	2.88	2.83	84.85

Figure 5.1 shows that when the data collected on perceptions of Indian business school librarians is plotted as a bar chart, with value of library (column 1 of Table 5.3) on the x axis and the mean and SD values on the y axis, we can clearly see that value no. 7 (adds value to the overall academic culture of the institution) is rated highly with little variation.

In the section where responses were sought on whether the librarians considered calculation of ROI for libraries possible, most of them felt that it was difficult to measure ROI and stated the need for development of a model for ROI. Some of them indicated that partial measurement was possible with measurement of resource usage, user satisfaction and research output. This question and the response to it form a critical part of this study. It was in light of this perception that I propose a framework for calculating ROI in business school libraries.

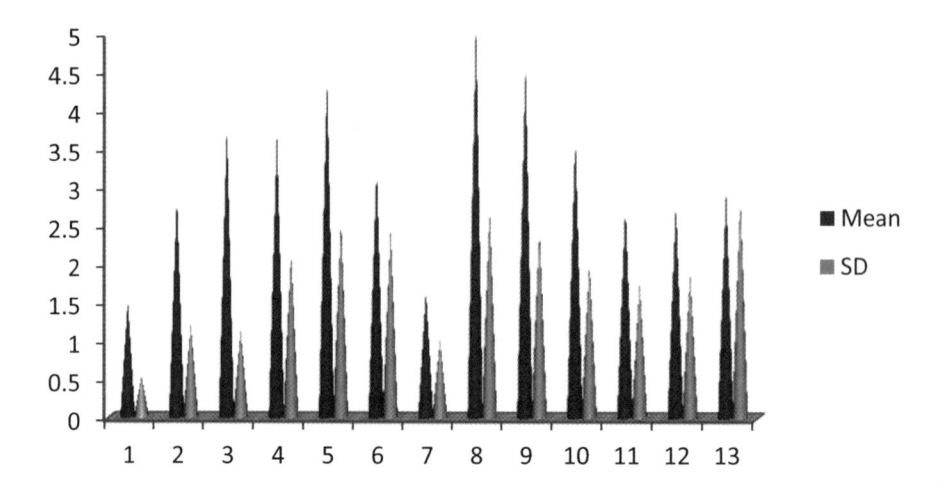

Figure 5.1 Perceptions of Indian business school librarians

In response to the question on the relevance of libraries in future, all librarians responded positively. Some suggested re-engineering their role and functions through personalized and relevant services and providing credible, validated and organized resource materials.

THE PROPOSED FRAMEWORK

It is quite evident from the literature review and the survey conducted that the need for calculating the ROI is pertinent. Existing models need to be further researched and evolved to address the needs of various libraries. Some may consider this increased interest on ROI as madness (Neal, 2011) and advise restraint. Different contexts and perspectives need to be explored, if we look at different types of libraries (public or academic). Even within one campus we may need to look at various groups of users differently. For instance, undergraduate students would use and derive value from a library that is quite different from a doctoral student within the same institution. In business schools, the needs vary with the users who may include participants of long-term, short-term or distance programmes and external users. So far as existing studies are concerned, there are hardly any that have an Indian context.

At the outset, one may attempt to look at ROI as a means to establish the fact that library value can be expressed in monetary terms. The fundamental premise of calculating ROI is that management has invested x amount in making the library operational and expects returns, if not directly in terms of money, in terms of impact or value generated that is then translated into the terminology of money.

The existing ROI studies on academic libraries have resorted to calculating either the financial value or the impact value. Financial value has been derived by simply dividing the monetary value of benefits by the monetary value of cost. This can also be termed as cost–benefit analysis. In the second approach, the library's impact on its users is measured in terms of outcomes or benefits that may have been derived. A combination of calculating the financial values of cost and benefits and indentifying the library's impact through a survey of perceptions may be useful.

The value of a library, on adopting a simple approach, would mean the benefits received against the cost incurred. In case of the cost incurred, the tangible part can easily be calculated, but there may be issues in calculating the intangible cost. Some intangible costs incurred include faculty and 'other-than-library' staff time in library governance, cost of the institution's goodwill in procuring materials or dealing with external agencies and so on. The cost factor in a library (Hanumappa, 2011) would generally include:

- resource identification cost: identifying relevant resources
- resource procurement cost: purchase and acquisition
- resource maintenance cost: preservation and providing access
- resource management cost: creating systems to manage the resources
- resources needed to achieve all the above, including people, infrastructure, technology, institutional overheads and so on.

While library budgets in India typically provide cost details of resources to be procured, it is difficult to ascertain other costs through library budgets. Keeping this in mind, to review the cost incurred in operating a library it would be necessary to include direct costs and indirect costs. The direct costs will include the items listed in the library budget, such as cost of procuring the resources and technology needed to manage and provide access to these resources. One would also need to add the salaries of the staff, library maintenance, electricity consumed, institute overheads in supporting the library operations and other expenses incurred like tax, cost of real estate and so on. The indirect costs would include unnoticed costs such as costs incurred in managing external visitors to the library, cost of faculty time and administrators in facilitating library operations and so on. Therefore, ascertaining actual costs incurred on libraries is complex but very possible.

On the other hand, benefits or value derived from a library can be broadly categorized into two sections based on the users of the library:

1. internal users
2. external users

Internal users

The benefits of the library to internal users could be at two levels, institutional and individual. They are further elicited as follows.

Institutional level
At the institutional level the benefits may include:

- students' choice, retention, parents perception
- research and publication outcomes
- faculty choice, retention, satisfaction
- staff choice, retention, satisfaction
- brand-building – rankings, international partnerships, accreditation, placements, linkages to industry and public (academia, government, industry)
- savings accrued through purchases for the library through negotiation, sponsorship, identifying content overlap and avoiding collection duplication, consortia participation and ILL services.

Individual level
At the individual level each category of user may have different set of benefits and could be described as:

- faculty: publishing (cases, working papers, papers, research books, textbooks, conference proceedings, newspaper articles, teaching, research guides), faculty development, consulting, institution-building, invited talks, collaboration, promotion and so on
- students
  - MBA – grades, placements, learning: assignments (reports, summer course and so on), class discussions, peer learning, summer placements (remote logins), higher education, research and publication, entrepreneurship
  - doctoral: grades, research processes and understanding, publications, interaction with faculty, networking, teaching assistantship, higher education
  - executive education: learning, assignments, class discussions, peer interactions and so on
  - faculty development programmes: learning, teaching, research, publication, administration.
- research assistants/academic associates: support and assistance to faculty, publication, higher education, jobs
- interns: completion of projects, learning, impact in mainline of education
- academic visitors: research, teaching, publication, learning and administration
- staff: attracting and retaining specialized staff and their growth
  - computer professionals
  - library staff

- physical education staff
- other professional staff.

External users

The benefits derived by external users are also important for a library. In the Indian context, especially for the Indian institutes of management that were established by the Indian government, one of the objectives is to support similar Indian institutions and further the cause of businesses and also management education in the country. In this context, the external users who could benefit from the business school library are:

- corporate users
- PhD students
- faculty and researchers
- 'only reading' users: doctors, consultants, entrepreneurs and similar
- general public, including foreigners, architects, amongst others
- potential stakeholders such as students and faculty
- libraries that are active in our ILL programme
- academic institutional members
- management and decision-makers of other institutions
- alumni
- government.

It may be useful to note some of the possible outcomes in relation to the value a library derives by serving its external users:

1. connection to alumni, leading to facilitation in placements and raising endowments and sponsorships for the business school
2. improved position in international and national accreditation and rankings
3. alignment with the business school's overall mission
4. intangible outcomes:
   - improved ambience to academic setting
   - improved visitor perceptions
   - user goodwill
   - promotion of entrepreneurship in the region
   - display of institute output, such as faculty publications, student reports and publications, news items on library noticeboard.

When we consider different categories of users it may be useful to look at the varying levels of importance of the library as perceived by each type of user. We may have to develop a model that looks at varying weightings for each type of user. For instance, a faculty may find use of library far more important and critical than a MBA student, and a doctoral student's perception of the library's value must be different from that of an executive attending a short-duration programme at the business school. It may also be important to differentiate the value derived by a faculty while preparing a grant proposal versus teaching a course. And this could well be extended to use of the library by a faculty to prepare a session for a training programme versus a doctoral programme. Therefore, it would be too simplistic to not consider these complexities before assigning an overall value for library use.

The other complexity in calculating value or ROI of a library would be the types of use of the library by various categories of users. These may include:

1. walk-in and browsing
2. issue/return of library materials
3. referencing the resources in the library
4. self-study or group study of resources
5. use of computers and Internet
6. virtual or online use of library resources
7. discussion by students/faculty (for example, for class preparation, assignments and so on)
8. seeking individual guidance in using the library resources.

While researching on the value of libraries it may also be worth looking at the contribution of the library staff in activities beyond serving the immediate users and consider these when calculating the library's ROI. As an illustration, some of the initiatives and activities that my library is currently associated with are as follows:

- curriculum development, teaching courses, visiting lectures, talks/papers in conferences, selecting interns and trainees and so on for library and information science (LIS) schools
- publication of papers in national and international journals and presentation of papers and lectures in national and international conferences
- contributing to the library profession through the Ahmedabad Library Network and Management Library Network, and professional talks and meetings with LIS students
- contributing to LIS, architecture and design students' projects
- mentoring/guidance to start-ups in the domain of radio frequency identification, open source software, e-book reader software and publishers
- membership of the institute's staff evaluation and development committee, computer services committee, website committee, chair of staff grievances committee and staff welfare committee
- Organizing management conferences, contributing as a faculty in the management development programme – Innovating for Excellence (a programme for deans and directors of business schools) – designing and delivering a management development programme for publishers

- developing library orientation and information literacy sessions for students of various programmes – MBA, doctoral (internal and external) and faculty development (internal/external)
- contributing to the public cause through involvement in government initiatives like MJ Public Library, Sachivalay (government of Gujarat) Library, Sardar Patel Institute of Public Administration Library, Knowledge Consortium of Gujarat (government of Gujarat), organizing book fairs and founding member of the International Institute for Entrepreneurship.

These contributions by library staff could be considered as irrelevant as they were not planned for when the library was conceived. However, when looking at calculating a library's ROI, it will definitely be desirable to include all such known, unknown, direct, indirect, intended or unintended benefits to users, which may include internal and external benefits.

CONCLUSION

We may not have an agreed and mature model for calculating the ROI of a library, let alone the business library. However, contributions to the body of ROI literature are increasing, with an emphasis on ROI becoming inevitable for library professionals. It may be worth developing models that are relevant to various contexts. This chapter has attempted to elaborate the Indian situation in regard to business schools.

As seen from the survey of the perceptions of Indian business school librarians undertaken in this chapter, there is a great need to develop a model for calculating ROI, although most respondents felt that ROI is only partially measurable. Measuring resource use, satisfaction surveys and measuring research output in business schools were suggested as some of the approaches towards developing a model for calculating ROI. However, when calculating a library's ROI, it will definitely be desirable to include all known, unknown, direct, indirect, intended and unintended benefits to internal and external users.

Within these two categories – internal and external users – we may find many types of user, such as students, faculty, researchers and so on. For each type of user the need and benefit may be different and has to be factored into the ROI model that we build. In addition, for an internal user like a faculty member, their research paper may benefit from the reference resources subscribed to by the library, or from the faculty member just browsing the shelves when they walked into the library, or by borrowing a book. Similarly, if we look at students, it may become very important to look at the type of programme the student belongs to, their purpose in using the library and then the actual use made.

Hence, when calculating the returns of a library, one needs to consider assigning values to each type of use based on the user, purpose and use. In addition to use of the library by users, it may also be necessary to include outcomes of library staff engagements outside the primary domain of the library. Once the returns have been calculated it will be easier to calculate the ROI.

In conclusion, a business school library could use existing models of dividing the returns by cost incurred and project a ROI figure. But, to do this, one has to consider all costs (tangible and intangible) and all returns (tangible and intangible). In the process of calculating the returns, the individual library will have to assign values to the user, use and purpose, depending on the mission of the school or institute. More studies of this kind may help in the development of a standard model for calculating the ROI of a business school library in the future.

REFERENCES

Aabo, S., 2009. Libraries and Return on Investment (ROI): A Meta-Analysis. *New Library World*, 110(7/8), 311–24.

ACRL, 2010. The Value of Academic Libraries: A Comprehensive Research Review and Report [online]. Association of College and Research Libraries. At: http://www.acrl.ala.org/value/ (accessed 7 August 2012).

Brown, J., 2011. Developing a Library Value Indicator for a Disciplinary Population: Proceedings of the 3rd Annual Library Assessment Conference [online]. Association of Research Libraries. At: http://digitalcommons.library.unlv.edu/lib_articles/102 (accessed 7 August 2012).

Cain, D. and Reynolds, G.L., 2006. The Impact of Facilities on Recruitment and Retention of Students. *Facilities Manager*, May–June, 54–60.

Chadwell, F.A., 2011. Assessing the Value of Academic Library Consortia. *Journal of Library Administration*, 51(7–8), 645–61.

Cornell University, 2013. Library Value Calculations [online]. At: http://research.library.cornell.edu/value (accessed 21 April 2013).

Eakin, L. and Pomerantz, J., 2009. Virtual Reference, Real Money: Modeling Costs in Virtual Reference Services. *Libraries and the Academy*, 9(1), 133–64.

EBSCO, 2013. At: http://www.ebsco.com/ (accessed 20 April 2013).

Fonseca, T., 2010. Speaking in the ROI-al We: On the Need to Create a Return-on-Investment Calculator for Academic Libraries of Community Colleges and Regional/Undergraduate Four-year Institutions. *Codex: The Journal of the Louisiana Chapter of the ACRL*, 1(2), 80–99.

Grzeschik, K., (2010). Return on Investment (ROI) in German Libraries: The Berlin School of Library and Information Science and the University Library at the Humboldt University, Berlin – A Case Study. *The Bottom Line: Managing Library Finances*, 23(4), 141–201.

Hanumappa, A.K., 2011. Return On Investment (ROI) from Libraries. In: Jagdish Arora et al. (eds), *Towards Building a Knowledge Society: Library as Catalyst for Knowledge Discovery and Management.* Proceedings of VIII International CALIBER. Ahmedabad: INFLIBNET, 479–88.

Imholz, S. and Arns, J.W., 2007a. Worth Their Weight: An Assessment of the Evolving Field of Library Evaluation. *Public Library Quarterly*, 26(3–4), 31–48.

Imholz, S. and Arns, J.W., 2007b. Worth their Weight: An Assessment of the Evolving Field of Library Valuation [online]. Americans for Libraries Council. At: http://www.ala.org/research/sites/ala.org.research/files/content/librarystats/worththeirweight.pdf (accessed 29 April 2013).

Jackson, H.L. and Hahn, T.B., 2011. Serving Higher Education's Highest Goals: Assessment of the Academic Library as Place. *College & Research Libraries*, 72(5), 428–42.

Kaufman, P.T., 2008. The Library as Strategic Investment: Results of the Illinois Return on Investment Study. *Liber Quarterly*, 18(3–4), 424–36.

Luther, J., (2008). *University Investment in the Library: What's the Return? A Case Study at the University of Illinois at Urbana-Champaign* [online]. Library Connect, Elsevier. At: http://libraryconnect.elsevier.com/sites/default/files/lcwp0101.pdf (accessed 5 January 2012).

McClure, C.R. et al., 2001. *Economic Benefits and Impacts from Public Libraries in the State of Florida* [online]. Information Use Management and Policy Institute. At: http://dlis.dos.state.fl.us/bld/Research_Office/final-report.pdf (accessed 5 January 2012).

Mays, R., Tenopir C. and Kaufman, P., 2010. Lib-Value: Measuring Value and Return on Investment of Academic Libraries. *Research Library Issues: A Biomonthly Report from ARL, CNI, and SPARC*, 271, 36–40.

NCES Public Library Peer Comparison Tool. At: http://nces.ed.gov/surveys/libraries/ (accessed 21 April 2013).

Neal, J., 2011. Stop the Madness: The Insanity of ROI and the Need for New Qualitative Measures of Academic Library Success. In: *Declaration of Interdependence: The Proceedings of the ACRL 2011 Conference.* Philadelphia, PA: Association of College and Research Libraries.

OCLC, 2003. *Environment Scan: Pattern Recognition.* [online]. Online Computer Library Center]. At: http://www.oclc.org/reports/escan/toc.htm (accessed: 12 April 2012).

OCLC, 2005. *Perceptions of Libraries and Information Resources* [online]. Online Computer Library Center. At: http://www.oclc.org/reports/2005perceptions.htm (accessed 2 February 2012).

OCLC, 2010. *Perceptions of Libraries: Context and Community* [online]. Online Computer Library Center. At: http://www.oclc.org/reports/2010perceptions.htm (accessed 12 April 2012).

Sarnikar, S., 2010. Growth of Higher Education in India: Regulatory Complexity and Funding Policy Ambiguity. *The FedUni Journal of Higher Education*, 5(3), 7–23.

Sidorko, P.E., 2010. Demonstrating ROI in the Library: The Holy Grail Search Continues. *Library Management*, 31(8–9), 645–53.

Steffen, N. et al., 2009. *Public Libraries – A Wise Investment: A Return on Investment Study of Colorado Libraries*. Denver: Library Research Service.

Stone, G., Pattern, D. and Ramsden, B., 2012. Library Impact Data Project: Hit, Miss or Maybe. In: *Proving Value in Challenging Times: Proceedings of the 9th Northumbria International Conference on Performance Measurement in Libraries and Information Services*. York: University of York.

Strouse, R., 2003. Demonstrating Value and Return on Investment: The Ongoing Imperative. *Information Outlook*, 7(3), 14–19.

Tenopir, C. et al., 2010. *University Investment in the Library, Phase II: An International Study of the Library's Value to the Grants Process* [online]. Library Connect, Elsevier. At: http://libraryconnect.elsevier.com/sites/default/files/2010-06-whitepaper-roi2_0.pdf (accessed 5 September 2012).

ULC, 2007. *Making Cities Stronger: Public Library Contributions to Local Economic Development* [online]. Urban Libraries Council. At: http://www.urban.org/UploadedPDF/1001075_stronger_cities.pdf (accessed 10 January 2012).

White, L.N., 2007. An Old Tool with Potential New Uses: Return on Investment. *The Bottom Line: Managing Library Finances*, 20(1), 5–9.

CHAPTER 6

TECHNOLOGY CHALLENGES FOR THE BUSINESS SCHOOL LIBRARY

JONATHAN EATON

INTRODUCTION: TECHNOLOGY AND THE GROWTH OF THE BUSINESS ECOSYSTEM

Our working and personal lives are dominated today by technologies that make information, communication and entertainment more readily accessible than ever before. We live in the age of globally pervasive, instantly available network connections, of data and applications that live in clouds, and a rapidly expanding range of devices that suit our differing access needs, wherever we may happen to be, at any time. Technologies have clearly converged: no longer do we have a Sony Walkman for music and a Palm Pilot for our address book. Instead, our homes, streets and workplaces bristle with devices able to handle media and data formats easily and reciprocally, way beyond those for which they were originally designed. We can browse the web using a games console; watch TV on a smart phone; Skype a friend on a smart TV screen. Moreover, convergence is not limited to technology – this is the age of media convergence, typified by the interactions now possible between broadcasters, publishers and socially contributed content, creating infinitely varied, composite, edgeless communication flows. Ray Ozzie (Microsoft's former Chief Technology Officer) memorably summarized the new information and communications technology (ICT) frontier as 'three screens and the cloud' (Ozzie, 2009). By 'screens' he meant not mainly a conventional desktop or laptop PC but more the new breed of appliance-type devices like a smart phone, a tablet, a TV, all connecting to a central data and applications store. Ozzie thus vividly identified the impact of technology and media convergence as the consumer's requirement for solutions to be delivered in a coherent way, across different kinds of devices. The old technology moulds are now broken: digitized information can now escape its former media and format boundaries.

THE IMPORTANCE AND IMPLICATIONS OF BUSINESS ECOSYSTEMS FOR LIBRARY TECHNOLOGY

Convergence is also the defining characteristic of the modern business world. The term 'business ecosystem' emerged some two decades ago (Moore, 1993) and is now widely used to describe the continuously evolving and interdependent ways in which organizations of all kinds are now linked together (both competitively and also cooperatively) to deliver their services or products, using technology. This contrasts sharply with the former post-war era in which companies sought to achieve market dominance individually in a head-to-head battle within their peer sector. The ecosystem model has proved so compellingly effective that the dominant technology-based companies of the modern era have all used it to build and extend their business strategies. It's a dynamic paradox: the dominance of the world's great technology companies relies not just on a global mass user base, but also critically on their interrelationships with the many individual, much smaller firms that create complementary applications and services. Google started with search, but now provides a cloud-based personal information environment driven by its Android devices. Apple's paradigm-shifting hardware also relies on the iTunes and Apple Store infrastructure. Amazon started with online retailing but now additionally offers corporate-grade cloud storage and computing platforms. Not to be outdone, Microsoft is giving chase, with its Windows 8 operating system extending to smartphones and tablet devices, thus joining up its Azure cloud-based data and applications.

Business libraries similarly exist as part of these wider ecosystems, both in respect of their own organizations and in their relationships with information suppliers and patrons. As a more specialized branch of academic libraries, they typically deal directly with some of the biggest and most influential vendors in the global corporate marketplace, whilst still forming part of the professional library services ecosystem represented by the familiar online information suppliers, publishers and aggregators, together with the specialized array of service and management tools, including: library management systems (LMS), Discovery services, OpenURL resolvers, proxy servers, federated access management and e-resource management systems. In the past five years major changes to the electronic library infrastructure market have resulted in a decisive shift away from the overheads and complexities of local hosting towards cloud-based applications accessed via a web browser, along with an increasing focus on support for mobile devices. It would therefore seem that all the technology signals are set in broadly the 'right' direction for improving customer experience and streamlining library digital services management processes. But whilst this might be broadly true of the wider academic library in general, for business libraries in particular there are instead some very real and present technology challenges to address. This chapter will outline some major problem areas for service and productivity, and investigate what kinds of practical steps can be taken to address or mitigate them. The technology challenges facing business libraries stem mainly from the corporate-grade information products and services they must license, integrate and support within their e-resources portfolios to deliver the kinds of high-quality, current and diverse business, economic and financial data that their students, professors and researchers expect and require.

The content, functional and operational attributes of these commercial business data services are frequently out of step and incompatible with the more general e-resource management tools now widely used to activate content access, store licence information, record usage and calculate return on investment. They also typically offer negligible support for the kinds of direct or deep linking often required by virtual learning environments (VLEs). Whilst the pedigree and integrity of top-brand business data services is never disputed, in their current incarnations and lack of compliance with widely adopted library and publishing industry technology standards, they can pose many problems which in turn not only affect the academic user experience, but also involve the business library and its IT department colleagues in extended and often ongoing maintenance work, with consequent productivity implications. As we shall see, not all of these identified issues are insoluble, but to address and overcome them will require a combination of short-term local library contingency effort and a longer campaign of wider community-based lobbying with suppliers and other participants in the business information ecosystem.

FINANCIAL MARKETS DATA: THE MAJOR TECHNOLOGY DIFFERENTIATOR

To fully support their student patrons, reflecting their prior and future career destinations, business libraries must offer highly specialized and high-cost business and financial online information services (both numeric and textual) that are widely used in the corporate sector. For financial markets and economics data, this typically means subscribing to products based primarily around the Windows desktop application software model, such as: Bloomberg Professional; Thomson Reuters' Datastream Advance, EIKON and SDC Platinum; FactSet; and Haver Analytics' Data Link Express (DLX). Each requires a substantial software application to be locally installed, configured and maintained; each has its own idiosyncrasies and operational differences that carry local support, training and maintenance overheads. Of course, any software will eventually need updating, and here wide variations in methodology and frequency are found. Using a background process invisible to the user, Bloomberg's Professional software client updates automatically each month, but if for any reason the updates fail or are not manually implemented, after three months the installation will expire, rendering it useless until a manual update to the latest version is performed. Haver Analytics' DLX application differs from the client-server model of its peers (where the application is locally installed and connects to remote servers to access data) by using filespace on the local PC or network to store, dynamically retrieve and expand its data series compressed using a proprietary protocol.

There are undeniably many functional benefits derived from this desktop application model. These applications are complex but effectively fully maximize the facilities of the Windows operating system and the processing power of the local PC environment to support a variety of powerful and flexible access models, including Excel add-ins and application programming interfaces (APIs) that enable other analytics tools, such as MATLAB or SAS, to integrate with them. However, the model remains strictly Windows-based, with the overarching design assumption that access will always be localized to a fixed and physical environment – backed up by local installation and maintenance resources – and that users will continue to accept this limitation despite their wish to use devices of their own choosing that may run different operating environments. For business libraries that need to offer a combination of these Windows-based applications, decisions may need to be made whether to run all of them on one PC to offer maximum flexibility at the risk of potential conflicts and added complexity, or to dedicate PCs to specific applications to help pre-empt and isolate any technical issues. To provide these financial applications on any more than a handful of PCs requires considerable IT deployment support, ideally using applications package management tools such as Microsoft's Systems Center Configuration Manager (SCCM).

It is clear that the strengths of these highly localized, Windows-based corporate financial information applications can also become serious weaknesses for service delivery and training in the business library context. Highly proprietary, individually licensed services like Bloomberg have a very sophisticated ecosystem for immediate online support and on-demand training, but this relies entirely on the user being privileged to access a physical PC and to be actually running the application and logged in. Again, the access model favours the more fortunate full-time student able to visit campus frequently (or live locally in costly central city locations) and apparently disenfranchises their part-time or more distant counterparts. But the corporate marketplace is itself now increasingly demanding more flexible access solutions from its business applications suppliers – so how have the financial data services vendors responded?

The major financial data suppliers – Bloomberg, FactSet and ThomsonReuters – have all committed resources to improving their support for more mobile users, in differing ways. Bloomberg and FactSet both provide 'thin-client' versions of their PC workstation applications in Bloomberg Anywhere and FactSet Connect. With both these variants, the user's PC can be running Windows, Macintosh or Linux, and with a Citrix thin-client installed, can then use a web browser to access the Windows desktop application running on a centrally hosted server provided by the supplier. There are numerous advantages to the thin-client model, not least the centralized management architecture (where the application is always updated by its own supplier) and the hugely increased flexibility of access to remote users on non-Windows environments. However, the shortcomings include network sluggishness or 'latency' (a typically slower and less responsive user experience due to the thin-client access model) and, for Bloomberg Anywhere, a restriction of a terminal licence to a single named (and biometrically authenticated) user. Thomson Reuters has opted to build a web-based version of its Datastream application, called

Datastream Professional, although this is based on Microsoft technology and so is not truly device-independent.

Corporate-grade financial and economic desktop software-based services will continue to pose technical challenges for business libraries both now and into the future, because of their long history as localized applications designed expressly for Microsoft Windows, which is a strategy that itself reflects the embedded nature of Windows within corporate IT. A still more pressing library management issue remains linked with these kinds of resources – the relative paucity of usage data (typically, due to financial markets compliance protocols) that suppliers may provide. This is particularly problematic given the high costs of subscription and the increasing internal pressure to justify spending against clear evidence of e-resource use. We will return to this in a later section where we look at usage data and standardization issues in more detail.

HOW THE APPLICATION PROGRAMMING INTERFACE (API) MODEL HELPS UNLOCK PROPRIETARY FINANCIAL SOFTWARE TOOLS

Although they may seem to swim against the technology mainstream of 'three screens and the cloud', in fact the top-grade financial markets and economics software applications are already positioning themselves within the overall trend to communicate with other, customer third-party applications by providing their own APIs and ready-made add-ins for Excel integration, which offer users alternative ways to access data, serving in practice to streamline much of the otherwise more complicated and proprietary workflows of the native Windows desktop interface. This in turn can help reduce training overheads for business library support staff. For more sophisticated users, the API potential is further enhanced when tools such as MATLAB and its DataFeed Toolbox are implemented on the same PC. Because MATLAB provides both a numerical computing environment and a powerful programming language, its DataFeed Toolbox (which integrates with a wide range of historic and real-time markets and economics series data suppliers, including Bloomberg, Datastream, FactSet, Haver Analytics, Reuters MarketData System and even Yahoo! Finance) enables users not only to make simple connections and queries to these systems from within the MATLAB application environment, but also to integrate this data within MATLAB applications of their own.

However powerful and flexible this kind of integration, it is still dominated by the Windows PC desktop as the native APIs for services like Bloomberg are installed with the standard client software – hence Mac users of MATLAB can't directly benefit within the Mac OS. So it seems that financial and numeric markets and business data are still locked into a Windows-desktop, localized platform environment to which the only remote access solution is the less fully functional thin-client alternative.

Currently, for non-Windows and mobile devices, these suppliers offer useful but nonetheless rather functionally limited applications: well suited to users on the move but not yet a realistic proposition replacing their Windows desktop counterparts.

ALTERNATIVE FINANCIAL DATASET ACCESS MODELS: ACADEMIC AND CORPORATE

There is a highly successful, long-established academic finance research datasets application paradigm that has none of the remote access or multiple operating system or device limitations, and is ideally suited to the business school and academic business library world. Wharton Research Data Services (WRDS) is ideally placed to address and overcome many of the challenges we have already identified. Begun at the Wharton School, University of Pennsylvania, in the 1990s, first as an in-house research tool and then successfully developed into the leading international academic finance research platform, WRDS is subscribed to by over 250 business schools, universities and research institutes. The WRDS designers looked at the then current model (which involved loading datasets files licensed from commercial vendors onto local minicomputer systems for terminal access or FTP use), then at the web browser (already in its first incarnations) and envisaged a future for finance research freed from the need for complex proprietary Windows desktop applications that moreover were used only as a conduit to download data for post-processing elsewhere. This platform could be accessed by anyone with a web browser, and a WRDS user account would also still provide traditional character-based console-type access for more specialized use cases. A further key refinement for power users is the ability to connect directly to WRDS datasets from within numeric analysis tools such as PC-SAS to perform complex programmatically-driven queries that join data queried from multiple different datasets into one results table.

The rapid success of WRDS, and its prominent position in academic finance research, owes much to the fact that it was originally designed in the mid-1990s by finance researchers, for finance researchers, and that it neatly combines the new environment (web browser querying using standardized forms, and delivery of data for download within the same browser session) and the older terminal session model for users needing to develop and run programs of their own. By creating a novel, centralized solution, it effectively turned the old paradigm inside out, to provide a unique and primarily web-based service that dissolved physical access boundaries. It's no exaggeration to state that WRDS in its own way has anticipated and pioneered cloud-type finance data applications at least five to ten years before the current web titans began to adopt this model. And that it has created its own ecosystem by successfully partnering with commercial information suppliers, standardizing the user experience for data access, querying and output, and delivering this reliably on a web platform that means all major

OSs and tablet devices are supported. For library administrators, the additional, delegated responsibility of locally managing a WRDS accounts lifecycle has to be offset against the many benefits of a web-based usage reporting tool – another area for which, as we will shortly see below, WRDS offers significant advantages over the desktop-based corporate equivalents.

One main historical issue for WRDS has been that its pre-eminent role in finance research has until very recently been confined to academia and non-profit organizations. In one significant respect, this lessened its attraction for business school students (as opposed to faculty and PhD students) because their WRDS experience could no longer continue in the corporate domains into which they graduated. Unlike, say, experience of Bloomberg or Capital IQ gained during business school programmes, WRDS exposure rated lower on the CV because it was not available in a commercial environment. But that situation may soon begin to change, as from 2012 WRDS has taken the strategic step of marketing a corporate version.

Thomson Reuters, the giant financial data services player, has developed a platform of its own that addresses some of the issues that WRDS originally set out to overcome. Thomson Reuters faces the self-induced challenges created by its various different Windows desktop applications effectively creating and perpetuating a series of multiple datasets silos, when many of its corporate customers also actively desire the WRDS-like freedom to access different datasets within a single, integrated access environment. To tackle this, Thomson Reuters developed its Quantitative Analytics platform (TQA), which integrates both its own data and that from other third parties, along with customers' own, but adds a unique identifier to create a single, normalized massive database. This in turn can be queried through a variety of client applications, including a proprietary client and also linked to MATLAB and other statistical packages such as R and SAS. Whilst potentially attractive as a consolidated access environment, Thomson Reuters Quantitative Analytics in its current incarnation does not use the same WRDS-like cloud model of centralized access, nor is there any built-in, browser-based query environment. Instead, it's effectively a big database composed of sub-databases that needs to be implemented and updated on a customer's own enterprise-grade Microsoft or Oracle Structured Query Language (SQL) platforms. This, of course, ideally suits hedge funds and other investment clients, because their use of data locally hosted in Quantitative Analytics remains fully private and entirely opaque to the supplier, but the significant long-term local IT resource overheads the platform involves, combined with the lack of web client access, make it potentially far less attractive or viable for the academic business library.

STANDARDIZATION ISSUES, BUSINESS LIBRARY PRODUCTIVITY AND THE USER EXPERIENCE

Web-based numeric and textual information services designed for the global corporate marketplace, but which have to be licensed by business libraries in the same formats, pose a series of access management challenges and issues that can adversely affect both the customer experience and also e-resource management workflows and productivity. We can group these issues and challenges under two main headings: user access (the way in which users must log in to use the resource) and usage statistics (once logged in, what data evidence is then available to help business library managers evaluate the use of that resource). We will examine first how the vendors' failure to incorporate compatibility with the latest developments in federated access to e-resources in turn creates significant local overheads for business libraries, particularly for services that are personalization-based. Then we will look at the issues surrounding the problems of obtaining usage statistics and then trying to integrate them with the e-resource management (ERM) tools normally used to collate and analyse e-journal, e-book and textual database usage that rely on data standards adopted by academic and professional publishers. In both these problem domains, we'll see how business libraries struggle with significant lack of information industry standards compliance and innovation apparent in some major areas of the business and professional publishing sectors. This wide variance within the supply chain for key operational functions and reporting processes indicates that this particular business ecosystem is affected by some systemic and persistent problems.

PERSONAL USER ACCOUNTS LIFECYCLE MANAGEMENT OVERHEADS

Personalization of the user experience, providing the options to customize searches and views of data, and to receive email-based alerts, is a staple feature of many textual and numeric-based information services. In the business library arena, examples include: Capital IQ, E-Financial News, Forrester, FT.com, Roubini and WRDS. There are workflow issues around both initial registration and overall lifecycle management, for whilst initial registration is normally conducted via the supplier's existing online process, in many cases shortcomings and inefficiencies exist in the data management tools that suppliers may (or may not) offer to their subscriber's designated administrators.

User access validation typically depends on current academic status, but in business schools and universities the volume of users that has to be managed poses a continuing problem when the personalization-based service does not support an automatically applied expiration data attribute for each user's account. Many academic environments have a high 'rollover' frequency several times a year as students graduate at different times. However, many of the personalization services user account administration tools lack the data triggers to automatically expire accounts at a predefined date aligned to graduation. Moreover, most do not support any kind of batch deletion functions, making both the identification and account deletion process a laborious, repetitive clerical task that has to be undertaken relatively often. Essentially, for services designed primarily for the corporate market, many of the supplier tools for user account management currently offered are poorly designed to cope with these academic scalability issues. WRDS represents an exception because its design originates in the university environment, and it uses a hierarchy of roles (Masters' programme student, PhD student, faculty member, researcher and so on) in combination with account expiration dates that can be adjusted by administrators as needed.

The proliferation of different individual user login accounts so clearly evident in the corporate model of personalized information services consequently adversely affects both users (who must remember, store and recover their credentials) and business library subscribers themselves when staff are required to provide ad hoc support in addition to the productivity-reducing task of account maintenance in multiple vendor systems. The typical scenario whereby a username based on email address combines with a user-chosen password is one that originated nearly two decades ago, and which is itself only reproducing the ancient username/password model dating from a time when only a small handful of computer systems were used by a small number of highly privileged users. Self-evidently, it is only viable for a relatively small number of services; when these scale up across today's typically diverse e-resources service portfolios, it becomes a serious technology-induced burden.

Information professionals are rightly frustrated by this technically and operationally stagnant status quo – the more so since recent developments in user access models now becoming widely adopted within higher education worldwide offer a clear opportunity to apply standards-based technologies and protocols to resolve the issues outlined above. There is already a way for both suppliers and library subscribers to benefit, and that is by using federated authentication techniques as an additional or alternative personal login solution that fully addresses the needs of the academic marketplace.

Federated authentication provides a flexible and secure way for eligible users to access a highly disparate range of computer systems and services but without the need for multiple sets of different credentials. Whereas the widely used username and password model relies on a 'shared secret' (the user and the remote system they log in to both have to store and present a password), federated authentication instead uses a more indirect and flexible technique of checking 'attributes' released from a local authentication system where the user enters their primary local login credentials. Accordingly, one main user account can provide a 'single sign on' experience for many different services, but by releasing trusted information about the user that doesn't involve exchanging the shared secret of the password. Whilst this might seem too restrictive to allow personalization services to work (because a service provider must record a user's email address), the underlying data standards and protocols of federated authentication already cover this contingency. A user can be asked if they wish to disclose more specific personal information (for example, their email address jdoe@rummidgeuniversity.edu, as well as first and last names), and this can then be added to the package of attributes released to the remote service as part of the login and user authorization process. Lastly, in its most basic form, federated access provides the same kind of generic eligibility validation for a data service provider ('this is a user from customer Rummidge University') as the very widespread method of IP address range authentication, but with the added customer and library management benefit of not requiring proxying to extend access to off-campus users. Additionally, an attribute is released that uniquely (but opaquely) creates a unique identifier (computed on a per-user, per-service basis) that the service provider's system can consume and process to support basic user personalization functions (such as displaying items viewed in previous sessions), all without the need to disclose any personal details.

Federated access accordingly delivers many best-practice benefits for personal identity and access data management: a user's information remains securely controlled and updated by their home institution as part of normal business and lifecycle processes. This significantly reduces or even removes the need for exchanging, storing and duplication often quite extensive personal information (users' personal names, email addresses and so on) spread across a range of external systems outside the home institution's direct control and scrutiny. Federated access can deliver significant improvements across the board: making users' lives simpler, reducing data overheads on the supplier, and improving library staff productivity whilst streamlining licensing compliance. Yet it is noticeably not implemented by the majority of specialized numeric and textual information services that sell into the business library segment of the academic market. This is a key differentiator and technological challenge for the business library, when most of the main academic online aggregators (such as EBSCO, ProQuest, Ovid) and many publishers (Elsevier, Wiley Blackwell), already support federated login.

There are several reasons why take-up of federated access is so poor inside the information industry sectors that business libraries most commonly deal with. The principal factors are currently complexity, cost and lack of wider corporate, market-driven demand. The drive to implement federated authentication has come from academic technology funding and policy-making bodies such as JISC in the UK and Internet2 in the USA. But there is a much more fragmented and less focused interest on the business IT domain, despite the initiatives of Liberty Alliance (now Kantara) to bring leading commercial technology vendors together. Federated authentication brings its own challenges at both ends of the supply chain: vendors and library subscribers alike must grapple with the initial technical complexities of implementing service and identity provider services (since it is a specialized IT skills domain), and bear the continuing soft and hard costs of maintaining hardware and software For many information providers, the business case is complicated and less attractive due to key technical challenges deriving from retrospectively adding federated access as a new project to a business system where it was never previously within scope. Unless and until the majority of business customers begin to implement federated access, then business libraries will remain tied to the default and familiar status quo methods of either IP address range authentication (and proxying for remote use) or traditional proprietary username and password. It is only by joining forces to create the needed critical mass effect of customer scale, that business libraries will stand any chance of convincing commercially-oriented information suppliers to adopt federated authentication.

BUSINESS INFORMATION PUBLISHING AND THE CHALLENGES FOR E-RESOURCE MANAGEMENT

A lack of standards compatibility leads inevitably to discontinuities and anomalies within the supply chain. Business libraries are particularly vulnerable because they typically have to license online information resources from suppliers whose main marketing and support operations focus on the corporate sector and whose publishing activities may not use globally unique identifiers such as print and e-ISSNs or -ISBNs or even digital object identifiers (DOIs). This means that a significant proportion of a business library's e-resources expenditure is placed with data suppliers that operate entirely outside a now increasingly well-defined and highly integrated e-resources management (ERM) model whose processes and tools are commonly adopted by libraries worldwide for both content activation and usage cost–benefit analysis. Issues consequently arise in two main areas: the knowledge bases (KBs) used to populate OpenURL resolver and Discovery services, and usage statistics. In an era of continuing financial uncertainty, stringent cost controls and pressure on library budgets there is a consequent requirement to manage the spectrum of subscribed e-resources wherever possible within the same range of ERM tools and processes. These ERM environments in turn rely on a suite of data standards and protocols (including DOI, Open URL, KBART, ONIX, COUNTER and SUSHI) for textual resources developed through extensive collaboration between key players in the supply chain: libraries, publishers, information aggregators and platform vendors.

The unfortunate reality for business libraries is that the technology platforms for ERM are designed to work primarily with publishers and suppliers of textual resources that conform to the standardized environment of unique content identifiers. This means that e-journals and e-books are well covered, but other kinds of important business, financial and economic content, including investment research, market research reports, country analysis, numeric data amongst others, which comprise key parts of business libraries' service propositions, are immediately incompatible with the main ERM tools for both content activation and usage analysis. Some simple examples will illustrate the gulf between general academic content and more specialized practitioner-oriented business literature:

- The top-ranked peer-reviewed academic journal *Administrative Science Quarterly (ASQ)* is available in different forms (current and archival volumes) through a wide variety of channels and can be quickly activated for OpenURL resolvers and Discovery systems as it will already have multiple knowledge-base entries. The pivotal identifiers for *ASQ* as a 'content object' are its unique print and electronic ISSNs which support a common key for data-tracking and analysis in multiple systems used within the ERM ecosystem.
- Moreover, usage of this journal can be quickly and easily tracked over time across different channels using COUNTER statistics. These can be consolidated in a COUNTER-based analysis tools such as ExLibris' UStat or Serials Solutions' 360 Counter.
- The e-journal subscription costs for the latest publisher-hosted volume can be configured in the COUNTER analysis tool, to provide cost analysis per downloaded article.
- In the European private equity field, the monthly practitioner journal *Real Deals* is influential. To access current and historic content requires a subscription to the publisher's website, but there is no ISSN assigned to this journal, nor will the publisher undertake to supply usage statistics.
- To activate the title in a KB to appear in an e-journals A–Z list involves manually creating an entry, but no usage data can be linked to its annual subscription cost for further (comparative) analysis.

Similar problematic examples can be found with market research publishers, where, even if reports are published within a series, identifiers such as ISSNs, ISBNs or even DOIs are not used.

Consequently, the ERM workload for business libraries is significantly increased within the textual publication domain, since typically each specialized business practitioner content publisher will generate its usage statistics in a proprietary way. This effectively creates a two- or even three-speed ERM workflow scenario which actively disrupts and protracts the collection management process by fragmenting usage data and actively obscuring actual levels of use (or non-use) of content:

- Academic e-journals and e-books that use globally standardized identifiers can be readily managed within an ERM system for content activation and usage analysis based on COUNTER statistics.
- Practitioner business reports and other similar content published online with no standardized identifiers require usage to be analysed offline in multiple spreadsheets outside an ERM system.

Numeric (financial and economic datasets) resources delivered as Windows desktop applications will necessarily require yet another series of offline, non-standardized and fragmented usage analysis workflows. Some suppliers (for example, Bloomberg) will not release any service usage data, due to markets compliance issues. Others (for example, Thomson Reuters) can supply number of series downloaded or types of analysis run. It might seem unrealistic to require three such very different information genres to be compatible with current ERM tools, given their inherently very different attributes. But when business libraries are faced with internal reporting tasks such as balanced scorecard analysis, the ability to impose some form of standardization for usage data becomes more urgent. Faced with such a range of highly proprietary reporting practice within its resource portfolio, what wider community initiatives and techniques can a business library harness to address this lack of standardization?

One approach is to start with the most basic usage statistic dimension – the user session. If vendors prove unwilling or unable to supply this data, then it must be captured at the local point of origin. This can be harvested from service links in library e-resource web pages, institutional portals or (where access is managed via an EZproxy server or federated access identity provider service), via logfiles analysis using the open-source RAPTOR software project. RAPTOR provides a web-based administrative 'dashboard' to identify individual resource usage, which can then be downloaded to Excel or as a PDF.

It may be desirable to enforce standardization on non-standard e-resource usage data by means of a coercion technique to reformat it to the best-fit report in the COUNTER Code of Practice. This has the advantage of ensuring that the resulting usage report file can be loaded and analysed in an ERM system alongside native COUNTER reports from fully compliant data suppliers. If considering both textual and numeric data services, then the COUNTER JR (Journal Report) and BR (Book Report) series are incompatible, as they rely on identifiers (print or e-ISSNs/ISBNs). The pragmatic choice is the COUNTER Database Report 1: Total Searches and Sessions by Month and Database, which can report on usage for a database or content module within an overall publisher or platform system namespace. The COUNTER DB1 report format thus provides some means for business libraries to help consolidate and standardize usage data from non-COUNTER-compliant information services, within an ERM system, to reduce the burden of fragmented statistical collection that otherwise adversely affects the reporting process.

E-BOOKS

E-books currently represent a major problem domain for library e-resource managers in that they present multiple simultaneous challenges, not least because technology issues for use and service management are closely bound up with the vagaries of different publisher and aggregator business models and strategies. Business libraries inevitably share many of these format, delivery and access platform issues with their academic and public library counterparts, but a key factor in e-book management in the business library environment is frequently the most basic: availability in online form. As part of the broad 'professional' content marketplace, business book publishing is typified by low print runs, frequent edition updates and consistently very high costs for the most popular specialized texts set as recommended course readings. The result is the business library service paradox that sees many of the most popular materials remain locked in a print format, with all the attendant discomfort factors, such as remote access, weight and bulk, proving problematic for students who need to travel long distances to campus, or whose contact time is limited.

The dense and often complex formatting of print business books, particularly the more technical financial and accounting kind containing exhibits and mathematical formulae, may actually translate less successfully to the online or digital format than simpler manuscripts found in the consumer or leisure markets. This is particularly true when little genuine new user value is added to the digital textbook proposition, such as the ability to interactively view underlying data (as is increasingly common in online academic journal articles). There is evident publisher reluctance to allow library customers to cherry-pick their most popular print titles as e-books; instead, a graduate business school may be offered only a bundle containing a mixture of some high-value titles that match its mission but also others of little direct relevance because they are aimed at undergraduates. The anecdotal experience of business librarians confirms that business and technical publishers are still highly reluctant to abandon a print model, where professional topic books may retail between $100 and $200 each, for a digital format where the consumer and leisure e-book markets (driven by the massive ecosystems of Apple and Amazon) have primed users to expect e-books to sell for a tenth of those sums.

At present, the topic of e-book management across multiple devices points to a period of huge divergence rather than convergence, such is the bewildering array of proprietary devices and platforms available. Any effective e-book management and delivery technology solution will have to engage and solve the problems not just of cost and availability, but also of formatting, access across different devices for the same or multiple users, and the need for synchronization of lecturer and student annotations. VitalSource's BookShelf e-textbook delivery platform (strong in the medical field) provides one such example.

'BIG DATA' AND THE BUSINESS LIBRARY

For all kinds of libraries, the tracking, collation and analysis of subscription content usage statistics represents another manifestation of the well-known 'big data' problem (Naughton, 2012). Our customers' usage ('activity') data is itself an essential organic part of the e-resources management ecosystem: library managers are challenged to use this data for collection analysis and improving the user experience. Notwithstanding the problems identified and outlined above with business information resources that are currently non-compliant with activity usage data standards like COUNTER, there is a huge untapped potential for surfacing our usage data for the benefit of users and representing it in new ways to help them better understand the content available.

COUNTER journal usage data can directly support more effective, evidence-based decision-making for business library e-journal collection management purposes, particularly when local activity data can be compared with aggregated usage generated by a wider community. In late 2011 the London Business School Library needed to review its options for renewing a five-year academic consortium agreement for Elsevier ScienceDirect-hosted journals. Our own Elsevier COUNTER usage data identified our most heavily used titles (which in turn determine which titles we contractually needed to 'retain') over the outgoing agreement period, but we could additionally and very effectively augment that evidence with the community-aggregated top 100 and top 250 titles by volume usage, from the UK academic peer group of other Elsevier ScienceDirect-subscribing libraries. This example shows how such large-scale, community-based activity data pooling can deliver significant benefits for e-resource collection decision-making, not least because the aggregated usage dataset helps individual smaller institutions identify and offset possible statistical distortions in their own data, as may be introduced by side-effects of the Law of Small Numbers (Kahneman, 2011).

A fuller discussion of the opportunities and challenges of activity data collation and analysis is beyond the scope of this chapter, but a recent UK report (Kay and van Harmelen, 2012) provides a useful high-level summary with case studies from universities in the UK and the USA. One of the latter includes discussion of the Pennsylvania State University Libraries' MetriDoc initiative. A technology framework for library usage activity assessment and analytics, MetricDoc is notable for its ambition to collect data from as many different activity sources (library management systems, COUNTER, resource authentication logs) as possible. The MetriDoc project goals highlight the substantial current and future problems involved in trying to collate, store, normalize and then analyse the very wide range of data observations that libraries collect from their portfolios of different resource management systems.

Much of the practitioner discussion of activity data centres on its use in analytics (that is, how it can generate actionable outcomes) for business intelligence, shaping key decisions on e-resource subscriptions and refining or even transforming services and workflows. However, one further potential application of content usage data (where it is available at a detailed level for textual services) could be to build innovative data visualizations as part of business libraries' continuing user education, training and communications processes – for example, dynamically generated heat- or tree-map-type graphical usage reports that showcase activity against content available within specialized information services. This is particularly relevant given that the systems architecture of many such services cannot support direct linking of the kind powered by OpenURL and DOI within academic publishing systems, thus making it difficult to create dynamic recommendation-based services.

The big data effect (combined with the long-term impact of the global economic crisis on higher education funding, and the rapid development of cloud computing) is also manifesting itself in other solutions to technology challenges that academic libraries face. It is well known that the e-resources business ecosystem poses many data management issues, and some recent initiatives are emerging on the shared services model to harness community resources and expertise to deliver new solutions. In the UK, the KnowledgeBase Plus (KB+) pilot project aims to improve workflows for e-journal (and e-book) subscription management, and works closely with the US-based Global Open Knowledgebase (GOKb) to provide open, high-quality publication information about e-resources.

CONCLUSIONS

Predicting technology futures with high degrees of accuracy is an undertaking fraught with risk. Many famous industry names have been notoriously and amusingly caught out by hindsight – notably Bill Gates when in charge of Microsoft (Pogue, 2012) – proving perhaps that even those apparently closest to the levers of change may sometimes know the least. This chapter has sought to focus on the present reality at the expense of discussing more nascent or even glamorous technologies, including, but not of course limited to, such marvels as online avatars for user reference and guidance encounters, e-paper, augmented reality – as identified in one recent study of personalized library services in higher education (Wales, 2012) – that may yet help transform the service proposition. These may soon prove as commonplace as the formerly bizarrely futuristic notion of a palm-sized device that would enable its user to watch real-time streamed media clips on a telephone when travelling through city suburbs or the open countryside.

Technology challenges for the business library have been outlined in this chapter against the backdrop of now widespread technology trends: the 'consumerization' pressure represented by the bring your own device (BYOD) phenomenon (McLellan, 2013), whereby users increasingly expect that their personal device (whether a smart phone, tablet, laptop PC or netbook) can consistently access the same sophisticated corporate-grade services found on desktop PCs, from any location. Accordingly, business libraries receive students armed with Apple Mac PCs, iPads, iPhones, Android phones and tablets; Amazon Kindles and other proprietary e-book devices, who expect to access business information data services seamlessly on these platforms, not just on fixed-location Windows desktop PCs. Although business libraries self-evidently need to reflect the commercial organizational world in their e-resource subscriptions, this should not mean that we remain satisfied with the status quo shortcomings evident in Windows desktop applications and outdated authentication methods.

Whilst Discovery services are helping integrate diverse kinds of e-content into a single search-and-access environment, business libraries will inevitably find that their portfolios cannot thus be fully integrated into a single platform. A major challenge is to harness technology to improve the communication with users and stakeholders to better surface proprietary content and help maximize its effective use. Because the established protocols of Discovery web-indexed search and document linking remain, for the present, beyond the scope of many text and numeric business information services, we need to focus on innovations in our resource presentation environment, ideally using appropriate data visualization techniques based on the 'big data' our individual and peer institutions usage profiles will generate.

The challenges we face represent another aspect of the kind of convergence in technology outlined at the start of this chapter. However, we need to see this in terms of personal professional development. The global financial crisis of recent years has imposed staffing constraints on organizations of all kinds, forcing employees to develop cross-domain skills in response to this changing climate and increasing pressure to deliver service improvements with fewer resources. So, for example, a librarian specializing in e-resources must rapidly acquire a statistical facility to cope with the increasing demands for ROI and balanced scorecard analysis to be generated from wildly varying and often un-normalized usage data. And when working with colleagues to deliver e-resource collection analysis, support and training, the statistical role needs to be further developed into data visualization, to help summarize patterns and trends and then to communicate these in ways that can be immediately understood, whether by peers, senior managers or customers.

Keeping track of the extensive range of actual and potential information and communications technology solutions, protocols and standards represents a continuing skills and competencies framework challenge. The commoditization of technology and the creation of massive, globally and instantly accessible *de facto* shared services for general information storage and communication, driven by Google and Facebook amongst others, suggest that we no longer need to rely on local library-oriented systems and programming expertise because the former complexities have disappeared as part of the great Web 2.0 paradigm shift. However, business libraries will continue to need a professionally-experienced, applied technology and data management skills backbone, just like any other kind of library, to evaluate, select and implement the most appropriate and effective combination of components in line with mission and business need.

Business libraries stand apart from the academic library mainstream by virtue of their engagement with corporate-grade specialized information services which typically remain incompatible with many of the ERM tools and processes that help streamline service delivery and business analysis. To assure the current and future health of our own business ecosystem, the business library sector must continue to press suppliers to maximize opportunities to utilize specialized technology standards, protocols and workflows wherever possible to improve productivity within the entire supply chain.

REFERENCES

Kahneman, D.J., 2011. The Law of Small Numbers. In: *Thinking, Fast and Slow*. London: Penguin, 112–13.

Kay, D. and van Harmelen, M., 2012. Activity Data: Delivering Benefits from the Data Deluge [online]. JISC At: https://repository.jisc.ac.uk/5010/1/JISC_Activity_Data_singlepages.pdf (accessed 10 February 2013).

McLellan, C., 2013. Consumerization, BYOD and MDM: What You Need to Know [online]. ZDNet. At: http://www.zdnet.com/consumerization-byod-and-mdm-what-you-need-to-know-7000010205/ (accessed 22 February 2013).

Moore, J.F., 1993. Predators and Prey: A New Ecology of Competition. *Harvard Business Review*, 71(3), 75–86.

Naughton, J., 2012. Big Data: Revolution by Numbers [online]. *Observer*, 18 November. At: http://www.guardian.co.uk/technology/2012/nov/18/data-analysis-applied-business-science (accessed 22 February 2013).

Ozzie, R., 2009 Three Screens and the Cloud [online]. At: http://www.youtube.com/watch?v=CbdvMxMgyC4 (accessed 4 January 2013).

Pogue, D., 2012. Use It Better: The Worst Tech Predictions of All Time [online]. *Scientific American*, 18 January. http://www.scientificamerican.com/article.cfm?id=pogue-all-time-worst-tech-predictions (accessed 20 February 2013).

Wales, T. (2012). Library Technologies for Boutique Services. In A. Priestner and E. Tilley (eds), *Personalising Library Services in Higher Education: The Boutique Approach*, Farnham: Ashgate, 63–86.

Products and websites referenced

360 Counter. At: http://www.serialssolutions.com/en/services/360-counter (accessed 22 September 2013).

Authentication World. At: http://www.authenticationworld.com/Authentication-Federation/ (accessed 20 December 2012).

Azure. At: http://www.windowsazure.com (accessed 20 December 2012).

Bloomberg. At: http://www.bloomberg.com/professional/tools-analytics/mobile/ (accessed 20 December 2012).

COUNTER. At: http://www.projectcounter.org (accessed 14 October 2012).

COUNTER DB1 report. At: http://www.projectcounter.org/r3/Release3D9.pdf (accessed 14 October 2012).
DOI. At: http://www.doi.org/factsheets/DOIKeyFacts.html (accessed 14 October 2012).
EZproxy. At: http://www.oclc.org/ezproxy (accessed 15 October 2012).
FactSet Connect. At: http://connect.factset.com (accessed 20 December 2012).
GOKb. At: http://gokb.org (accessed 13 February 2013).
Haver Analytics. At: http://www.haver.com (accessed 20 December 2012).
Internet2. At: http://www.internet2.edu/ (accessed 10 January 2013).
Joint Information Systems Committee (JISC) UK Federated Access Management. At: http://www.jisc.ac.uk/whatwedo/themes/accessmanagement/federation.aspx (accessed 22 September 2013).
Kantara. At: http://kantarainitiative.org/ (accessed 10 January 2013).
KBART (Knowledge Base And Related Tools). At: http://www.niso.org/workrooms/kbart (accessed 10 February 2013).
KnowledgeBase Plus (KB+). At: http://www.jisc-collections.ac.uk/knowledgebaseplus/ (accessed 13 February 2013).
MATLAB DataFeed Toolbox. At: http://www.mathworks.co.uk/products/datafeed/ (accessed 20 December 2012).
MetriDoc. At: http://metridoc.library.upenn.edu/ (accessed 10 February 2013).
ONIX. At: http://www.editeur.org/8/ONIX/ (accessed 10 February 2013).
OpenURL. At: http://www.niso.org/apps/group_public/project/details.php?project_id=82 (accessed 10 February 2013).
R. (R Project for Statistical Computing). At: http://www.r-project.org/ (accessed 20 December 2012).
RAPTOR. At: http://iam.cf.ac.uk/trac/RAPTOR (accessed 10 January 2013).
SAS. At: http://www.sas.com/technologies/analytics/statistics/ (accessed 20 December 2012).
SCCM (Microsoft System Center Configuration Manager). At: http://www.microsoft.com/en-us/server-cloud/system-center/configuration-manager-2012.aspx (accessed 10 January 2013).
ScienceDirect. At: http://www.sciencedirect.com/ (accessed 22 September 2013).
SUSHI (Standardized Usage Statistics Harvesting Initiative). At: http://www.niso.org/apps/group_public/project/details.php?project_id=111 (accessed 10 February 2013).
Thomson Quantitative Analytics. At: http://thomsonreuters.com/products_services/financial/financial_products/a-z/QA_Direct/ (accessed 10 January 2013).
Thomson Reuters Datastream Professional. At: http://thomsonreuters.com/datastream-professional/ (accessed 10 January 2013).
Thomson Reuters EIKON. At: https://thomsonreuterseikon.com/ (accessed 10 January 2013).
Thomson Reuters SDC Platinum. At: http://thomsonreuters.com/sdc-platinum/ (accessed 10 January 2013).

UStat. At: http://www.exlibrisgroup.com/category/SFXforLibrarians (accessed 22 September 2013).
VitalSource. At: http://www.vitalsource.com (accessed 22 February 2013).
Wharton Research Data Services (WRDS). At: http://wrds.wharton.upenn.edu (accessed 30 September 2012).

CHAPTER 7

OPEN ARCHIVES IN FRANCE: AN OVERVIEW OF THE ACADEMIC SECTOR

AGNÈS MELOT AND SOPHIE FORCADELL[1]

INTRODUCTION

At the end of the 1980s the world of research and libraries faced a significant increase in the cost of subscriptions to scientific journals. At the same time, the arrival of the Internet gave rise to new methods of communicating information. These two phenomena merged together and the concept of open access was born: free, immediate access to research results. By making their publications accessible online to all web users, researchers are enabling the dissemination of their research amongst other researchers all over the world, whatever the information budget of their own institution.

Open access is categorized into two different routes: the 'gold route' and the 'green route'. The first is the route by which publication is no longer financed 'downstream' by subscriptions but 'upstream' by publishing charges paid for by the author's institution. The second 'green route' is only dependent on engagement by researchers and their affiliated institutions. This route encompasses so-called 'open archives': websites in which authors deposit their articles before or after publication so they become easily and freely accessible. Two major types of open archive exist: subject/sector repositories or institutional repositories. The latter are defined by the Couperin Consortium (2013) as: '... an institutional archive bringing together the entire output of an institution (research, heritage, teaching and administration ...)'. In this chapter we will only be focusing on the green route, or open archives. Rigeade provides a brief summary of their history:

> The first open archive, ArXiv, was conceived by the physicist P. Ginsparg in 2001. It inspired Stevan Harnard's 'subversive proposal' that urged authors to deposit their pre-prints and post-prints in an institutional server. In February 2000, the PubMed Central archive was launched to provide access to research results. The adoption of the OAI-PMH protocol in July 2001 was an important

---

1   Chapter and quotations from sources translated from the original French version by Tim Wales.

step in the development of open archives. It enables interoperability between all the open archives in the world through the exchange of metadata. At the same time the final versions of the two main Open Source software platforms for Open Archives were released: GNU EPrints and DSpace. Still in the same year, researchers committed to the development of open access met in Budapest to finalize the 'Budapest Open Access Initiative' which encourages researchers to self-archive their works. University and research libraries played an important part in this movement. In 2002, IFLA published the 'IFLA Internet Manifesto' supporting open access and many library associations signed up to the 'Budapest Open Access Declaration'. (Rigeade, 2012, p. 15)

In 2004 the UK House of Commons Science and Technology Committee published a report, *Free for All?*, recommending the self-archiving of all published articles by British researchers. A European Commission report was published two years later, also recommending mandatory self-archiving after an embargo period (European Commission, 2006). The Commission, following the UK's lead, recommended free and rapid access to public research in compliance with author and other rights. European Union involvement followed in the form of the DRIVER project, which brought together different universities, research associations and the Centre National de Recherche Scientifique (CNRS) in France. DRIVER's aim is to create an open repository infrastructure for articles and a common-access interface across archive networks. Today, the DRIVER portal includes 295 repositories from 38 countries. Built using the DRIVER infrastructure, OpenAIRE facilitates compliance with the deposit mandate for public research outputs agreed by the European Commission and European Research Council. In France, the Couperin Consortium manages the OpenAIRE project interface.

The French model's uniqueness comes from it being a dual model based on a national open archive called HAL and a network of local institutional archives. HAL was developed in 2000 by the Centre pour la Communication Scientifique (CCSD), reporting to the CNRS. It went live in 2006 following the University Vice-Chancellors' and Grande Ecoles' conferences which had both signed up to the open access movement. A multidisciplinary open archive, HAL is '… intended for the deposit and dissemination of scientific research-grade articles (published or unpublished) and theses, originating from French or foreign teaching and research establishments, public or private laboratories' (HAL, 2013). Registered researchers are able to deposit their publications directly into HAL, provided that the documents are one of the types described above. The deposit process occurs in four stages, during which researchers can be assisted by a librarian: provision of descriptive metadata; author metadata; file transfer and verification followed by source-checking. Note that there is no quality-checking of the publication or its scientific level – the CSSD does not perform editorial control. Once a text has been deposited in HAL it cannot be withdrawn; on the contrary, the platform accepts multiple versions of the same article – which is one constraint of this platform. A second constraint is linked to the fact that HAL does not harvest other archives reciprocally and so requires direct deposit – that is, depositing a document in an institutional repository does not lead automatically to the deposit of the same document in HAL. Berthaud (2012) provides some statistics for HAL:

- As of 2012 HAL comprises 93 gateways, or 213,319 scientific articles available in full-text of which 42,276 fall within the humanities and social sciences, 32,549 theses in TEL (*theses en ligne*) and more than 600,000 authors referenced.
- Of the 39,589 full-text deposits made in 2012m 16,627 were self-archived. The distribution by type of publication is as follows: 6,067 pre-print; 12,282 articles in journals with editorial boards; 1,183 book chapters; 95 books; 6,777 papers from conference proceedings; and 6,708 theses. In 2012, 2,763 translations and 2,635 links were made with ArXiv, 1,736 translations made with RePEc and 465 with PubMed.
- Numbers of accesses rose in 2012 to 173,415,492: 13,424,181 files and 3,004,995 theses downloaded.
- Ten new gateways were launched in 2012, one of which was the HAL-Audencia Business School, as well as 485 open access collections.
- The most recent global rankings for open archives (CSIC, 2013) puts HAL in sixth place overall and TEL in eleventh place. Despite this good showing, HAL is still only accounting for a relatively small coverage rate of 10–15 per cent for French scientific publications. Institutional archives are faring better.

Institutional archives developed from the outset, in parallel with HAL, as services dedicated to researchers. Their number increased in France, from 31 in 2008 to 81 in 2009. Several recent studies have tried to estimate the number of French open archives as distinct from the number of institutional open archives. This was recently attempted by Rigeade (2012) in her dissertation. The author carried out an empirical study of 101 institutional archives in France: 36 institutions (including Paris Dauphine University) decided to create a local open archive and 65 institutions opted for a 'collection label' (an institutional gateway presence) on the national archive platform, HAL. This latter option makes available all publications by researchers at the same institution within the same collection and it is the preferred option for four business schools, including HEC Paris.

The following two sections study in more detail:

1. the role played by university libraries and French Grandes Ecoles (including business schools) in the development of open archives in France;
2. two case studies: the Paris Dauphine University open archive and use of the SSRN network in two business schools: INSEAD and HEC Paris.

THE ROLE OF UNIVERSITY LIBRARIES AND FRENCH GRANDES ECOLES

In order to understand the open-archive situation in France within the academic sector and the consequent role played by libraries, it is worth noting the results of a recent study on the subject.

The 2012 enquiry into open archives in France

This was conducted on behalf of four major players, Couperin, the Association des Directeurs et Personnels de Direction des Bibliothèques Universitaires et de la Documentation (ADBU), the Institut National de la Recherche Agronomique (INRA) and the Institut National de Recherche en Informatique et en Automatique (INRIA), in the first quarter of 2012. The inquiry, which followed on from an initial Couperin study carried out in 2008, had the aim of establishing an overview of French open-archive projects and achievements. It considered every type of teaching and research institution: EPST, EPIC, university or Grande Ecole, capable of producing an open archive, whether an institutional repository or a HAL-hosted collection.

The first important point to note is the high number of institutions responding (178), making this study very representative of the open-archive landscape in France. Of these 178 responses, 145 institutions indicated that they already had a live archive or an archive project underway, twice as many as in 2008. We note in passing that 92 per cent of the respondents to this survey were linked to libraries and that this extensive library involvement can be found throughout the results of the study.

Open archives as a prominent part of organizational identity
A primary characteristic of open archives in France is the small number of 'inter-institutional tools': 23 per cent of systems in place at present. This number is even smaller for those universities connecting up (or in the process of connecting up) to the PRES 'mega-structures', numbering 26 in 2012.

Institutional repositories are considered to positively reflect an institution's identity because they make a strong contribution to its development. Purposes behind the decision to embark on an open-archive project are often, first, research development or institutional development followed by the creation of a heritage archive (as opposed to supporting peer review which is seldom cited).

The same characteristic is true in differentiating between the institutional archive projects and those using the HAL platform. For those open-archive projects designated as pilot projects, 75 per cent are institutional archive projects while the projects using the HAL platform are much less prevalent. At the end of the day, open archives must be communication tools for the institution as well as for the researcher who prefers to maximize the visibility of his work rather than collect bibliometric indicators.

Cost: an important aspect in the choice of open access tool
Of the 155 open archives currently available, 46 are institutional archives and 53 are archives on the HAL platform (10 of these consist of regular direct deposits into the HAL archive without an institutional portal and six are integrated into subject open archives).

In terms of costs, the principal difference between an institutional repository and a HAL archive comes down to a technical level: purchase of computer hardware in the first case costs around €10,000 on average (but with large variations) while the technology costs for a HAL portal project come to around €625 on average. So, apart from the fundamental consideration of the institution's strategy in the subject area, its budget situation plays a very important part.

Finally, concerning the systems used, the most prevalent system at present is ORI-OAI (44 per of respondents), followed by EPrints (145), custom developments (11 per cent) and DSpace (9 per cent).

Theses are the most commonly available document type in open-archive repositories
Unsurprisingly, most open archives in France hold theses (72 per cent of responses). Lest we forget, legal deposit of theses is mandatory in France and henceforth in electronic form, too (but distribution by Internet is not mandatory). Pre-print articles and conference proceedings are the next most common types. Overall, deposits have risen 71 per cent between 2008 and 2012.

It is also not surprising that full-text documents are more prevalent in institutional archives than in HAL archives: 80 per cent of institutional archives house 100 per cent full-text documents compared to 37 per cent of HAL archives (with very noticeable disparities).

Library staff are at the heart of the system
Library staff are the most frequently cited personnel dedicated to open archives, way above IT staff, whatever phase the project has got to. Scientific and technical publishing support services staff are next, followed by researchers, but in a very small minority.

And what role do librarians have specifically? This is centred on the deposit process (59 per cent in 2012 against 63 per cent in 2008) but it has since evolved towards metadata management (74.4 per cent in 2012 compared with 59.3 per cent in 2008). We also note that, in 2008, 16.3 per cent of librarians took on a scientific moderator role while only 9 per cent carry out this role today. These results tend to show that library staff today are refocusing and specializing in their roles, but any appeals to researchers to manage their own deposits themselves are not guaranteed success.

Researchers are at the heart of reported problems
This last point has been shown in the various challenges reported by open-archive managers. Even if the difficulties are fewer today than they were in 2008 (see Table 7.1), the main challenge four years on remains the lack of researcher engagement.

Table 7.1   Open archives management challenges

Challenges reported	2012 (Insignificant)	2008 (Insignificant)	2012 (Significant)	2008 (Significant)
Insufficient institutional communication	25.0%	7.0%	26.0%	18.4%
Insufficient researcher/author engagement	15.0%	6.1%	30%	19.4%
Insufficient technical/information skills	63.0%	23.5%	4.0%	7.1%
Budget constraints	70%	24.3%	2.0%	6.1%
Lack of staff resource	37.0%	9.6%	19.0%	19.4%
Insufficient political will	34.0%	15.7%	20.0%	16.3%

Source: ADBU Couperin (2012).

In order to overcome this lack of researcher engagement, judged weak or below average by 40 per cent of respondents, 'face-to-face' communication is preferred. Is this because the lack of any other means of communication to complement this one leads to an image problem with the system on the part of decision-makers and researchers?

A mandate (or strong incentive) to deposit is one of the solutions to this problem most often cited today. According to the results of this survey, it remains seldom used but is used more often with institutional archives compared to deposits in HAL.

The conclusion to this survey found that the open-archive landscape in France is still heterogeneous. Institutional archives, on account of their higher cost and their role in supporting institutional strategies, are more likely to be subject to volume and quality controls relating to: the types of documents deposited; the proportion of full-text documents or the existence of a mandate or incentive to deposit. On the other hand, management of HAL portals varies considerably from one portal to another, and this global system still lacks coordination and sharing of best practice.

The management of open archives in French business schools

The survey discussed above has shown that scientific disciplines covered by the open-archive movement in France are very varied but that it is the 'hard' sciences (cited in 78 per cent of responses) that dominate followed by law/economics/management disciplines (52.4 per cent), arts and humanities (48.6 per cent) and medicine/pharmacology (32.4 per cent). In order to understand in more detail the picture relating to management science open archives, it is worth focusing on French business schools, which represent a large proportion of research in these disciplines.

ACIEGE members, representing French business schools
ACIEGE is an association founded in 1993 to promote the sharing of best practice amongst member institutions. We surveyed this sample of 37 teaching institutions of varying sizes on their open-archive systems or projects. The survey, circulated on the association's electronic mailing list, included around 10 questions on working or planned repositories in member institutions, the type of documents archived and the challenges faced.

Libraries are originating archive projects
Out of the 13 libraries responding, only one did not know whether an open archive existed in its parent institution. All the others have either new or existing tools or projects. Amongst those business schools not having a repository at present or having one in development, the main reason provided was the lack of interest shown by the academic body in increasing the visibility of researchers' research outputs. Existing repositories or those in development were all started by libraries but no institutional archive was cited: open archives were exclusively portal-type systems in HAL.

Still very few full-text documents
Contrary to the national survey mentioned in the first section of this chapter, our survey surfaced the virtual absence of full-text deposits. At a national level, those institutions depositing in HAL achieved a 37 per cent full-text deposit rate whilst for ACIEGE institutions, the proportion is statistically insignificant. Business schools put this down to the reticence of researchers to deposit their full-text outputs even if this is permitted by publisher agreements. On the other hand, the strong incentives in certain institutions for their researchers to publish in a prescribed and restricted set of journals do not favour full-text deposit either. One solution adopted by these libraries is to deposit the research papers of their researchers [themselves].

Legal issues remain an obstacle
Whilst editorial policies concerning pre-print, post-print and final-version deposits are starting to become clearer and more flexible, notably thanks to the SHERPA RoMEO database, librarians say that they still spend far too much time checking potential deposits in terms of permitted archiving or author rights. Taking into account the fact that these libraries are often relatively small in size, the time spent on such activity is often to the detriment of other essential library operational activities.

CASE STUDIES: PARIS DAUPHINE UNIVERSITY'S OPEN ARCHIVE AND THE USE OF SSRN IN TWO FRENCH BUSINESS SCHOOLS

Case study 1: Paris Dauphine University's open archive – a pioneer in management sciences in France[2]

Paris Dauphine University specializes in the hard social sciences (management, law, economics, political sciences, sociology, applied mathematics and decision sciences). It has an intake of 10,483 students each year in higher or executive education programmes of which 3,685 are undergraduates, 5,580 taught postgraduates, 452 PhD (50 per cent foreign students) and 1,324 in executive education. The staff body comprises 527 researchers (of which 110 are university professors), 225 assistant professors, 1,666 adjunct faculty drawn from the professions and 444 tenured or contract non-academic staff (librarians, IT engineers, administrators, technicians, estates staff).

Its international credentials are evidenced by the fact that 30 per cent of its students are foreign, coming from 110 different countries. The university also has 231 student exchange agreements in place with 51 countries and offers 20 combined honours programmes in 10 countries.

So it was in this context that the Dauphine institutional archive was created in 2009. Its purpose was to support the university in giving greater visibility to the works of its researchers. The strong strategic imperative of the university manifested itself through:

- the decision of its Scientific Council to create a publications database for its researchers
- the Paris Dauphine University Library joining the Nereus European Consortium in 2006 (comprising 19 large European universities) and Project NEEO, which led to the creation of the Economists Online database.[3]

---

2   The authors acknowledge the assistance of Christine Okret-Manville, Assistant Director of Paris Dauphine University Library with this section.
3   Ceased operation in January 2014.

From the very beginning, the library has been associated with (and was expected to set up) the open archive. It selected the DSpace open-source software to host it. This was for three main reasons: first, because the software is very flexible and easy for the library to master; second, because it is a widely used tool in the university sector; and, third, because it offers a complete workflow for creating a quality bibliographic database with deposit and validation by librarians.

The researchers' publications database or university institutional repository was named BIRD. It has offered, since 2009, direct deposit of publications by researchers, harvesting of data from external databases (laboratory databases and HAL, the national open archive) and researcher profiles created by librarians. Librarians check copyright notices, correct errors, add Dewey classification and add JEL codes required by the Nereus consortium for the Economists Online database. They research and add full-text versions (pre- or post-print), having checked the policies of the various publishers in the SHERPA RoMEO database. BIRD contains more than 10,700 documents (articles, conference proceedings, books, book chapters, theses, reports, working papers). 5,300 of these documents were created in the last five years. About 50 per cent are full-text, 40 per cent are English-language and the remainder are in French. They cover the following academic disciplines: management, economics, law, social sciences, mathematics, computer science and linguistics.

In order to validate its institutional repository (BIRD), the Dauphine University made the strategic decision to make it accessible from the university website and to register it in OpenDOAR (Directory of Open Access Repositories). BIRD is also deep-indexed by Google and Google Scholar, is registered with ROAR and with ISIDORE (the French CNRS gateway to open access humanities and social sciences academic resources). BIRD also provided regular data feeds to the Economists Online database run by the Nereus Consortium.

Usage statistics show this institutional archive, which forms part of the national archive, in a good light. Since October 2013 there have been more than 60,000 downloads each month. This success contributed to Paris Dauphine University's reaccreditation by EQUIS in 2012.

This example shows that the library can participate actively in developing a university's research and international profile, not only administering the publication database of its researchers but also, in collaboration with the Research and Development office, the university's electronic thesis deposit project. At Dauphine this work is the responsibility of a team, which at the time of its formation and launch, consisted of eight people devoting a third of their time. At the request of the University President, a Research Indicators Committee has been created. The library is represented on this committee, the objective of which is to establish bibliometric indicators that can measure the impact of Paris Dauphine University's research development policy more precisely.

Case study 2: the INSEAD SSRN portal

Several French business schools have been using the SSRN network to disseminate the research outputs of their academics, either according to a specific strategy decided by the school's senior management or as a substitute for an institutional repository. Some researchers have been pioneering the deposit of pre-prints and post-prints in SSRN in a personal capacity well before their research office took an interest in it. Libraries also anticipated that this network would meet the needs of researchers, and so some have created an SSRN institutional portal.

INSEAD, which has one of its three campuses at Fontainebleau (not far from Paris), created its own SSRN institutional portal in 2007. This brings together INSEAD's research papers collection of about 130 papers per year. The INSEAD portal contains two main categories of research paper: pre-prints and post-prints (taking into account copyright restrictions). The school has set up a very simple intranet-based system for research professors to flag up their work for inclusion in the INSEAD research papers collection. The researcher simply uploads his or her document and, with one click, authorizes it to be uploaded to SSRN. It then goes to the library team responsible for checking copyright and if, for example, the paper has been submitted for double-blind review, the portal administrator will be made aware and will only publish the document after the review process is complete.

The benefits of the portal came sooner than expected. The Dean claims that it has brought much visibility to the school and its researchers. The researchers appreciate the flexibility of the tool in particular: revisions to, and suppression of, a full-text version of an article can be made very quickly.

The download statistics are very encouraging. Some researchers say that they are in the top 10 downloads for their discipline. Furthermore, the institutional portal has only served to increase the visibility of their publications. When a paper has been personally uploaded by a researcher, who subsequently allows it to be deposited in the institutional portal as well, the same URL is used for both, thereby increasing the individual download statistics for the author. Finally, citation figures shown in SSRN are included in the Google Scholar profiles of those authors who have set it up, increasing their external visibility further still.

Case study 3: The SSRN portal of HEC Paris

Many researchers deposit their research papers in SSRN personally, and it was only at the beginning of 2013 that the Research Office, working with the library, undertook the creation of a school institutional portal. As with INSEAD, HEC Paris is seeking to increase the visibility of its research and validate many quality works, whether they are submitted or not. It also decided to open up the institutional portal to doctoral students so that they can rub shoulders with big-name researchers when developing their academic research profile. Here are a few quotations from a small sample of HEC Paris researchers about SSRN:

> *I have been uploading my papers on SSRN over the last 10 years – the first of my academic career. This is because it is the reference outlet for scholarship (also) in my field: law. (Alberto Alemanno)*

> *It is a website that gets a lot of traffic in terms of hits from other top schools and a common platform where most scholars showcase their work. (Gonçalo Pacheco De Almeida)*

> *It's the best way for me to make my working papers known. (Thomas Åstebro)*

These authors are undoubtedly acknowledging the effectiveness of this network in disseminating their research, increasing their visibility and numbers of citations. Professor of Law Alberto Alemano indicates that he has even broken into the top 100 global rankings of legal authors, something which, up until then, was essentially the preserve of professors in American institutions. On the other hand, researchers are undecided on the potential to publish their most recent works. Whilst some of them see it is a good way of signalling the fact that they are focusing on a certain subject, others prefer to wait until the paper is formally accepted in order to avoid unjustified attempts to appropriate their ideas.

Although institutional repositories in France seem to be the response to university strategies formulated by senior managers, the SSRN network seems to be a response to the true needs of researchers. Researchers' own deposits in SSRN, complemented by an institutional presence on the same network, increase the benefits of the system and research management tenfold, with researchers also benefiting from the dual visibility.

CONCLUSION

Evidence from an economics researcher

We had the opportunity to interview Nicolas Vieille to glean further material for our subject. Nicolas is a well-known economics researcher who has published in some very well-known journals such as *Econometrica*, *Annals of Statistics* and *Operations Research*.

For him, research outputs should be deposited as early as possible in open archives, even before formal submission, so that he can share the subjects on which is he is working with his peers. He compares this to a kind of patent submission process. Not only is he sharing the primary results of his research in this way, but he is also giving visibility to the subjects on which he is working and is in a position to express himself at the heart of his global research community.

The speed at which a researcher can deposit his initial work on a subject is so critical that it often renders institutional repositories less effective. Although Nicolas recognizes the value of an institutional repository in promoting an institution, especially to the world at large (journalists and so on), this type of archive is not dedicated to the needs of researchers themselves who need to go straight to the source, to see directly who has published what in their subject.

The SSRN network received a big vote of confidence from Nicolas. Besides its visibility and known flexibility, he values the information on numbers of downloads and citations generated by each of his deposited works. Generally speaking, he is convinced of the need for him and his peers to disseminate their work as widely as possible. He finds it excessive that certain journals still forbid the dissemination of post-prints but he remains optimistic about the eventual softening of editorial policies, especially with the arrival of open access journals.

The future of open archives in France

The French government's view of the future of French open archives was recently revealed by the Minister for Higher Education and Research during an open access conference organized on 24 January 2013. Geneviève Firoaso (2013) reaffirmed the government's support for the principle of open access to scientific information and for open archives. This support will manifest itself in the months to come through the following seven initiatives:

1. Develop green open access within the French BSN framework, consulting with publishers about the duration of embargoes (which will be allowed to vary by discipline).
2. Facilitate the evolution of gold open access with licence negotiation and cost control for those communities choosing it.
3. Promote the development of an innovative and lasting third [open access] route dubbed 'platinum open access'. This route will see the development of open access publishing which enables authors and readers to access scientific publications free of charge thanks to a strong alliance between all the stakeholders in scientific publishing: researchers, publishers, libraries, and platforms, using hybrid economic models. This will be the least restrictive route for authors and readers.

4. Improve the shared services HAL platform by actively encouraging researchers to deposit their publications in the national open archive and by facilitating connections with existing institutional open archives.
5. Offer researchers a national model publishing agreement preserving the rights of the author.
6. Start to reflect on the role of scientific outputs in research assessment frameworks.
7. Work with national publishers to support their international activities (for example, support for the translation of co-publications to preserve some form of editorial diversity).

The Minister has therefore announced a relaunch of the HAL national archive (point 4) and the signing of a new agreement between HAL and the various French institutional open archives. Under the terms of this agreement, the partners undertake to:

- encourage their researchers to deposit in open archives
- agree a communications strategy based on the creation and dissemination of best practice concerning free access to scientific results
- connect institutional archives to HAL
- respect the technical and procedural constraints of HAL, notably in terms of interoperability tools

The CCSD will facilitate the implementation of the convention by making those procedures and protocols available to those of its partners that have gained credibility in the international open-archive community. The partners, by dint of being present in HAL, will be able to benefit from HAL's perpetual archiving as well as connections to ArXiv, PubMed Central and RePEc.

FINAL REFLECTIONS

France continues to maintain its unique 'two-headed' archive model. Our survey of French business schools and universities has shown that they have become fully conscious of the need to create and manage an open archive of research publications.

Finally, an overview of the two surveys and two case studies covered in this chapter confirms the findings of the SAGE Publications and British Library report (Harris, 2012) on the roles increasingly being played by libraries in the progressive adoption of open access in scientific information. These are as follows:

- communication with researchers for whom open access is still too often associated with notions of 'paying to publish' and 'dubious quality of published results'

- building bridges between the different services in order to establish the [effective] distribution of tasks (managing an institutional deposit, for example) and make the links clear between free access and the entire publishing cycle (from producer to end user)
- implementation of open access management tools
- management of metadata at web scale to enable the identification of different versions of a publication
- working together/creating shared services to realize economies of scale.

REFERENCES AND FURTHER READING

ADBU, 2013. At: http://adbu.fr/ (accessed 27 April 2013).

ADBU Couperin, 2012. Enquête archives ouvertes 2012 [online]. At: http://bit.ly/ZOnjgF (accessed 27 April 2013).

Berthaud, C. 2013. Eléments de la politique nationale pour les archives ouvertes [online]. Webcast CC-IN2P3/CNRS, *Journées Open Access*. Couperin. 25 January. At: http://webcast.in2p3.fr/videos-elements_de_la_politique_nationale_pour_les_archives_ouvertes (accessed 27 April 2013).

Couperin Consortium, 2013. At: http://www.couperin.org/ (accessed 27 April 2013).

CSIC, 2013. The Ranking Web of Repositories [online]. At: at: http://repositories.webometrics.info/en/top_portals (accessed 27 April 2013).

European Commission, DG Research, 2006. *Study on the Economic and Technical Evolution of the Scientific Publication* [online]. At: http://ec.europa.eu/research/science-society/pdf/scientific-publication-study_en.pdf (accessed: 27 April 2013).

Fioraso, G., 2013. Position de la France sur l'Open Access. Webcast présenté à Journées 'Open Access' organisées par Couperin, 24 January 2013 [online]. At: http://webcast.in2p3.fr/videos-position_de_la_france_sur_l_open_access (accessed 27 April 2013).

HAL, 2013. At: http://hal.archives-ouvertes.fr/ (accessed 27 April 2013).

Harris, S., 2012. *Moving Towards an Open Access Future: The Role of Academic Libraries* [online]. Sage Publications. At: http://www.uk.sagepub.com/repository/binaries/pdf/Library-OAReport.pdf (accessed 27 April 2013).

House of Commons Science and Technology Committee, 2004. *Scientific Publications: Free for All? Volume 1: Report* [online]. At: http://www.publications.parliament.uk/pa/cm200304/cmselect/cmsctech/399/399.pdf (accessed 27 April 2013).

Rigeade, M., 2012. *Archives ouvertes institutionelles en France – état des lieux et perspectives (Les)* [online]. Masters dissertation, University of Lyon. At: http://www.enssib.fr/bibliotheque-numerique/notice-56708 (accessed 27 April 2013).

Schöpfel, J., and Prost, H. 2010. Développement et Usage des Archives Ouvertes en France. 1e partie: Développement [online]. At: http://archivesic.ccsd.cnrs.fr/sic_00497389 (accessed 27 April 2013).

WEBSITES

ACIEGE, 2013. At: http://www.aciege.org/ (accessed 27 April 2013).
ArXiv, 2013. At: http://arxiv.org/ (accessed 27 April 2013).
BIRD, 2013. At: http://basepub.dauphine.fr/ (accessed 27 April 2013).
BSN, 2013. At: http://www.bibliothequescientifiquenumerique.fr/ (accessed 27 April 2013).
DSpace, 2013. At: http://www.dspace.org/ (accessed 27 April 2013).
Economists Online, 2013. At: http://www.economistsonline.org/home/?lang=en (accessed 27 April 2013).
EPrints, 2013. At: http://www.eprints.org/ (accessed 27 April 2013).
Google, 2013. At: http://www.google.com/ (accessed 28 April 2013).
Google Scholar, 2013. At: http://scholar.google.com/ (accessed 28 April 2013).
HAL Audencia, 2013. At: http://hal-audencia.archives-ouvertes.fr/ (accessed 27 April 2013).
INRA, 2013. At: http://institut.inra.fr/en/ (accessed 27 April 2013).
INRIA, 2013. At: http://www.inria.fr/en/ (accessed 27 April 2013).
ISIDORE, 2013. At: http://www.rechercheisidore.fr/ (accessed 27 April 2013).
Nereus, 2013. At: http://www.nereus4economics.info/about-us.html (accessed 27 April 2013).
OpenAIRE, 2013. At: http://www.openaire.eu/ (accessed 27 April 2013).
OpenDOAR, 2013. At: http://www.opendoar.org/ (accessed 27 April 2013).
ORI-OAI, 2013. At: http://www.ori-oai.org/ (accessed 27 April 2013).
Project NEEO, 2013. At: http://www.nereus4economics.info/projectneeo.html (accessed 27 April 2013).
PubMed Central, 2013. At: http://www.ncbi.nlm.nih.gov/pmc/ (accessed 27 April 2013).
RePEc, 2013. http://repec.org/ (accessed 27 April 2013).
ROAR, 2013. At: http://roar.eprints.org/ (accessed 27 April 2013).
SHERPA RoMEO, 2013. At: http://www.sherpa.ac.uk/romeo/search.php (accessed 27 April 2013).
SSRN, 2013. At: http://www.ssrn.com/ (accessed 27 April 2013).
SSRN HEC Paris, 2013. At: http://www.ssrn.com/link/HEC-Paris-BSR.html (accessed 27 April 2013).
SSRN INSEAD, 2013. At: http://www.ssrn.com/link/INSEAD-Business-School.html (accessed 27 April 2013).
TEL, 2013. At: http://tel.archives-ouvertes.fr/ (accessed 27 April 2013).

CHAPTER 8

COLLABORATION IN BUSINESS LIBRARIES: CAREERS AND ENTREPRENEURSHIP

MARCELLA BARNHART AND CATHY OGUR

Universities and colleges are experiencing increasing pressure from students and other stakeholders to demonstrate a positive return on investment (ROI). Students expect learning experiences, tools, and services that will help them become gainfully employed after graduation. As noted by Sokoloff (2012, p. 16), "We academic business librarians work in a challenging and unique time, where higher education is increasingly perceived as a means to an end, where the job market for our graduates is highly competitive, and where all kinds of business information flows freely online." At an institutional level, universities are leveraging their unique environments to incubate new business ideas from faculty, students, staff, and their surrounding communities. The concept of the "entrepreneurial university," encompassing entrepreneurial science, enterprise creation. and social entrepreneurship, is considered critical to universities' ability to play a role as a larger innovative force in the world (Thorp and Goldstein, 2010). This increased focus on entrepreneurial thinking and its applications is evidenced by the recent growth in entrepreneurship education. Entrepreneurial classes and programs have proliferated, with "more than 2200 classes at over 1600 schools, 277 endowed positions, 44 English language refereed academic journals and over 100 centers" (Katz, 2003, p. 284) in the USA alone.

These changing demands have created new opportunities for developing business school library services, and new constituencies for those services. In order to achieve the best outcomes, business librarians cannot act alone in developing and marketing these services. Strategic partnerships with career development offices and entrepreneurial programs are critical to successful program development and sustainability. This chapter reports on the results of a survey of academic business librarians, providing a snapshot of the state of current practice in partnering with career development offices and entrepreneurial programs. It also includes a brief case study focusing on career and entrepreneurial research support efforts at the authors' institution.

BACKGROUND AND LITERATURE REVIEW

Libraries have a long history of providing collections and services to assist the job-seeker. In an academic environment there is a natural fit between a student's information needs when exploring careers, job-hunting and interviewing, and the business librarian's expertise in company and industry research. Earlier articles written about support for career research focus primarily on collections, rather than exploring the potential for relationship-building with career services staff or with students or other patrons. Anderson (1989) outlines the wide range of materials that libraries collect to support career research and provides guidance for career counselors in locating those materials. Lorenzen and Batt (1992) discuss the development of the library within a career services office as it changed from an ad hoc collection managed by career counselors to a more robust collection managed by a librarian associated with the university library. In this case, the emphasis was on building a collection, making it accessible, and training counselors to use it, rather than working directly with students. Abel's (1992) survey of cooperation between librarians and career planning staff found that respondents from the two groups did not regularly share information about their services and collections, and did not promote the other groups' resources.

DeHart (1996) discusses a multi-pronged approach to supporting career development through a separate career-oriented collection and workspace, guides for looking for information about specific companies participating in on-campus recruiting, and integrated instruction programs with career development. Hollister (2005) used an iterative approach to relationship-building, beginning with co-teaching classes and using the rapport and trust from that experience to expand services to provide satellite reference support in the career services office, as well as assisting with the collection development and overall collection organization in their library. Dugan et al.'s (2009) efforts focused on working with career services offices to develop a collaborative, collective career exploration and knowledge portal called CareerWiki. In addition to working together to create and maintain CareerWiki, promotion was a joint activity, leading to increased use, and a shared funding model among the library, career development offices, and the business school was adopted for certain resources.

Besides its obvious intent to assist students in reaching their career goals, career research instruction can have a positive impact on students' overall research skills. One case study found that students who attended career services workshops provided by the library were more confident in their abilities to research effectively, and expressed greater likelihood of using library resources in the future than those who had participated solely in course-integrated instruction (Song, 2005). Joranson's and Wider's (2009) collaboration with their MBA career services group provided opportunities to help students develop their critical thinking skills, which would allow them to ask better questions and provide more thoughtful answers in an interview setting.

Developing relationships with career services staff can be challenging, as the variety of career services offices existing at a single institution can be extremely complex; Dugan et al. (2009) mention 35 different offices having a career services function at Purdue University. However, the abundance of academic departments, research centers, programs, and projects which fall under the umbrella of entrepreneurial programs makes this area no less complex. The types of research requests received from students, researchers, and practitioners related to entrepreneurial projects can vary greatly, creating challenges of scale in assisting with these requests.

The broad range of requests makes it difficult to develop in-depth subject expertise in a field. Likewise, repeat questions are rare, making it challenging to remember and build on past research. In a typical week, one client will need to know the size of the North American market for Internet routers and another will diagram a chemical reaction and ask if similar processes have been patented (Fitzgerald et al., 2010, p. 192).

Support for entrepreneurial activities has become an important enough topic that the *Journal of Business and Finance Librarianship* devoted a special double issue in 2010 to services and collections supporting entrepreneurship, primarily focusing on case studies. Several articles in this special issue (Leavitt et al., 2010; Martin, 2010; Pike et al., 2010) describe the boundary-stretching activities of public university business libraries in Michigan, Ohio, and Alabama, respectively, as they collaborated with privately and publicly funded incubators and business development support networks in economically distressed areas. Chung's (2010) work at North Carolina State University involved building relationships with a new interdisciplinary "Entrepreneurship Initiative," including course-integrated instruction using an active learning approach.

The idea of embedded librarians is a common theme in articles that focus on services for entrepreneurial research. Business librarians are working within public–private technology incubators (Fitzgerald et al., 2010), making efforts to determine the value or ROI of library support based on staff time and resource cost calculations, as well as serving in more traditional academic environments embedded within project teams in entrepreneurship classes (Kirkwood and Evans, 2012). Library school students have also been embedded within a student-run consulting organization that provided assistance to small business clients, providing an experiential learning environment for both those students and MBA students (Holler, 2008).

METHODS

It is clear from the literature that many academic business librarians have recognized the value of partnering with career development offices and entrepreneurial programs. Most of the prior literature uses a case-study approach, making it difficult to identify broader trends in collaboration. In order to determine how prevalent such partnerships are, and to get a better understanding of how they have progressed, we conducted an environmental scan using a survey. The survey was sent out as a weblink to several electronic mailing lists targeted at business librarians. These included the following members-only mailing lists:

- Academic Business Library Directors (North America and Canada)
- European Business School Librarians' Group
- Asia-Pacific Business School Librarians' Group
- Management Library Network (India)
- CLADEA library directors' group (Latin America).

In addition, the survey was sent to the broader lists:

- BRASS-L – Business Reference & Services Section of the Reference and User Services Association of the American Library Association
- BUSLIB-L – list for practicing business librarians, oriented toward providing assistance with difficult research questions
- SLA-BF – Special Libraries' Association Business & Finance Division.

As part of the survey, we asked respondents if they would be willing to discuss their answers with us in more detail. We conducted telephone interviews with several of the respondents as a result. For the purposes of our survey, we used the following definitions for career services and entrepreneurial programs:

- *Career services*: a department/office on campus responsible for coordinating on campus recruiting, for helping students with career planning, including exploring career-related interests, and with developing strategies for pursuing full-time employment, internships, or other experiential learning opportunities. Campuses may have multiple career services offices.
- *Entrepreneurial programs*: a broad umbrella term that may include, but is not limited to, research centers, majors/concentrations, academic departments, small business development centers, business plan or innovation competitions, business incubators, and student groups, focusing on the research and practice of entrepreneurship.

RESULTS AND DISCUSSION

Institutional demographics

There were 71 responses to the survey. Not surprisingly, based on the places we distributed the survey and the fact that the survey was in English, almost 50 percent of responses were from US business librarians. The geographical distribution of respondents is shown in Figure 8.1.

Where is your institution located?

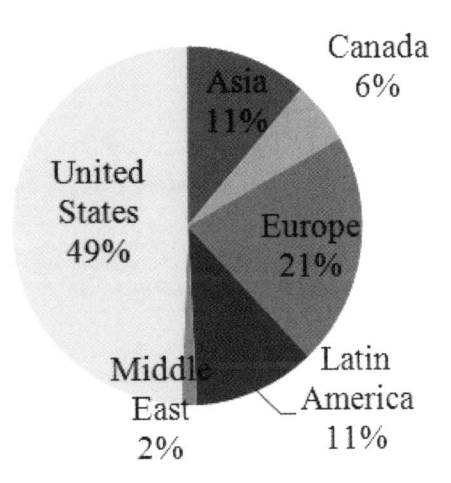

- United States 49%
- Asia 11%
- Canada 6%
- Europe 21%
- Latin America 11%
- Middle East 2%

Figure 8.1 Geographical distribution of careers and entrepreneurship support survey respondents

The distribution of respondents by institutional size was fairly even, with roughly one-third of working at institutions between 500 and 5,000 full time equivalent (FTE), one-third between 5,000 and 20,000 FTE and one-third at greater than 20,000 FTE. There was a broad representation of degree programs, as illustrated in Figure 8.2, with the MBA degree most highly represented (96 percent). In order to gauge the size of business library operations, participants were also asked how many FTE librarians at their institution were primarily focused on working with business students, faculty and staff—that is, research and instructional services, or with business materials (collection management, technical services, access services). The number of FTE librarians ranged from a high of 16 to a low of one; the mean was 3.67, the median was 2.25, and the mode was 1.

Degree programs chart

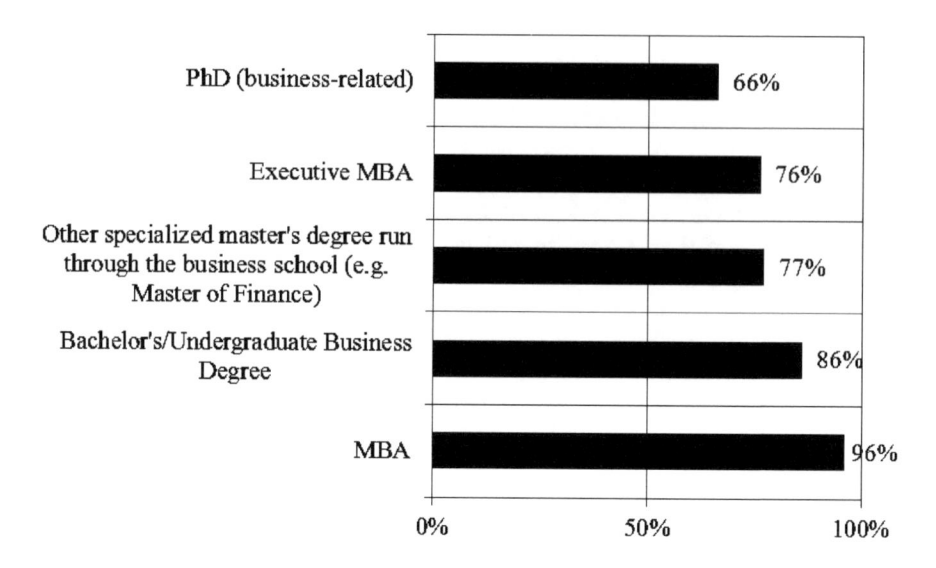

Program	Percentage
PhD (business-related)	66%
Executive MBA	76%
Other specialized master's degree run through the business school (e.g. Master of Finance)	77%
Bachelor's/Undergraduate Business Degree	86%
MBA	96%

Figure 8.2 **Degree programs supported by careers and entrepreneurship survey respondents**

Collections and resources

Most of the survey questions focused on services, rather than on collections and resources or specific tools developed to help students, faculty and staff access resources. However, there were two questions that asked about library collections and research guides related to entrepreneurship and career research. Eighty percent of respondents actively collect materials related to career research, while 94 percent actively collect materials related to entrepreneurship. Given the growth of entrepreneurship as an academic discipline within business schools, as well as cross-disciplinary programs, this is not unexpected: "We have an entrepreneurship program so of course we purchase to support that." A few people who explicitly commented on the fact that they do not collect career-related materials mentioned that these materials were collected elsewhere on campus: "The only reason I personally don't collect materials for 'Job & Career Research' is that I know the Career Center in the Business School does this."

Providing career research guides, bibliographies or pathfinders was commonly mentioned in case studies in the literature as a way in which business libraries were supporting students' job-seeking efforts, although Abels and Magi (2001) only found references to career research materials on 20 percent of the library websites of 20 top business schools. We reviewed the websites of those same 20 business school libraries and found that approximately 80 percent offered research guides specifically for career research and 70 percent for entrepreneurship. Similar to the results of that review, a substantial majority (68 percent) of respondents to our survey had created a research guide or similar tool such as LibGuides to assist students in this area. The corresponding figure for entrepreneurship research guides was somewhat higher at 74 percent.

In examining the examples that respondents were willing to provide, there were often several guides in each category. For instance, for entrepreneurship there might be a general overview guide and specific guides for particular classes, as well as guides for emerging areas such as social entrepreneurship. Similarly, for career research, there might be an overview guide as well as guides specific to particular careers or industries. These results suggest that trends in providing research guides in these areas that were identified by Lyons and Kirkwood (2009, p. 341) have continued. In their review of 75 academic business library websites, they found that 44 percent included at least one career research guide, with 93 guides in this category across 29 libraries; 44 per cent included at least one entrepreneurship guide, with 48 guides across 29 libraries. Given the fairly recent growth in entrepreneurial programs in business schools, they considered the prevalence of entrepreneurship guides to be an indicator that "business libraries are making an effort to keep their guides relevant and dynamic and that they are responding to changes in the business schools they serve."

Instruction

Following a pattern similar to the collection responses in the previous section, among our survey respondents, entrepreneurial research sessions were more prevalent (66 percent) than job and career research sessions (52 percent). Content analysis of the free-text responses about who teaches classes related to career and entrepreneurial research yields some interesting results about collaboration, or lack thereof, in this area. For job and career research, the respondents provided examples of workshops developed and run by the solely by the library, as well as collaborative sessions. The respondents who mentioned entrepreneurship in relation to instruction directly referenced visits to entrepreneurship classes and workshops through a small business development center (SBDC) or similar group. No one mentioned independent programming by entrepreneurial programs staff. In general, responses could be grouped into five clusters: librarians only, career services staff only, librarians and faculty (cooperatively), librarians and career services staff (independently) and librarians and career services staff (cooperatively).

Table 8.1   Types of instructor for career research and entrepreneurship courses

Instructor type	Number of responses
Librarian(s) only	22
Career services staff only	2
Librarians and faculty, cooperatively	2
Librarians and career services staff, independently	8
Librarians and career service staff, cooperatively	5

Cooperative sessions were much less prevalent than sessions taught solely by librarians, suggesting that there is not much co-development at the instructional level. This may be a missed opportunity. DeHart notes that students' attendance at, and interest in, jointly developed sessions with career services were much stronger than those taught exclusively by librarians: "The library presentation receives an introduction by and the full support of the career counselor. The library, when discussed in the physical surrounding of the placement office, is perceived as an integral part of the job search process" (1996, p. 79). Joranson and Wider (2009) also stress the increased value to the student of attending workshops that leverage the varied expertise of both librarians and career services staff. Representative responses to the "who teaches?" question include:

- "A librarian provides instructional sessions highlighting research sources and strategies for entrepreneurial projects. In career prep classes, a librarian also presents research strategies that students can use to find jobs and prepare for interviews. In addition, the career services department offers more extensive services and info for career prep but they may not highlight library services."
- "Usually 2 librarians lead the workshops. One subject specialist and one who works with the Vault/Wetfeet databases. We invite the staff member from Office of Career Services who are involved in that industry or the one who works with the MBA class. This helps to bring several types of expertise together for the benefit of the students."
- "Our career services center does for its own programming, and I (as the campus business librarian) provide active learning workshops for many ENT classes (and help teach one core research-intensive ENT class) as well as career-related workshops for classes with career-related research projects."
- "Librarian works with entrepreneurship teaching faculty to offer course-integrated instruction sessions."

Some unique methods of instruction are in action at the University of Arizona. Each MBA student is enrolled in a library module through their online course software.

There, Jason Dewland is developing side-by-side video tutorials for library resources and using software to assess skills learned through quizzes (Dewland, 2012). At Wharton, we also teach using synchronous webinars for entrepreneurship and career services resources, primarily presented to our executive education students.

Promotion of resources and services

Respondents were asked to write about their library's activities related to promoting career and entrepreneurial resources and services. This question was open-ended with no guidance provided about potential promotional methods or activities. Like the instruction information above, the responses were analyzed and grouped into categories (see Table 8.2). Respondents generally listed multiple promotional activities, and if more than one activity was included, the response was coded for each activity. For example, a response like "Communication with faculty: email, in-person conversations Students: Blackboard discussion boards" was coded as falling into the email, word-of-mouth/individual consultation and courseware/course guide categories.

Table 8.2 Promotional methods for career research and entrepreneurship resources/services

Category	Number of responses
Subject guide	16
Word-of-mouth/individual consultation	12
Library website	8
Email	7
Instruction sessions	6
Courseware/course guide	5
Physical displays/handouts	4
No special promotional efforts for these areas	4
Clubs/student groups	3
Social media	3

Responses about unusual promotional techniques included:

- "There is an online map of the career research section."
- "A column in the Recruiter newsletter published bi-weekly by the Undergrad Center for Professional Development."
- "I show up at the major and minor events related to entrepreneurs held on campus, and then network as much as possible. I promote the idea of meeting with me, the business librarian, during my office hours or by appointment."
- "We have a physical career research corner at the Business Library."

In addition to direct marketing efforts by the library, we asked participants whether career services and entrepreneurial programs provide promotional support for the library's resources and services. Forty-eight percent of respondents replied that their career services offices provided this support, while the remainder (36 percent) were unsure about promotional activities; only 13 percent definitively stated that the career services does not assist with promotion. On the entrepreneurial side, the numbers were similar: 52 percent provided support, 25 percent were not sure, and 17 percent did not provide support. As with the library's own marketing activities, respondents had the opportunity to provide free-text explanations about the types of promotion which were coded for multiple activities when appropriate. For example: "The Entrepreneurial Studies program faculty promote the library by including the librarian in the course management system, bringing classes to the library for instruction more than once a semester, promoting the librarian as the person to consult when any difficulty arises" was coded as courseware, class invitation and in person/in class.

Table 8.3 Promotional methods used by career services and entrepreneurial programs staff to promote library resources/services

Category	Number of responses
In person/in class	15
Class invitation	7
Website	5
Courseware	5
Email	5

Representative responses include:

- "Career Services links to library databases and research guides. Entrepreneurial programs invite me for presentation; personal consultations."
- "They promote contacting the Information Specialists for advice re: using library resources for this kind of work. They are about to start using some widgets to put library search onto their careers pages in our intranet."
- "The Entrepreneurial Studies program faculty promote the library by including the librarian in the course management system, bringing classes to the library for instruction more than once a semester, promoting the librarian as the person to consult when any difficulty arises. There is an emphasis on the importance of learning how to manage information as part of the business plan process."

Cost-sharing

Sharing the cost of subscription resources between the library and other programs and departments was not a common occurrence; only 17 percent and 14 percent of respondents indicated that they share the cost of resources with career services and entrepreneurial programs, respectively. The extent of cost-sharing varied from "Less than $1,000 for ebooks" to "Career services purchase the Vault online service and the library purchases the Wetfeet guides." A bigger issue may lie in a difference of perspective between librarians, who tend to try to disseminate information and resources as widely as possible, and staff in other departments who tend to focus on the needs of a narrower constituency and may not realize the relevance of their resources for others. Resources may be licensed for a small group, or simply not promoted or made available in a way that would lead to wider use. Comments included:

- "Not all vendors license beyond the SBDC staff, consequently, some resources they have aren't available on the library website."
- "Career Services has resources not listed on our library database page. I feel strongly that anything subscribed to on campus should be shared for the greater good. Unfortunately, that does not always occur."

In a post-survey interview, Suzanne Bell of the University of Rochester, USA, expressed positive experiences in sharing costs for entrepreneurial resources. For different resources, different models of funding have emerged. One database is funded three ways, by the library, by a professor's research budget, and by the business school. Another database is funded through a partnership with a department. Yet another resource is partially funded through an endowment, and that resource was built into the fundraising goal. Suzanne finds that subscriptions to "professional grade resources" enhance the students' work in a manner that faculty recognize and are subsequently willing to subsidize (Bell, 2012).

Collaboration through training

Providing training on library resources for career services and entrepreneurial programs staff is one way in which the library may be able to extend its support to a broader community. However, this type of training was relatively uncommon among our survey respondents. Only 34 percent of respondents said that they provide training for career services staff, while 25 percent provide training for entrepreneurial programs staff. Several respondents indicated that training was generally done via individual consultation, rather than in groups—for example, "The training is usually one-on-one, often for new hires." In certain cases, such as working directly with faculty, individual consultation may be particularly appropriate: "For Entrepreneurial Studies professors, the business librarian has helped with course and assignment design and also meets with new faculty to introduce library resources for their own research as well as for the students." Others mentioned specific circumstances in which group training does occur: "I offer a workshop on what's available every couple years or so, when there's significant staff turnover. These are usually during their department meetings. I'm the one who usually approaches my contact within the organization and asks if they would like me to talk."

Extending reach: support services to those outside the university community

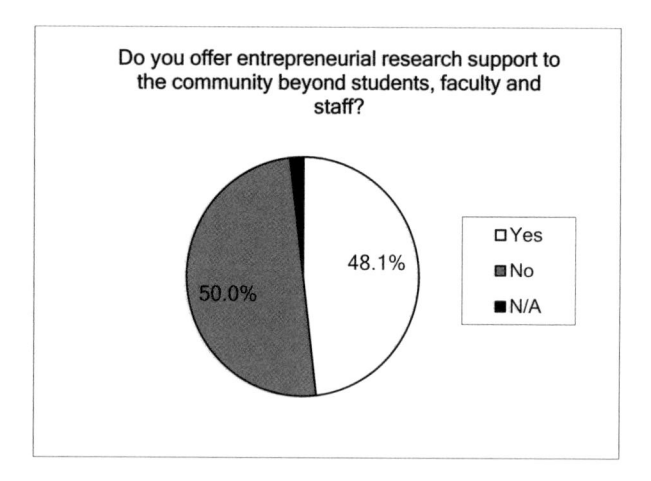

Figure 8.3 Percentage of survey respondents offering wider entrepreneurial research support

Respondents were split almost evenly in their support—or non-support—of the entrepreneurial research needs of people outside the university community (see Figure 8.3). This may partially be a function of licensing restrictions for resources available to assist non-university-affiliated users; as noted by one respondent, "To some extent. The community can come in and get access to our databases. but it does get a bit, again, tricky, because these resources are NOT supposed to be used for commercial purposes. aggh. Very murky area." Several respondents noted that they are required to provide assistance because they work at public institutions. The most common constituencies mentioned were small business development centers and alumni. Our survey did not include a question to assess career support to those outside the university community, which could be a method of building town-and-gown relationships.

Focus on career services

Career development offices are different from other student service organizations in that they often have some type of library or resource center as part of their operation (Hollister, 2005). Half of our respondents indicated that there was an independent library as part of career services offices at their institutions. Of those separate libraries, 15 percent were staffed by a librarian. Several responses mentioned the size of the career services collection—for example, "It's a small collection of guides and periodicals"—or the modality of the collection—for example, "The career services library is a virtual library, not a physical one"—as explanations for the lack of librarian staffing. In addition, 75 percent of respondents indicated that subscription materials purchased by career services were available to the broader campus community, while 25 percent indicated that at least a portion of the resources were limited in some way to business school students. Even when resources might be open more broadly, the location of the resources or the marketing of those resources could limit their use. For example, one respondent noted, "They don't check your ID at the door, but my sense is that really only the b-school folks use it." Fifty-two percent of respondents indicated that they have access to their career services recruiting schedule, which has great potential for identifying opportunities for proactively developing news and resource feeds related to the companies who are coming on campus to recruit.

Focus on entrepreneurial support

In conversations with survey respondents, solid relationships with the entrepreneurship faculty were the stepping-stones to the integration of library support to the programs. For Diane Campbell at Rider University, USA, that pathway was initiated while completing her MBA degree (Campbell, 2012). She approached a faculty member to be an advisor to her independent study project which bloomed into a co-authoring relationship. For Suzanne Bell at the University of Rochester, being newly appointed was an open door to establishing faculty relationships, and enthusiastic faculty integrated her into entrepreneurial classes and programs (Bell, 2012). Hal Kirkwood at Purdue University, USA, has been involved with entrepreneurial programs at the curriculum level, participating on the advisory board for their undergraduate Certificate in Entrepreneurship (Kirkwood, 2012). Purdue librarians have also been involved in working with rural entrepreneurs through Purdue's extension offices, as well as an entrepreneurship "bootcamp" for veterans.

At Cal Poly, USA, Mark Bieraugel was able to leverage his previous experience working with three start-ups and his willingness to attend a wide variety of entrepreneurial campus events, to provide consultation and instruction services for many groups operating outside the classroom, including a business incubator (SLO Hothouse), small business development center, and senior projects. Because of the relationships he developed with these groups, he has been brought into new projects, such as working with Kauffman FastTrac TechVenture when Cal Poly hosted one of their programs (Bieraugel, 2012). For Gwen Gray at the University of Missouri, USA, her attendance at an evening meeting on campus that was open to the community presented an opportunity to mention resources to the Vice Chancellor for Research, the Director of the Business Incubator and to a Biodesign Fellow (Gray, 2012). Being open to networking opportunities beyond traditional outreach can lead to productive relationships.

Perceived relationship strength

Most of our survey questions sought to elicit information about the different approaches business school librarians are taking to provide support for career and entrepreneurial research. We also asked respondents to rate their level of cooperation with career services and entrepreneurial services on a 1–5 Likert scale, where 1 indicated no collaboration and 5 an extremely strong relationship. As shown in Table 8.4, most respondents felt that their relationships with both groups rated a 3 or higher.

Table 8.4 Ratings for library cooperation with career services and entrepreneurial programs

	Percentage of respondents					
	No collaboration (1)	2	3	4	Extremely strong relationship (5)	N/A
Career services	18.2	21.8	20.0	27.3	9.1	3.6
Entrepreneurial programs	10.9	21.8	16.4	21.8	**23.6**	5.5

It is interesting to note the differences at the top and bottom of the scale—overall respondents perceived stronger relationships with entrepreneurial programs and were more likely to report no collaboration with career services. Given that entrepreneurial programs, or at least elements of them, are academic programs, these results are not particularly surprising. Librarians are more accustomed to working with this type of program in traditional library liaison work, while developing similar relationships with career services staff may require a different set of skills. Those who included comments about their interactions generally indicated that they would like to do more to develop relationships, with both constituencies, although there was one very enthusiastic response:

> *I feel extremely lucky and grateful that from day one (and I only assumed these responsibilities a little less than 1 year ago), I have been treated like a member of the E. faculty: I go to every faculty meeting including the annual day-long retreat, every monthly luncheon, have given a presentation at that*

luncheon, am invited to present in all the E. classes, etc etc etc. In short, I'm treated as a full member of the team, and it's *wonderful*!!

CASE STUDY: LIPPINCOTT LIBRARY OF THE WHARTON SCHOOL

In 1929 Dorothy Bemis, the librarian at Lippincott Library of the Wharton School at the University of Pennsylvania corresponded with Dr. Emory Johnson, a pioneer for the business curriculum at the school and said: "… the problem now confronting us seems to be to 'sell' the library … There are comparatively few who know the extent of its resources and who are therefore enjoying to the full its opportunities and advantages" (Bemis, 1929).

The challenge of marketing our libraries still remains today. The students passing through our campuses require constant outreach. We make persistent efforts to build strong relationships with faculty members and staff within our institutions. With career research and entrepreneurial support services, we see a chance for academic business libraries to be relevant in real time to students and to significantly impact on their academic experience beyond their coursework. Wharton recently introduced a new brand platform, "Knowledge for Action", and library support for career services and entrepreneurship matches this strategic initiative.

Undergraduate students and MBA students at Wharton tend to move into full-time employment after graduation. Preliminary results from the 2012 "Career Plans Survey Report" indicated that 88.1 percent of students were employed and 4.8 percent were in graduate school as of August 2012 (*Wharton Undergraduate Class*, 2012). The "Career Reporting Overview" for the class of 2012 MBA students outlined that as of 30 September 2012, 92.1 percent of students were seeking employment, were returning to a previous employer or were starting their own business; and 1.2 per cent were continuing their education (Wharton School, 2012). Since employment is generally the next step after an undergraduate business or MBA education, how can the library offer the best support and services to students for that process?

Generally, our library supports career research for all University of Pennsylvania students through a career research guide, offering workshops and, of course, answering direct questions from students. Recently, our efforts to increase our reach to students have directly focused on our workshops. From 2005 through 2007, we offered one workshop at the beginning of the fall semester titled "Job Search Research" which had an average attendance over the three years of five students. In the 2008–2009 academic year, we began to offer one workshop each semester for career research with similar attendance rates. In the spring of 2011 our model for career support expanded by increasing the number of library workshop sessions, but despite trying to time the sessions with key recruiting events on campus, attendance continued to be disappointing. To promote the workshops, a link to registration existed on the homepage for the Lippincott Library, and our reach to students with these tactics was definitely limited, although we continued to utilize a space that could seat 60 people. Our breakthrough came in the spring of 2012, when we partnered with Penn Career Services to market our workshops and co-present with us. We believe the simple act of promotion via email through the career services office, coupled with the students' increased desire to find a job during the spring semester, caused a significant rise in workshop attendance. For one of our workshops, 43 students attended a single presentation, and we are extremely pleased with the results of our partnership with Penn Career Services.

In the fall of 2011 Wharton MBA Career Management (MBACM) approached us with the idea of developing an event, and we leapt at the opportunity. We now participate in a presentation titled "Keys to Company & Industry Research" which is held twice on one day in the beginning of the fall semester in the building where MBA students have classes. The presentation is a true joint effort between MBACM and our library. We meet several times to develop content and to practice. The event is promoted by MBACM and is open to all Wharton MBA students. A video recording of the presentation and the corresponding slide deck are uploaded onto the Wharton MBA Career Management website for viewing by those unable to attend in person.

Our relationship continues to evolve with career-related services across campus. We:

- are invited to present with Penn Career Services at workshops;
- hold information training sessions with career office staff members;
- seek out opportunities to support career services offices, such as suggesting library resources to highlight on their websites;
- share materials with the physical library at Penn Career Services by passing along past copies of publications when we acquire the most recent editions;
- promote the resources and services of career services offices on our research guides.

Moving forward, we are exploring ways to fine tune the timing of our services and looking to expand our presence to support career services on campus. Questions for further examination include:

- Can we schedule presentations to more optimally correspond with student needs during on campus recruiting?
- Can we attend additional presentations held by career services office staff?
- Is there some way we can offer support to students attending career fairs?
- How can we support recent graduates still seeking employment, given the contractual restrictions on many of our electronic resources?
- How can we be more proactive and anticipatory of student needs?

Approximately 20 percent of Wharton MBA graduates pursue entrepreneurship at some point in their careers, and Wharton Entrepreneurship is an umbrella to multiple initiatives on campus to support entrepreneurial research and endeavors. The Wharton Entrepreneurship program is part of the Management Department and, along with classes and other programs, includes the Wharton Business Plan Competition, the Venture Initiation Program, the Entrepreneur in Residence Program, the Wharton Small Business Development Center, and the Sol C. Snider Entrepreneurship Research Center. Our library has a liaison librarian for the Management Department, but due to the increased interest in entrepreneurship on campus, a second librarian provides outreach specifically to this specialized area.

Within Wharton Entrepreneurship, our library has developed particularly good relationships with the Wharton Business Plan Competition (WBPC) and with the Wharton Small Business Development Center (WSBDC). Beginning in 2009, our library was invited to conduct a WBPC workshop to assist entrants. The session is promoted by the WBPC, and it is recorded and made available on the event's website alongside workshops presented by Wharton professors. Once semi-finalists for the competition are announced, we now reach out to each one individually to offer customized research guidance for business plan development. In 2011 a librarian worked directly with seven of the eight finalists, and in 2012 a librarian worked directly with four of the eight finalists.

Our support of the WSBDC has also grown substantially over the past few years. The WSBDC utilizes undergraduate and MBA students as consultants in its High Impact Growth Consulting Program. The library provides training and research guidance to those consultants, along with precise instructions on how library resources may be used on their engagements in accordance with our vendor contracts. Our librarian is truly embedded in this program as a liaison who holds office hours on a weekly basis in the WSBDC office. When engagements are in full swing, the librarian may be asked to participate in client meetings, attend mid-point presentations by consultants to the WSBDC managing practice leader, and function as a senior advisor. In this setting, the expertise of the librarian and the library's resources and services are highly regarded. Beyond the WBPC and WSBDC, we also offer entrepreneurial research workshops in the library, maintain an entrepreneurship and small business research guide, and attend the Wharton Entrepreneurial Open House.

The prospects to further engage with entrepreneurship efforts on campus are numerous, partly because of their interdisciplinary nature but also due to growth in popularity. For example, students from communications studying future business models for newspapers to students in the University of Pennsylvania's Integrated Product Design Program all touch on entrepreneurship. Reaching these programs and students will require monitoring campus news sources and more outreach to faculty and students, perhaps in creative ways we have not yet imagined. Although we are a business library, we support the entire campus in business-related endeavors. Beyond expanding our traditional constituency, we continue to work on some obvious inroads, including:

- aligning our services with coursework
- creating scalable research support in the form of guides and tutorials
- outreach to students' groups, competitions, research centers, departments and faculty
- capitalizing on opportunities to be provide support outside the library building
- developing methods to push content instead of reacting to requests, such as the utilization of social media.

Our library strives to develop an entrepreneurial mindset to generate ideas to ensure that our services and resources are reaching students and faculty in relevant and meaningful ways.

DISCUSSION AND CONCLUSION

The academic environment is dynamic, with frequent student, staff and faculty changes. As illustrated by our own experience, and the experiences of our survey respondents, the challenge of promoting academic business library services and resources to entrepreneurs and job-seekers on campus lies in our ability to "institutionalize such efforts through existing organizational structures" (Walter and Eodice, 2007, p. 222). Excellence in outreach for career research and entrepreneurial support could lead to considerable challenges in sustainability and scalability. Already, academic business libraries are providing research guides, FAQs, online tutorials, office hours, workshops and individual assistance, and yet we face the same marketing roadblocks of the librarians of the 20th century. If our current practices are not enough, how can we elevate them to a higher standard?

Academic business librarians supporting students with career research and entrepreneurial endeavors presents an opportunity for measurable results of real-world application of library resources, but how can we measure these efforts? Assessment will require planning and collaboration with others on campus. Our career services office delivers a post-graduation employment survey to students. The chance to include questions about use of information resources in the job search and on the job through that survey could provide insight. Similarly, employers recruiting on campus may be willing to share which resources are utilized within their enterprises to assist in our providing relevant experience to students; Sokoloff's (2012) experience in interviewing employers about the information competencies of former students may be useful in informing these conversations or surveys. The process of gathering input from these groups cannot happen through the library alone, so building relationships with career services staff will be critical.

On the entrepreneurial side, some of the librarians we spoke with post-survey are involved in review panels for client projects or business plans, which allow them to directly see the impact of library resources and services on a finished product. While Au (2012) reports that the projects in which students have taken advantage of consultation services "present a more developed plan, while the others are more touchy feely," he notes the difficulty in developing an assessment rubric. In addition to examining project work, some feedback could be gleaned from alumni entrepreneurs. What resources provided the best foundation for their ideas? From their perspectives, to what additional information could we provide access to support student entrepreneurs on campus? Answers to these questions could provide a starting-point to assist in assessing currently promoted resources. Again, this will require building relationships with entrepreneurial groups outside the library, both on campus and off. The next step could be to demonstrate the relevance of the resources with outreach that is timely and to track the usage trends of resources following their promotion. A loop of feedback and assessment is a chance to become more in sync with the needs of our on campus job-seekers and entrepreneurs. Being in step with information needs and trends in the working world can only help us in demonstrating the relevance and impact that successful use of library resources can have in career planning and entrepreneurship.

REFERENCES

Abel, C., 1992. A Survey of Cooperative Activities between Career Planning Departments and Academic Libraries. *The Reference Librarian*, 16(36), 51–60.

Abels, E.G. and Magi, T.J., 2001. Current Practices and Trends in 20 Top Business School Libraries. *Journal of Business & Finance Librarianship*, 6(3), 3–19.

Anderson, B., 1989. Working With Your College Library. *Journal of Career Planning and Employment*, 49(4), 46–9.

Au, K., 2012. Personal interview. 30 November.

Bell, S., 2012. Personal interview. 28 November.

Bemis, D., 1929. Letter to Emory R. Johnson. 25 July 1929.

Bieraugel, M., 2012. Personal interview. 7 December.

Campbell, D.K., 2012. Personal interview. 29 November.

Chung, H., 2010. Relationship Building in Entrepreneurship Liaison Work: One Business Librarian's Experience at North Carolina State University. *Journal of Business & Finance Librarianship*, 15(3–4), 161–70.

DeHart, B., 1996. Job Search Strategies. *The Reference Librarian*, 26(55), 73–81.

Dewland, J., 2012. Personal interview. 30 November.

Dugan, M., Bergstrom, G., and Doan, T., 2009. Campus Career Collaboration: "Do the Research. Land the Job." *College & Undergraduate Libraries*, 16(2–3), 122–37.

Fitzgerald, K., Anderson, L., and Kula, H., 2010. Embedded Librarians Promote an Innovation Agenda: University of Toronto Libraries and the MaRS Discovery District. *Journal of Business & Finance Librarianship*, 15(3–4), 188–96.

Gray, G., 2012. Personal interview. 28 November.

Holler, C.M., 2008. Building Bridges Early: Embedding Future Information Professionals in an MBA Student Consulting Organization [online]. Special Libraries Association. At: http://www.sla.org/pdfs/2008CP_Holler.pdf (accessed 28 November 2012).

Hollister, C., 2005. Bringing Information Literacy to Career Services. *Reference Services Review*, 33(1), 104–11.

Joranson, K. and Wider, E., 2009. Librarians on the Case Helping Students Prepare for Job Interviews in an Uncertain Economy. *College & Research Libraries News*, 70(7), 404–7.

Katz, J.A., 2003. The Chronology and Intellectual Trajectory of American Entrepreneurship Education: 1876–1999. *Journal of Business Venturing*, 18(2), 283–300.

Kirkwood, H., 2012. Personal interview. 30 November.

Kirkwood, H. and Evans, K., 2012. Embedded Librarianship and Virtual Environments in Entrepreneurship Information Literacy: A Case Study. *Journal of Business & Finance Librarianship*, 17(1), 106–16.

Leavitt, L.L., Hamilton-Pennell, C., and Fails, B., 2010. An Economic Gardening Pilot Project in Michigan: Libraries and Economic Development Agencies Collaborating to Promote Entrepreneurship. *Journal of Business & Finance Librarianship*, 15(3–4), 208–19.

Lorenzen, E.A. and Batt, S.J., 1992. The Career Center Library: A Special Library in an Academic Setting. *Reference Librarian,* 36, 61–74.

Lyons, C. and Kirkwood, H., 2009. Business Library Web Sites Revisited: An Updated Review of the Organization and Content of Academic Business Library Web Sites. *Journal of Business & Finance Librarianship*, 14(4), 333–47.

Martin, J.A., 2010. A Case Study of Academic Library and Economic Development Center Collaboration at the University of Toledo. *Journal of Business & Finance Librarianship*, 15(3–4), 237–52.

Pike, L. et al., 2010. Library Outreach to the Alabama Black Belt: The Alabama Entrepreneurial Research Network. *Journal of Business & Finance Librarianship*, 15(3–4), 197–207.

Sokoloff, J., 2012. Information Literacy in the Workplace: Employer Expectations. *Journal of Business & Finance Librarianship*, 17(1), 1–17.

Song, Y., 2005. Collaboration with the Business Career Services Office: A Case Study at the University of Illinois at Urbana-Champaign. *Research Strategies*, 20(4), 311–21.

Thorp, H.H. and Goldstein, B., 2010. *Engines of Innovation: The Entrepreneurial University in the Twenty-First Century*. Chapel Hill: University of North Carolina Press.

Walter, S. and Eodice, M. (eds) 2007. *Meeting the Student Learning Imperative: Supporting and Sustaining Collaboration between Academic Libraries and Student Services Programs* [Special Issue]. *Research Strategies*, 20(4), 219–321.

Wharton School, Full-Time: Career Reporting Overview [online], 2012. Wharton MBA Career Management, University of Pennsylvania. At: <http://mbacareers.wharton.upenn.edu/statistics/full-time.cfm> (accessed 13 March 2013).

Wharton Undergraduate Class of 2012: Career Plans Survey Report [online], 2012. University of Pennsylvania Career Services, September. At: http://www.vpul.upenn.edu/careerservices/files/WHA_2012cp.pdf (accessed 13 March 2013).

CHAPTER 9

REVITALIZING LIBRARY SPACES FOR A SUSTAINABLE FUTURE: A HONG KONG PERSPECTIVE

LAI FONG LI

INTRODUCTION

The traditional role of the library as an acquirer and preserver of collections has changed dramatically over the past few decades. The introduction of the Internet and ubiquitous mobile technologies, in addition to advances in wireless networks, has significantly altered the delivery model of scholarly information. The digital library nowadays provides access to a wealth of information via full-text databases and other electronic resources such as e-journals and e-books. Users can find information anytime and anywhere without physically entering the library. The success in building virtual learning spaces reinforced perceptions of the library's diminishing importance as a physical space (Carlson, 2001). In contrast, Scott Bennett indicated that 'some of the social dimensions of learning cannot be fully realized or substituted for in virtual space. These include, for instance, the learning opportunities that come with racial, ethnic, religious, and economic diversity' (2007, p. 16). Physical library spaces are still needed even as virtual learning spaces have become increasingly important. How academic libraries can revitalize their spaces in response to fundamental changes in students' learning modes and move to an innovative, user-centred approach has become a great challenge in the 21st century. This chapter discusses the library as a learning space in general and is not restricted to business libraries. It introduces the current trends and practices of Hong Kong academic libraries, with a special focus on how the Chinese University of Hong Kong Libraries revitalized their spaces by adopting the Learning Commons Model. The planning and strategies for creating the Learning Garden and Research Commons in its Main Library extension are explored.

TRANSFORMING LIBRARY SPACE

New ways of learning

The younger generation today is referred to as 'digital natives'. Lizabeth Wilson aptly said: 'Today's digital kids think of information and technology akin to oxygen.

Interactivity is a hallmark of their lives. They live in a collaborative world that does not exist for most of us – hyper-linking, gaming, multi-tasking, always on, always interacting' (2004, p. 344). The net-generation students are highly social and accustomed to being connected to each other via smart phones and the Internet all the time. They differ from previous generations in terms of needs, expectations and learning behaviour. Furthermore, the curriculum has shifted from the traditional lecture to new pedagogy that is more focused on interactive and cooperative learning for both teachers and students. Group work, discussions, peer teaching and peer critique are now regarded as important learning activities. Social interaction and group learning have become the preferred learning modes for the current generation of students. The physical library can no longer serve as solely a book repository or self-study space. Rather, we need to create a learning environment that fosters a diversity of learning activities.

The proliferation of electronic resources and networked information has also made information literacy instruction more important today. The library plays a significant role in teaching information literacy skills and assists students in transforming information into knowledge. The emerging importance of information literacy for lifelong learning has repurposed the library space for teaching and learning. The technology and pedagogical changes, as well as the growth of electronic resources, are forcing libraries to transform their spaces to support collaborative learning, interaction, teaching and experiencing for a sustainable future.

Why Learning Commons?

As students require more dynamic and collaborative learning spaces, the library needs to be more flexible to support a variety of learning activities. The establishment of group study areas is increasing in popularity. At the same time, library instruction programmes are expanding, and these require the building of additional seminar rooms in the library. A central hub for learning, research and instruction, as well as technology- and information-rich spaces, is needed. In his *Libraries Designed for Learning*, Bennett (2003) recalled the long heritage of common rooms in higher education, where all members of the academic community met informally and shared their interests. Although the Information Commons and Learning Commons frameworks share the same origin, the former emphasizes knowledge-seeking, while the latter focuses on knowledge-created goals. As Bennett points out, 'the core activity of a learning commons would not be the manipulation and mastery of information, as in information commons, but the supporting collaborative learning by which students turn information into knowledge and sometimes into wisdom' (2003, p. 38).

Indeed, learning can take place anywhere on campus, including classrooms, laboratories, halls of residence and outdoor spaces. Then why do students still come to the library? The current findings of the Chinese University of Hong Kong indicate that there are four major advantages of libraries as learning spaces that attract students to come: 'convenient location'; 'quietness'; 'availability of books and reference materials'; and 'spaciousness and availability of seats' (Kwong et al., 2011). The library's traditional strengths of quietness and an ability to connect people to information are still relevant today. Students value libraries as learning spaces that offer services to support their learning. Libraries have a unique edge in providing space to further accommodate student-oriented learning activities.

The Learning Commons Model emphasizes a range of programmes and services to support student success. It requires the partnership between the library and academic units to foster wider community spirit for the benefit of students, bringing experts together into one central location for a range of learning activities (Beagle, 2004; Beagle et al., 2006). It becomes a new learning space where information and advice are found easily with the latest technology. In the Learning Commons, students can choose between quiet study, reflective learning, social engagement with peers in academic works, or to seek advice from experts. Over recent years, Learning Commons is being incorporated into many academic libraries, and the libraries in Hong Kong are no exception.

HONG KONG HIGHER EDUCATION REFORM

There are eight tertiary institutions in Hong Kong that are funded by the University Grants Committee (UGC), the advisory committee responsible for advising the government on the development and funding needs of higher education in Hong Kong. In 2012 higher education in Hong Kong experienced a major transformation from a three- to a four-year normative degree. The educational reform is known locally as 3+3+4 reform. Local universities are required to absorb the double cohort consisting of students from the last cohort of old seven-year secondary education alongside students from the first cohort with six-year secondary education in 2012. Overall, they need to provide a net increase of 14,500 places based on the current average student intake (Education and Manpower Bureau, 2005). Most universities are therefore investing heavily in their infrastructure to ensure that they can accommodate the double cohort of students. At the same time, large investments funded by the UGC were also made in the expansion of existing libraries.

With the introduction of new curriculum and pedagogy, as well as the increasing number of students, libraries in Hong Kong need to explore and adopt new service approaches to support the learning and teaching of students and staff. Many academic libraries, such as the University of Hong Kong (HKU), Hong Kong University of Science and Technology (HKUST) and the Chinese University of Hong Kong (CUHK), are incorporating the Learning Commons Model into their expansion projects. As there is no separate business library in Hong Kong's universities, the Learning Commons are built in their main libraries.

THE CHINESE UNIVERSITY OF HONG KONG

Founded in 1963, CUHK is a comprehensive research university and the second oldest university in Hong Kong. It is a bilingual (Chinese and English) and bicultural community with a total enrolment of 28,753 students, of whom 15,370 are undergraduate students and 13,383 are postgraduate students as at September 2012. There were also more than 2,700 (18 per cent) undergraduate students enrolled in business programmes (The Chinese University of Hong Kong, 2012a). In fact, CUHK Business School is a pioneer of business education in Hong Kong. It is the first business school to offer MBA and EMBA programmes, and is one of the first two business schools in Asia to achieve AACSB (Association to Advance Collegiate Schools of Business) accreditation.

The CUHK Libraries support teaching and research at the university by means of a campus-wide network of seven libraries with 200 staff. It consists of 2.4 million print volumes. Over 140,000 titles in the collection are business-related and housed in the main University Library. The CUHK Business School community has access to 65 business databases and myriad online resources, while benefiting from using the print collection in business and related subjects in the main library.

With a four-year normative curriculum, CUHK and its new outcomes-based curriculum expects students to graduate with additional attributes, including critical and creative thinking, problem-solving, self-managed learning, adaptability, and collaborative and communication skills (Centre for Learning Enhancement and Research, 2007). To meet the demands of this changing curriculum, CUHK needed to create new learning environments and spaces. The CUHK Libraries shared the same responsibility to provide new library learning spaces to enhance student learning, in reflection of the university's mission. We therefore proposed to establish the Learning Commons in the new library extension and in the newly established 'integrated teaching block'.

PLANNING

Understanding user needs

A good library design should be based on the needs of its users, particularly their independent and collaborative learning behaviour. During the planning process, we conducted a number of surveys on library services and space use.

To learn how students perceive and use libraries as learning spaces, an important study that included observation, short interviews and surveys was jointly conducted by the CUHK Libraries and the Centre for Learning Enhancement and Research (CLEAR) from 17 to 28 January 2011. The study focused on the use of the main

University Library and the branch library, Chung Chi College Library. During the two-week study, a total of 17,590 library users and their activities were recorded. In addition, a total of 421 users were interviewed, while 540 users completed the survey.

The study aimed to identify: the learning activities being conducted in the library; the students' learning preferences; how various design features such as table and chair settings influenced students' learning; use of technology in the library; and the strengths and weaknesses of the library as a learning space (Kwong et al., 2011).

- *Learning activities in the libraries*: The findings revealed that the library spaces were mainly used for learning activities – 81 per cent of the students in the interviews indicated that they were engaged in learning activities while staying in the library. The most common learning activity was reading (approximately 60 per cent) and revision/studying (approximately 40 per cent). More than half of students were reading with or without their computers. Reading or studying took place in the individual study carrels and large study-table areas.
- *Students' learning preferences*: Students were asked about their preferences for various library areas when carrying out learning activities (5-point scale; 5 being most likely to go). The results are shown in Table 9.1.
- It was interesting to note that the areas being planned (individual study rooms and a cafe) received higher scores than the existing areas, such as group study rooms. Obviously, access to food and drink are welcomed by students. We also observed that only around 50 per cent of the students in the discussion zones were actually engaging in group discussions or group work. In fact, furniture in these areas included big sofas, study carrels and large study tables, much like the other parts of the libraries. The furniture is too heavy to move around to form small groups for project discussion. The findings showed that fixed and heavy furniture may hinder collaborative learning.
- *Technology use*: Through observation and interviews, it was found that 53 per cent of the students were using computers in libraries. We found that 82 per cent of students who used their own computers in libraries had their computers connected to electrical sockets. Students were also asked about their preference in using library computers or bringing their own laptop computers to libraries. We found 53 per cent of students preferred to use library computers, while 38 per cent preferred to use their own laptops. Another 9 per cent of students had no preference. The main reasons for using library computers were the convenience and the need of network printing. The top features related to use of technology in libraries were: Wi-Fi connection, electrical sockets, computers with Internet connection and printing services.
- *Strengths and weaknesses*: Understanding the strengths and weaknesses of libraries is important for further development. Though the interviews, we identified four major advantages of libraries as learning spaces: convenient

location (21 per cent), quietness (17 per cent), availability of books or reference materials (15 per cent) and spaciousness and availability of seats (14 per cent). The traditional image of the library as a quiet and resource-filled place is still valued by today's net generation. The libraries' weaknesses that needed to be improved were computing facilities (21 per cent), noise (9 per cent), ventilation/air-conditioning (6 per cent) and lack of tables and seats (4 per cent).

Table 9.1   Students' preferences for various library areas

Areas	Mean
Individual quiet study areas	3.38
Information commons/PC workstation areas	3.31
Individual study rooms	3.19
Cafes	3.18
Group study rooms	3.18
Group discussion zones	3.08
Multi-seat quiet study areas	3.03
Late reading room	2.76
Outdoor reading areas	2.61

This study provides valuable information for our space planning in the new library extension. The availability of sufficient table spaces for students' study is important. Moveable furniture that allows students to redefine space use for group learning is needed. It is clear that the provision of Wi-Fi access, electrical sockets and wireless printing will encourage students to use their own laptop computers in the library. Balancing the space for collaborative learning with quiet space for study is also essential in space planning.

Furthermore, we learned a great deal about library use through LibQUAL and other surveys. For example, undergraduate students were more likely to visit the libraries than other groups of users. We found that 89 per cent of undergraduate students used library resources and facilities on a daily or weekly basis (Li, 2011). Business students were also an active group of library users, who provided over 200 written comments on library services and facilities. Overall, findings and feedback indicated that group study rooms, a comfortable environment and advanced computing facilities support study and learning. The results helped us to plan and implement the Learning Commons in the new library extension.

Learning from others

In the past few years we have explored how library spaces can be revitalized to facilitate many more needed student activities. Research on new learning spaces in academic libraries worldwide has identified the Learning Commons Model that provides students a range of services and facilities for individual and group work, supported by trained staff and long opening hours (Oblinger, 2006). Chaired by the Pro-Vice-Chancellor of CUHK, the Working Sub-group on Learning Commons was founded in 2009 to prepare an action plan on Learning Commons' designs and layouts. Members included the University Librarian, Head of Public Services and heads of other academic departments. Site visits and interviews with overseas experts were conducted to learn from the many libraries that had already created a Learning Commons. The visits were mainly to UK universities' Learning Commons, such as Glasgow Caledonian, Warwick and Sheffield. In addition, a consultant from the University of British Columbia was invited to give presentations about the Learning Commons to the university administrators and library staff, which enhanced the understanding of the Learning Commons concept, including its design, management, services and assessment.

Communicating with users

The CUHK Libraries have a formal communication channel with users through the Library User Group (LUG). The group members consist of the Librarian, Head of Public Services, eight teaching staff nominated by the faculty deans and six student representatives. The LUG meets at least three times a year to discuss matters pertaining to the use of the library. The architect and the Director of Campus Development were invited to attend the meeting to brief members on the planning of the new library extension and the Learning Commons. Discussions on initial installation, proposed improvements, delivering new services and so on were covered in the LUG meetings. Faculty and student comments and feedback were well received.

The library extension project was also made transparent to the university community through briefing sessions and presentations in the lecture hall. It not only allowed more students and staff to learn about the new library spaces and services, but also helped to create support and excitement among our users.

BUILDING THE NEW UNIVERSITY LIBRARY EXTENSION

The main University Library is located centrally on the campus, facing the popular University Square. The new extension adjoins the University Library on its adjacent car park. It is a five-storey building with a basement, with a height not exceeding that of the University Library. The new library complex integrates the library facilities on various floors of the University Library and the new extension, with easy accessibility. A central atrium was built between the new extension and existing building, bringing in natural light through the skylight.

The construction work on the extension commenced in 2009 and was completed in September 2012. The new extension provides a total of 11,000 square metres of floor area with an additional 1,200 reader spaces in a variety of environments with cutting-edge technologies.

The new library complex of approximately 22,000 square metres has been zoned for noisy, informal learning in the basement and on the ground floor, research study spaces on the first floor, and more quiet reading spaces on the upper floors. The building accommodates not only quiet reading and book stack areas, but also a large Learning Garden and Research Commons.

THE LEARNING GARDEN

By adopting the Learning Commons approach, the CUHK Libraries proposed to establish open, flexible, technology-rich 24/7 facilities, particularly to support undergraduate students and provide places where they can go before and after classes. The Learning Commons aims to provide a variety of expertise and services to assist students in their learning. We define the role of the Learning Commons at CUHK as:

- a home of learning
- a 24/7 environment
- a place to meet for group work
- a place for debate and interaction
- a place to make and trial multimedia presentations
- a quiet place for independent study
- a place to relax
- a place to get advice and help in project development
- a coalition of services to support learning
- a place to build community to complement university life.

The Learning Commons of over 2,500 square metres is located in the basement of the University Library's new extension. Although it is situated on the lower ground floor, natural lighting penetrates into the space through the water pools and garden of the University Square above. Given large open spaces and abundance of daylight, we have designated the Learning Commons facility a 'Learning Garden', where students can enjoy the outdoors and nature through the skylight while studying in this grand, open space (Pang, 2013).

The new Learning Garden is configured into a number of zones: collaborative learning zone, IT zone, open forum, refreshment zone and quiet zone. As the Learning Garden offers 24-hour access, a separate entrance is provided after normal library hours. The strategies for creating the Learning Garden included the following:

Variety of learning spaces

The collaborative learning zone is designed to be flexible to encourage student teamwork and collaboration. An innovative, unique feature is the creation of two winding tables referred to as the 'learning path'. The design concept is based on previous survey findings of the need to provide 'sufficient table spaces' for students' learning. The table is 50 metres long and multidimensional. Through its curved shape design and subtle variations in height and width, it creates a series of zones for different types of learning activities, from an individual working with a mentor to large group discussions, interacting. At the same time, the special design of the table with its ambiguity between public and private, openness and enclosure, allows for various activities and configurations of use. Further, the pebble-like mounds on the floor create an environment for leisure, reading and discussion. Other furniture is designed to be flexible and attractive, and can be moved around to create spaces that fit students' needs. This area provides a new way of learning and developing ideas.

Bubble group study rooms have a wide range of equipment installed, including laptops and LED screens. Students can also bring their own devices and connect into the system. Learning and teaching activities such as seminars, book talks and presentations can be conducted in the open forum which is a welcoming place that encourages students to join in the activities at any time. When the forum is not in use, students can sit on the forum steps for reading and discussion. Ample electrical sockets have been installed in the forum for easy access to power. The refreshment zone provides vending machines for snacks and drinks. It is a relaxing and friendly place where discussion and social interaction take place. A cafe located on the ground floor serves the same purpose. A variety of study spaces and facilities are available to bring students together and to encourage student engagement in learning.

Technology-rich environment

The Learning Garden is covered by wireless hotspots, facilitating the use of laptops and mobile hand-held devices. The IT zone provides advanced computing facilities, including PCs with software applications, iMacs and workstations with dual screens. Multifunction printers (MFPs) offering high-speed printing, scanning and photocopying are located throughout the library, including the Learning Garden. These MFPs collect charges via Octopus cards, which are the most popular stored-value smart cards used to transfer electronic payments in Hong Kong. This makes computing and printing facilities more convenient. Mobile interactive whiteboards to facilitate collaborative discussion are provided. To increase the number of computers available to users, a laptop loan service is offered. Wireless printing capabilities are also available for students to print from their laptops. More important, library staff and an IT expert roam these areas to provide information and technical support to enhance the students' experience and to enrich their skill development.

Collaboration

To support student academic success, it is crucial to engage experts from various academic departments and service units to provide new services and programmes that foster active and creative learning. Target partnerships include the Information Technology Services Centre, Office of Student Affairs, independent and language units, and student unions. For example, we invited the Independent Learning Centre to display the whiteboard poems of 'The Power of Words', a reading and writing event in the Learning Garden. Other programmes included cooperation with the English Language Teaching Unit to conduct presentations on controversial topics at the open forum, in which the walk-in audience could ask questions. In addition to such activities, we aim to bring expert help with technology, information, writing, advising and more to the Learning Garden. Through these collaborations, the new space can be a central learning hub where students get advice from librarians, tutors and IT assistants on their work.

THE RESEARCH COMMONS

Located on the first floor of the University Library, the Research Commons, with a total floor area of approximately 2,400 square metres, integrates the library facilities of the existing building and the new extension. It serves as a centre for a wide range of scholarly activities by integrating technology, scholarly resources in print and online, research help and instruction, as well as quiet individual study space. The primary audience is postgraduates, researchers and faculty, but other groups are not excluded from using the Research Commons. This new area also attracts business students because some research databases such as Datastream and FactSet are available in dedicated workstations there.

Renovations were made to the existing building to form part of the Research Commons. Some collections were relocated to release spaces for building doctoral study rooms and a computer zone. Research materials, including Hong Kong studies and government documents, are still kept on the first floor. The reference collection remains on the same floor but was reduced in size to fit the available space. After the renovation, the old reference room became a quiet reading room, lined with reference books and with a modern, light and welcoming ambience. With seating capacity of 140, the reading room provides an inspirational environment for quiet and contemplative study. Other facilities in the Research Commons include group study rooms equipped with LED screens, glass/interactive whiteboards and notebooks for group work and presentation practice. Ample electrical sockets and raised floors for easy access to wires or rewiring were installed to accommodate current needs and unforeseeable changes in technology. A multipurpose room serves as a seminar room for library instruction, special tutorial sessions and learning activities in which small classes on copyright, publishing, theses writing, data analysis, research methods and the like can be organized collaboratively by the library and various academic departments. The room is opened to students if it is not in use. Many individual study carrels are also available for quiet study.

An innovative 'idea exchange' was created around the corner. This place is designed for students and researchers to hang around to share ideas with peers, and includes sofas, moveable chairs and tables, sliding whiteboards, a mobile interactive whiteboard and a touch-screen TV with software to connect with Android tablets or notebook computers for capturing ideas. It creates an atmosphere for exploration and building knowledge across the disciplines. A research consultation room nearby is for subject librarians to provide one-on-one consultation by appointment and on demand. The reference service desk has been relocated to a more visible place for reference enquiries and research help. The Research Commons is not only a resources- and service-rich space, but also provides a meeting place for students and researchers to come together to share and discuss research projects. Further, a Research Commons librarian has been recruited with the responsibility for promoting services and organizing scholarly activities.

NEW SERVICE FOR NEW SPACES

To increase the visibility of the new learning spaces and library services, we launched the roving service in mid-September 2012. By merging the reserved books and interlibrary loan counter with the circulation counter, library assistants have been redeployed to provide roving help. Equipped with iPad, library staff roam the main University Library, reaching out to users proactively and offering assistance when needed. To make the service more visible to users, staff wear vests with the library logo and labelled 'Library Roving Service – We Can Help'. On the basis of the previously mentioned survey conducted by the CUHK Libraries and CLEAR, we decided to offer the roving service during the library's peak hours (12:00 to 17:30 from Monday to Friday). The new service has received positive feedback from users, and statistics for the first three weeks indicated that over 900 enquiries were answered by rovers. Many general enquiries, from locating an item to using computing facilities, are handled by roving staff, and more complicated questions are referred to the service desk and reference librarians.

Training sessions were provided before implementing the roving service. In fact, some staff are more proactive in their approach to users, whereas others seem to experience psychological barriers based on the perception that roving violates users' privacy. Library senior management provided support by conducting sharing sessions for roving staff. Professional librarians and library assistants were invited to share their experience and customer techniques. At the same time, senior management listened to rovers' concerns. This seems to be an effective way of offering peer support to those who lack confidence to rove.

In addition, roving staff are encouraged to attend regular workshops on customer service, communication skills, information search skills and so on, organized by the library and personnel office. Various technical training sessions on using advanced technologies were provided before launching the new service. The positive attitude of library staff towards the new service and their thorough knowledge of library resources and facilities helped them provide assistance at the point of need.

RECOMMENDATIONS

Plan for flexibility

In planning and implementing the Learning Commons Model at CUHK Libraries, we aim to create open and flexible spaces equipped with advanced technologies and moveable furniture to support a variety of learning activities. These spaces need to be easily reconfigured by users, depending on need. To create space for new facilities, we also shifted books around for the construction of the Research Commons and other learning spaces. Some books were relocated to compact shelving and remote storage. In fact, the JURA (Joint University Research Archive) project, a collaborative effort of all eight academic libraries in Hong Kong, is now being planned to remove the least-used materials to central storage to free up shelf space for future library expansion. Overall, flexibility is the main focus in our library space planning.

Staff development

New spaces also provide an opportunity to offer new services. The roving service is one example. In the Learning Garden and Research Commons, librarians no longer position themselves at the service desk and wait for users to approach them. Instead, they take a proactive approach to service, roaming throughout their areas and offering assistance when needed. We became 'blended librarians' who have knowledge of the traditional skill-set of librarianship combined with the technological and instructional skills to effectively support student learning (Bell and Shank, 2004). The library needs to provide more training and development opportunities for staff to assume new responsibilities.

Student helpers

To provide 24-hour access to the Learning Garden, we have recruited a team of student helpers to work after normal library hours. To create a sense of responsibility, their title is 'Part-time Library Assistant' and they receive formal training from the library. These student helpers not only gain experience from team work, but also improve their communication skills via social interaction and helping other students. It is another way of enhancing students' learning in and through work.

Partnerships and collaboration

While the design and implementation of the Learning Commons may be relatively straightforward, it is more challenging to bring experts into one central location to provide learning and research support. Librarians need to be more proactive to approach faculty and departments for cooperation opportunities. The establishment of the 800 square metres Learning Commons in the integrated teaching block is a successful example of the collaboration between the CUHK Libraries and the Information Technology Service Centre. We now share space, staff and resources, as well as providing access to information resources in an integrated environment. Strategic partnerships and collaboration between different stakeholders on campus is the long-term goal of the Learning and Research Commons in CUHK.

CONCLUSION

The year 2012 was a time for academic libraries in Hong Kong to make big investments in the renovation and expansion of their libraries due to the education reform. The CUHK Libraries took this unique opportunity to design a new learning space that provides facilities, technology, training, services and support to meet the present and anticipated future needs of students. After opening the new library extension in September, the gate count of the University Library increased 16 per cent from approximately 80,000 to 93,200 users, compared with the same period in the previous year. In October the gate count jumped to a record high of 113,806 users, a 22 per cent increase. The number of students entering the library is increasing steadily. They are choosing which zones and seating styles they prefer. Teaching staff also conduct tutorials and learning activities in multipurpose rooms and the open forum. A thorough assessment of the effective use of new library spaces and their impact on learning will be held in the near future. As libraries continue to evolve, librarians need to be more flexible to accommodate technological changes and evolving pedagogies to ensure that the library spaces can meet the changing needs of the university and its users for a sustainable future.

REFERENCES

Beagle, D., 2004. From Information Commons to Learning Commons [online]. Paper presented at the Leavey Library Conference, Los Angeles, California, 16–17 September. At: http://www.usc.edu/libraries/locations/leavey/new_at_leavey/conference/presentations/presentations_9-16/Beagle_Information_Commons_to_Learning.pdf (accessed 1 September 2012).

Beagle, D., Bailey D. and Tierney, B., 2006. *Information Commons Handbook*. New York: Neal-Schuman Publishers.

Bell, S. and Shank, J., 2004. The Blended Librarian: A Blueprint for Redefining the Teaching and Learning Role of Academic Librarians. *College & Research Libraries News*, 65(7), 372–5.

Bennett, S., 2003. *Libraries Designed for Learning* [online]. Washington, DC: Council on Library and Information Resources. At: http://www.clir.org/pubs/reports/pub122/pub122web.pdf (accessed 1 September 2012).

Bennett, S., 2007. First Questions for Designing Higher Education Learning Spaces. *Journal of Academic Librarianship*, 33(1), 14–26.

Carlson, S., 2001. The Deserted Library. *Chronicle of Higher Education*, 48(12), A35–8.

Centre for Learning Enhancement and Research, 2007. *The Development of an Outcomes-based Approach to Teaching and Learning at The Chinese University of Hong Kong* [online]. At: http://www.cuhk.edu.hk/clear/download/OBAwebsite_UGC_18April07.pdf (accessed 15 September 2012).

The Chinese University of Hong Kong, 2012a. *Statistics and Student Enrolment 2012* [online]. At: http://rgsntl.rgs.cuhk.edu.hk/rws_prd_life/re_menu/gn_100048555.asp (accessed 29 November 2012).

Education and Manpower Bureau, 2005. *A Message from Secretary for Education and Manpower* [online]. At: http://334.edb.hkedcity.net/doc/eng/main.pdf (accessed 10 September 2012).

Kwong, Z., Ho, E., Lam, P. and Leung, S., 2011. *Libraries as Learning Spaces – 2011 Study Summary Report*. Working Paper 7. Hong Kong: Centre for Learning Enhancement and Research.

Li, L.F., 2011. *The Chinese University of Hong Kong: LibQUAL Library Survey Report 2011* [online]. At: http://www.lib.cuhk.edu.hk/survey2011 (accessed 24 September 2012).

Oblinger, D.G., 2006. *Learning Spaces* [online]. At: http://www.educause.edu/research-and-publications/books/learning-spaces (accessed 15 September 2012).

Pang, A., 2013. *The Chinese University of Hong Kong Main Library Spatial Reorganization and Renovation*. Hong Kong Institute of Architects Annual Awards & Exhibition Submission, 11 January.

Wilson, L.A., 2004. What a Difference a Decade Makes: Transformation in Academic Library Instruction. *Reference Services Review*, 32(4), 338–46.

FURTHER READING

The Chinese University of Hong Kong, 2012b. *Expand the Library for '3+3+4': Preserve the Beacon for Posterity* [online]. At: http://www.cuhk.edu.hk/libraryextension/ (accessed 20 August 2012).

Council on Library and Information Resources, 2005. *Library as Place: Rethinking Roles, Rethinking Space.* Washington, DC: CLIR.

Dewey, B.I., 2008. Social, Intellectual, and Cultural Spaces: Creating Compelling Library Environments for the Digital Age. *Journal of Library Administration*, 48(1), 85–94.

Joint Information Systems Committee, 2006. *Designing Spaces for Effective Learning: A Guide to 21st Century Learning Space Design* [online]. At: http://www.jisc.ac.uk/media/documents/publications/learningspaces.pdf (accessed 5 September 2012).

Malcolm, B.B. and Lippincott, J.K., 2003. Leaning Spaces: More than Meets the Eye [online]. *EDUCAUSE Quarterly*, 26(1), 14–16. At: http://net.educause.edu/ir/library/pdf/eqm0312.pdf (accessed 20 September 2012).

Oblinger, D.G., 2005. Leading the Transition from Classrooms to Learning Spaces [online]. *EDUCAUSE Quarterly*, 28(1), 14–18. At: http://net.educause.edu/ir/library/pdf/eqm0512.pdf (accessed 10 September 2012).

Schader, B., 2008. *Learning Commons: Evolution and Collaborative Essentials.* Oxford: Chandos.

Sinclair, B., 2009. The Blended Librarian in the Learning Commons: New Skills for the Blended Library. *College & Research Libraries News*, 70(9), 504–16.

Working Sub-group on Learning Commons, 2009. *Final Report.* Hong Kong: University Library System.

CHAPTER 10

THE PHYSICAL LIBRARY IN THE BUSINESS SCHOOL OF THE FUTURE

KATHLEEN LONG

Academic libraries and librarians inhabit the intersection of three industries in the midst of massive disruptions—publishing, higher education, and academic libraries. As defined by Clay Christensen and Michael Radnor:

> ... *disruptive innovations ... don't attempt to bring better products to established customers in existing markets. Rather, they disrupt and redefine that trajectory by introducing products and services that are not as good as currently available products. But disruptive technologies offer other benefits— typically they are simpler, more convenient, and less expensive products that appeal to new or less-demanding customers. (Christensen and Radnor, 2003, p. 34)*

Over the past 10 to 15 years these disruptions to the academic library have continued and gained speed. In the academic library, all aspects of our operations have been affected, but one of the most obvious is the impact that these disruptions have had on the use of space in academic libraries and how we think about that space.

Most colleges and universities are grappling with a host of competing priorities for space on the central campus, and more and more of them are looking at the library and asking why it still needs so much real estate in the Internet age. As we redefine our libraries, the model of the "temple of learning," the grand centerpiece of the campus, is being called into question. In the minds of librarians the word "library" denotes a portfolio of content and services. Conceptions of libraries from people outside the library field, however, invariably involve a building and books. How many of us have heard the following words coming from our students and faculty? "I never visit the library anymore—everything is online"; "Do we really need all these books?" Most of them instinctively think of the library as a physical space housing physical materials.

More than a decade ago, C.W. Hartman noted: "Libraries today are in transition both as institutions and as a building type" (2000, p. 112). This statement applies even more so today.

Smith and Pickett comment:

> *If we are to retain a meaningful bricks-and-mortar component to our services, we must deploy our spaces with the aim of delivering to our patrons the room they need when they need it, instead of vast storage areas, or—when we are able to escape the warehouse paradigm—inflexible, single-purpose areas that lie fallow for large periods of time. Our emphasis must be on flexible, multipurpose space that is available 24/7, or as close to that as possible.* (Smith and Pickett, 2011, p. 43)

This is, I think, the minimum for library spaces in the future, and indeed, in the present.

SPACE TRENDS IN ACADEMIC LIBRARIES

The definitions and descriptions of academic business libraries today usually involve physical spaces. Over the past decade academic libraries, including business libraries, have responded to the questioning of the uses of library space in a number of ways. I will discuss several of the trends that have impacted on academic business libraries and which I think will continue to do so into the near future. I will illustrate some of these trends with some specific examples from academic business libraries.

So far, I have been using the term "academic business library," but this is a phrase that has many definitions, depending on which school we are discussing. So what do we mean when we discuss the business school library? As Tim Wales explains in the opening chapter of this book, organizationally there is no single type of business school or library. Most business schools are part of a larger college or university, but a few are not. Many business school libraries are part of the larger university library and operate a physical space as a branch of the university library and report to that entity; and their physical space is sometimes in proximity to the business school and sometimes is not. Some business school libraries are part of the business school and are funded and administered by that school. Some business schools support only graduate MBA programs, some support MBA and PhD programs, and some support an undergraduate business program, in addition to the graduate programs. Each type of program requires different spaces and puts different demands on the space. Each type of organization requires different sets and levels of staffing with differing demands on space. The main focus of this discussion is on the use of the public spaces and not on the space needed by the library for staff offices and behind-the-scenes operations. This should reduce the impact of the differences in organizational structures on the use of the space. For the most part I will focus on graduate education and the MBA programs. Schools with large undergraduate business programs will potentially have different needs and priorities.

Danuta Nitecki identifies three activity-based functions that define the university library, and I think that this framework holds true for business libraries as well:

> ... they will be categorized as the role of accumulator (of books, equipment, and other information carriers), service provider (for retrieving information and borrowing materials, instruction, and other customer assistance for assessing knowledge) and facilitator (through the design of environments and the nurturing of relationships that foster self-directed learning and the creation of new knowledge). (Nitecki, 2011, p. 31)

Although the focus of her article is library assessment, this framework will be useful for considering the recent changes in these roles in the library and in identifying the trends for the future.

The first and most obvious trend affecting all academic library space, including business libraries, is the move to electronic resources and away from physical resources. This change directly affects our roles as "accumulators." Libraries often occupy prime real estate on our campuses, and administrators are increasingly reluctant to devote a significant portion of that space to what some of them refer to as "warehousing books." Consequently, over recent years, more and more libraries are moving physical materials to high-density, typically offsite storage facilities. Materials are retrieved from storage as customers require and are delivered to either their workspace or a space set aside in the library for them to work with the materials. This frees up significant space for other uses on campus by both the library and other departments.

Most business libraries in the USA are significantly reducing their onsite collections. The proportion of collection budgets spent on electronic resources continues to grow, and, with few exceptions, the proportion devoted to physical materials will continue to shrink. The business school faculty is focusing increasingly on datasets which, while they present significant long-term storage challenges, do not require stacks in the center of campus. Business libraries that are part of the central library, but have space in the business school, are finding that space being eliminated or reduced and the library staffing and functions consolidated with other campus libraries. Business libraries that are part of the business school are under continual pressure to reduce the footprint of their collections and to accommodate other functions and activities in the library. This is reflected in Schonfeld's and Housewright's (2009) Ithaka survey of faculty which indicated the minimal importance given to the library building as a starting-point for faculty research.

The Academic Business Library Directors of North America (ABLD) compile annual reports from their members each year. In the report for the year 2000/2001, 10 out of 41 libraries reporting mentioned moving materials off-campus, repurposing space for other academic uses, or being moved to less desirable space. In the 2004/2005

Year in Review, 34 out of 42 libraries reporting mentioned some issue with space. Of these, 12 reported significant reductions of onsite collections, 12 mentioned renovations, redesign, and repurposing of space usually to provide additional study space for students; four were downsized; five mentioned in-process assessments of their space; and one library reported expansion. By the 2009/2010 report, 29 out of 47 libraries reported trading stack space for study space. Other changes reported that year included creation of an Information Commons at two libraries and repurposing of space to create event spaces, outdoor seating, and 24/7 space within the library building at four others.

As the academic library's role as accumulator decreased, the focus of most libraries increasingly turned to the library's role as service provider. People have always used the library for study and research, but now librarians have started to internalize and articulate the fact that the space they provided was perceived as a high-value service to their customers. Much of the space previously devoted to stacks was converted to student study areas, including group study rooms and designated quiet study. Many of the renovations that took place aimed to make the space more attractive and useful to the students. Spaces that facilitate discovery and learning on campus are critical, and libraries are expert at this (Bennett, 2011).

The Information Commons

Information or Learning Commons, with its focus on providing the students with seamless access to all the technology and offering assistance in an integrated way, started to appear in the mid-1990s and the early part of the 21st century. As computers and electronic resources proliferated in libraries, students expected to be able to get assistance from the library not only in finding materials, but also in using the tools and software they needed to organize and synthesize that content. They were looking for social and human resources to facilitate their ability to make sense of what they are learning (Beagle, 2006, pp. 3–10). Information Commons was a response to that student need. Information Commons projects involved collaboration between libraries and other parts of the university on a larger and more constant scale than in the past. Librarians needed to make joint staffing arrangements with other groups, typically IT, and deal with the organizational and cultural challenges that came with that territory. Most of these installations, which are prevalent in libraries today (see Lai Fong Li's chapter in this book for a recent Chinese case study), tend to be concentrated in undergraduate libraries. Most academic business libraries that focus on the MBA and PhD populations have not moved as aggressively in that direction. In some cases, this is because the graduate student demand for this service is not as strong as it is for undergraduates and, in others, it is a function of space. This type of service requires a larger physical footprint than most academic business libraries have. And students have access to other spaces like that on campuses.

Information Commons will continue to be popular in the near future, but changing technologies will affect the types of resources they provide. The evolution of this model will be shaped not only by more sophisticated and integrated discovery and synthesis tools, but also by the information-seeking behavior of the students. The role of the Information Commons in facilitating the use of the new forms of technology and in supporting the knowledge-creation and learning process will be still be key, but it is unclear what kind of space this will demand, if any.

LIBRARIES IN THE FACILITATOR ROLE

In the future of the Information or Learning Commons role, the library has the potential to evolve from its role as "service provider" to that of "facilitator" (designer of environments and the nurturer of relationships that foster self-directed learning and the creation of new knowledge) (Nitecki, 2011). How else might libraries step into this role in ways that will potentially affect their use of space?

One way in which libraries are starting to emphasize their roles as facilitator is through the use of embedded librarians. One example that I think business libraries could do well to study and decide if this model works for them is the example of the Welch Medical Library of the Johns Hopkins University in Baltimore. In 2012 the Johns Hopkins Medical School appointed the Committee for the 21st Century Welch Library, which undertook an assessment of the entire library operations and considered the physical space as one of the components of the services offered by the library. The committee had two missions. The first was to distinguish between the library as an information resource and as a building. The second mission was to ensure that the library serves the academic and patient care needs of faculty, students, and staff. It is this first mission—distinguishing between the library as a resource and the library as a building—that I think business libraries would be wise to consider as they plan for the future. When we work with our institutions to determine the future of our spaces, we need to make sure that the decision-makers we are working with understand the distinction between the physical space occupied by the library and the resources and services the library provides. We also need to make sure that we librarians do not remain entrenched in our traditional view and make the mistake of equating our space with our value and identity.

After the committee report came out, the medical school decided to eliminate the physical library, with the exception of the history of medicine collection. The space will be repurposed and renovated for use as a student center. A website and book and article delivery services will continue and the "informationist" (which is what the librarian role is called at Johns Hopkins medical school), is co-located with the particular community served. Kathleen Oliver (2005) cites several examples of the role that the embedded librarian can play in both the clinical and research environment. In each case she discusses, Welch Library developed two types of service to the various groups it supports—touchdown suites, which are both virtual points with relevant information and small physical spaces distributed around the campus, and multidisciplinary teams involving close collaboration between the informationist and the researcher or clinician.

As described on the Welch Medical Library website:

> *The embedded informationist service model comprises customized information services—delivered where you are, at your points of research, teaching and clinical care. By working with you wherever you are, and integrating ourselves into your workflows, we will be able to answer your questions faster, fill your information needs more effectively, and act as your information expert on research and care teams ...*
>
> *As your informationists, we'll be much better positioned to offer on-the-spot instruction/consultation and searching, create digital portals for you, develop Web 2.0 forums on your departmental sites, participate on systematic review teams, and collaborate on your projects as they evolve.*
>
> *To foster our relationships, we may ask to attend your open activities such as grand rounds and seminars, and to present our services at one of your departmental meetings. As we get to know each other and we work with you to assess your information needs, we may suggest any or all of the following: holding set "office hours" somewhere in your research or clinical space; participating in your journal club or case/residents' conference; participating on some of your committees. (Welch Medical Library, 2013)*

Is this a model that would work in business schools?

There are currently several examples of North American academic business school libraries providing an embedded service. At Yale University the business collections and the School of Management (SOM) Librarian have always been part of the social sciences library and located across the street from the main SOM. In 2012 a new combined science and social sciences library opened at Yale further away from the SOM. The business librarian at Yale now has a touchdown space in the business school and works there for one and a half hours over the students' lunch break two days per week. The touchdown space is located in one of the students' social spaces. The biggest drawback to the current configuration is the lack of a permanently designated table or place in the space for the librarian to set up shop, so the location will vary from time to time. When there is a table with a sign, the service is more visible and more used. In the first three months of the service there have been 26 questions, and, of those, approximately 25 per cent resulted in an appointment for a more extensive consultation.

At Yale, a new SOM building is slated to open in 2014. A donation was made for a library space in that building, and the library collaborated with the SOM in designing the service point. The library space will be in the front of the building, and there will be a permanent place for research consultations, as well as a limited selection of reference and print reserves materials. The SOM Librarian will spend time at the space, depending on student and faculty need. The service point will be staffed by a high-level support staff member who will be available for assistance with basic information questions and access services. Although targeted primarily at students, the space will also serve as a drop-off and pick-up point for materials requested by the SOM community from the Yale libraries, and interlibrary loan. In addition to the impetus given by the alumni donation, the SOM also wanted to be sure that research and information services were conveniently available for the MBA students and, as much as possible, part of their daily routine (Parchuck, 2013; Silkotch, 2013).

The University of Illinois at Urbana has also moved some of its business information services to an embedded model. In 2011 the university library convened a committee to investigate the consolidation of the business and economics library (BEL) into the social sciences library. The College of Business faculty did not want to lose the dedicated space, so the consolidation was put on hold. Early in 2012 the university library looked again at repurposing the space occupied by the BEL to expand their social sciences hub, and at this point decided to go ahead with the consolidation. In order to address the concerns of the Dean of the College of Business, the head of the BEL developed a digital research library concept, with the College of Business, providing a space in their building. The space includes four computers and chairs, with an area for either the faculty librarian or a graduate intern to provide consultation and service. Unlike the model at Yale, which targeted students, this service is targeted at faculty and doctoral students and has recently expanded to include undergraduates serving as faculty research assistants. The space is staffed five afternoons per week and the staff continue to market their presence and expertise to the faculty at the College of Business. The other faculty librarians who were part of the business information center are also embedded with other customer groups for some time each week—one with the experiential learning group and the other with the labor and industrial relations department. As the physical collections of the various department libraries are increasingly sent off-campus or consolidated in central libraries, the University of Illinois sees this as one potential future service delivery model (Smith, 2013).

Here at the Stanford Graduate School of Business, the MBA Liaison Librarian held office hours twice a week in the building housing the first-year MBAs for nine months in 2012. Through trial and error, she determined which times were the most productive and, while she built some excellent collaborative relationships with the students, she found the numbers (0–2 questions per 1.5 hours) did not justify the investment of her time. In 2013 she will move her office hours to the MBA lounge, which is a common gathering place for students between classes. Her hypothesis is that students between classes will be much more likely to be focused on academics at that time than students traveling to and from their rooms or on their way to dinner or to the gym. The initial measure for success will be at least two questions per shift and at least 25 per cent of turning into consultations.

A different example of integrating the library space and moving into the workflow of the researchers comes from Camp Library at the Darden School at the University of Virginia. Several years ago Darden was facing a space challenge. The number of research centers was expanding from three to five and was projected to grow by an additional five in the coming years. The campus therefore needed additional office and collaborative research spaces to support these centers and the additional research personnel required, such as research assistants, post-doctoral students, and visiting scholars. At the same time, additional offsite storage space became available for the library and the synergies of having the research centers located within the research library with proximity to the librarians, the data, and the collections could be realized. The school hired a consulting firm to look at the work of the centers and facilitate a series of meetings to determine what they did and what space they needed to support their mission.

As a result of this process (in which the library was closely involved), Darden decided to create a pilot research suite in the library space. Camp Library reduced its onsite collection from 75,000 items to 19,000 and devoted 2,000 square feet of that space to the research suite. The design of the research center allows for private spaces that are personalized for the researchers, but adjacent to other people so that they are conducive to communal activities and discussion. There is also space to allow for gathering "in the hallways" to facilitate the serendipitous exchange of ideas that results from proximity. The suite also includes a conference room for more deliberate meetings and collaborations, and all of the space is available 24/7. This presents an opportunity for the library to become an integral part of the research infrastructure of the school. Other advantages cited include: the development of more and better communication between the researchers and the library; the development of closer relationships and a shared sense of responsibility for research projects; and face time with the key players in the research process at the business school (King, 2012, 2013).

CASE STUDY: THE NEW LIBRARY AT THE STANFORD GRADUATE SCHOOL OF BUSINESS

The library here at the Stanford Graduate School of Business (GSB), Palo Alto, opened in 2010. It is an example of a library space that moved away from its accumulator role, increased and enhanced its service provider role, and is moving toward a facilitator role. As we worked on the project, our focus was on how to better integrate the library space into the daily life of the GSB.

When the GSB began to plan its new facilities in 2005, we had the opportunity to rethink our library spaces.[1] By that time it was clear that the use of the physical collection had decreased significantly and would continue to do so. The entrance to the library was equipped with a turnstile and required a university ID for entrance. MBA students used the space primarily as study space and for access to the items on course reserve. The library housed the only group study rooms on campus, and they were in high demand. Hours had been reduced over time because of staff cuts and limited use in evenings and at weekends, and the principal student complaints were about the loss of the space for study, not limited access to materials, either reserve or circulating. The students had access to a separate 24/7 computer lab, so although the library had a significant number of public computers, it was not the only source of computers. (Unlike most business schools in the USA, Stanford GSB does not have a laptop requirement for its MBA students, so the public computers were heavily used.) Faculty members were in a separate building and, with the increased availability of electronic journals and the library's document delivery service, they used the physical library less and less.

Starting in 2002, PhD students had been allowed unlimited 24-hour access to the library and continued to make use of it particularly when the library's evening hours were reduced in 2009. It is difficult to say, however, if the attraction was collection access or study space. The library was not part of the normal research workflow of either the faculty or the students. Over time the library space had been reduced from three floors to two, and the square footage was reduced from over 52,000 square feet in 1999 to around 34,000 square feet in 2005. Most of that reduction came from moving parts of the collection offsite. Between 2005 and 2011, when the new facility opened, additional library space continued to be repurposed with the addition of non-library staff offices to space formerly occupied by study tables and soft seating. The purpose of most of these changes was to accommodate additional business staff without costly structural changes, and there were challenges integrating this into the operation of the library.

Over the three-year planning process for our new space, several other events impacted on our planning and ideas for the new library. At that time the school introduced an ambitious new curriculum that focused on collaboration and community and required smaller, flexible settings for some of the new courses. Stanford University Libraries opened a new remote high-density storage facility and the business school library had an allocation for 130,000 items. The business school library had started to rethink its collection policies for the electronic era and was aggressively moving to improve cooperation and reduce overlap with other Stanford libraries.

---

1   All the libraries of the professional schools at Stanford – business, law and medicine – are funded by, and report to, their respective schools, not the university libraries.

Visions and missions

The vision for the Knight Management Center, which is the name of new Stanford GSB complex reflects:

> ... [a] commitment to creating space that enables collaboration between faculty and students, between Stanford GSB and the rest of Stanford University, and with the global business community ... The Knight Management Center buildings are designed to enable growth over the next century while responsibly using energy, water, and materials.[2]

The dedication reads: "Dedicated to the things that haven't happened and the people who are about to dream them up."

Our vision for the library was a space and an operation seamlessly integrated into the GSB campus and the GSB curriculum. As we designed the space, we thought about who our consumers would be. It was clear that, in the future, students would be the primary customers for the library as space, and we needed to make that space an integral part of their everyday lives. If you look at how our students currently use space, you can see that all aspects of their life are intertwined and that they prefer to move seamlessly from one activity to another without having to physically relocate. The goal of our new library space was to bring together resources, expertise, and technology in a comfortable, attractive, multipurpose space. We designed the space so that students could easily move between research, group discussion, collaborative presentations, and productions, taking a break and socializing as they wish.

The overall mission of the library is twofold: to foster information discovery, analysis, and management and to provide an environment for knowledge creation and incubation. We wanted to re-imagine the library space as an Intellectual Commons: a place where faculty, students, alumni, and outside scholars come together to build knowledge; a place that stimulates interaction and collaboration by increasing their access to one another and to the resources, expertise, technology that they need. The new GSB curriculum focused on collaboration and community, and we wanted the design of the library to support those goals.

Concepts

The library had been assigned prime real estate in the front of the main building of the school, the Bass Center. The building itself was conceived as the primary student space for study, computing, and research, but also as a facility that would have multiple meeting spaces for all members of the community. The library space is

---

2 http://www.gsb.stanford.edu/about/knightcenter/facts_features/vision.html (accessed 2 September 2013).

located on the main floor and the lower level and designed with open access, a single service desk, and the bulk of the collection in compact shelving on the lower level. The main floor includes a small reference collection and some display space along the walls for new popular business books and a few journal titles still being received in print—an area referred to as the "Makena Capital Traders' Pit" which includes Bloomberg terminals and computers with specialized services and software focused on financial data. That area also included two televisions tuned to the financial news station and a ticker board. This space is at the rear of the public space but visible from the main door. The other spaces on the floor have a combination of tables and soft seating, and there are a few public computers in standing carrels. The original plans for the Bass Center called for a welcome center for the entire GSB to be included in the front of the building to provide information and directions, but reluctance to staff the space and the potential for confusion by having two service desks opposite each other caused a change of direction. Currently, that space is equipped with an information kiosk for people seeking directions, campus maps, and dining options on campus and some soft seating, and it serves as a gathering place for potential students coming for class visits and campus tours. The library service desk, called the i-desk, also provides directions and information about campus events. The people staffing the desk were not initially happy about having this role added to their duties, but have warmed over time to their role as ambassadors for the school. While this is clearly a "non-library" service, it serves to better integrate our space with the daily workings of the school.

The second and third floors of the Bass Center, which are arranged around an atrium, include small group study rooms, some larger seminar rooms, a flat classroom, a space with multiple computers, study tables and soft seating. The fourth floor has a large reading room at one end with soft seating and study tables, as well as a balcony with outdoor seating and tables. At the other end of the building is a large boardroom used for various Stanford GSB meetings and events. In the previous library space, the library staff was responsible for allocating and managing the small inventory of group study rooms. In the Bass Center, the rooms can be booked online or at the door, and any issues are managed by the facilities department, which removes a significant pain point for the library staff. The reading room, called the General Atlantic Great Room, is for quiet study and, although under the control of the library, is largely self-managed by students.

Evolutions

In the year since we moved in there have already been two major changes to the space. The flat classroom on the third floor has been converted into a trading classroom with computers and some specialized financial software used in several classes. The conversion gives the library an ideal set-up for database workshops, while not having to worry about the utilization rate of specialized space elsewhere within the library. It also gives us more opportunities to collaborate with the finance faculty on the acquisition of specialized finance software and more access to their expertise.

The second alteration relates to the public area of the lower level where the GSB has constructed a distance-learning classroom linked with similar spaces in India and China. To accommodate this change we consolidated our collection by removing some of the compact shelving on one side and reconfiguring the remainder. Theoretically, we lost growth space for the collection, but the long-term trend continues to favor decreasing use of physical materials, so we do not think this will be a problem. We have not started to use the facility as yet, so do not know how the traffic from the classroom will impact on the use of library space. Before the construction this was a favored quiet study space because of the presence of tables with computers and the absence of traffic, and we still find people using the space now even without the tables. We view these changes as opportunities to integrate the physical library more closely into the school and to develop more fully the library's role as learning facilitator.

User behaviors and responses

One of the words that captured the experience of being in Jackson Library (the former name of the GSB library) is 'barriers'. There were physical and institutional barriers to entry, restrictions on bringing in food and drink, an extensive list of policies and procedures for using space and materials, barriers to the time of day that the space could be used, and barriers to using the group study rooms. In designing the new library we wanted to remove as many of these barriers as possible. Our new library space has open access, there are no restrictions on food and drink, and all of the study space is available 24/7. Although we wanted the space to be as open as possible, we did need to restrict access to the remaining collection when the library was not staffed. On the main floor we accomplished this by installing gates in front of the wall displays, the reference area, and the i-desk, which are closed when the library is closed. On the lower level, the doors at the bottom of the stairs are closed and locked when the library closes. They are key-carded and can be opened by faculty and PhDs who have after-hours privileges. This leaves the remainder of the facility, including the Makena Capital Traders' Pit and the General Atlantic Great Room, open to the GSB community. Most of the policies and procedures for circulation, access and issue of materials had been modeled on those of Stanford University Libraries and designed for a much different environment and a much larger collection. We took this opportunity to rethink all of these procedures and were able to eliminate or simplify the great majority of them.

Originally, we were concerned that the library did not contain specifically social space, such as a cafe. Over the past year, we have observed how the students use the more active space on the main floor and find that an area directly across from the i-desk and adjacent to the traffic coming in and out of the building is one of the most heavily used. It has the feel of an alcove and has soft seating for four people and a study table for six. During the day those seats are generally all filled by individuals, not by people working in groups. As Gayton (2008) discusses, students seem to come to the library looking not for social spaces, but for communal study spaces.

The response of the students to the space has been extremely positive; they tend to think of the entire building as the library, and the space is some of the most heavily used on campus. With the benefit of hindsight, we would have added more touchdown spaces with computers on the main floor. Our focus is to facilitate the student's learning experiences as much as possible by creating the various spaces and facilities they need to do this. Judging by the past, what they need today and what they will need tomorrow will not be the same. Any space in a business school needs to be as flexible as possible, and this includes the library spaces. Another thing we would have done differently is to reduce the footprint of the service desk and the space behind it. As the use of physical reserves continues to shrink and circulation of physical volumes continues to decline, we need less work space behind the desk. As we move into the future, we need to keep asking ourselves the question: "What do we want to happen in this space and who do we want to use it and how do we want them to use it?" We also need to observe closely how the use of the spaces evolves and be ready to adjust our footprint based on that.

LOOKING TO THE FUTURE

If we look at the current trends in both higher education and business education, we can see that most of the growth is projected to come from distance education, executive education, and more custom programs. Globalization and internationalization and the move to blended learning will continue (Hawawini, 2005). These are the areas on which our institutions are focusing. As we consider the academic business library of the future we will need to assess the library as place in terms of whether the library is perceived as supporting the business school's mission (Jackson and Hahn, 2011). We need to measure the use of our library space using institutional metrics rather than library metrics. Measuring the value of business libraries in these terms is not commonly done, and one of the challenges that academic business libraries will face in the future is to determine how to measure this value.

But I think that one question that we need to consider seriously for the future is: do we need a physical library at all? If we answer that question in the affirmative, what purpose will that space serve? If we answer that question in the negative, we need to devise strategies to insure that our products, services, and value to the institution are not equated to having a physical footprint.

What role does the physical space called "library" play in the modern business school and what role will it play in the future? Do we need it to serve the storage function? Will we continue to be accumulators? What role, if any, will library space play in the daily life and research process of the faculty? What role will it play in the daily life of the MBA student? The PhD student? The distance learner? Executive education students?

Students, both graduate and undergraduate, typically use the business library space for study rather than for research. Many MBA programs are focused on case-based learning, so the need for students to interact with any of the physical materials in the library is limited, and they expect any necessary research material or data to be available electronically. If we think of our physical study space as a service, does it have to be provided by or in the library? Studies of student preferences for libraries as study spaces indicate a preference for more traditional spaces (Applegate, 2009). As physical environments move further and further from that traditional look and feel, will a space called "library" be as attractive to them?

In any future we imagine for the business library, collaboration will be key to the library's success. We need to identify information partners, places at the school where our skills and expertise can contribute. Will that involve a physical presences called "library"? It is difficult to say, but we need to be open to opportunities to redefine the physical library and that could mean co-locating with other groups and sets of services as per the embedded librarian or Information Commons models previously discussed. One question to consider is: what is the most effective way to deliver the value we are offering?

Most of this discussion of space has focused on the role of library space in the life of the MBA student. Another question to consider is whether the library space will have a role in the research life and workflow of the faculty. The Darden School is experimenting with one solution co-locating research centers with the library. Some of the embedded models discussed above have a small allocation of space and that could continue. Since data and datasets will continue to become more and more central to the research of many of our faculty, should we designate some of our physical space to housing a resource center with the tools and expertise to work with faculty on their data projects? Or will cloud computing and future improvements in technology reduce the need for any type of central data center?

One of the most significant challenges academic libraries, including business libraries, face is that our identity is bound up in a physical building or space, even as the content, services, and value we provide are primarily delivered virtually. If our space disappears or changes significantly, what happens to our identity? This is not a question to which there is an easy answer, but it is one we must all grapple with as we move into the future. Smith's and Pickett's response is a fitting end to this chapter:

The computers and networks that link items and collections, the buildings that we inhabit, and the tools we offer are not primary to our purpose. Primary are the people who need and want these things. If we are going to sink costs somewhere, that is where we should sink them. If our focus shifts from serving individuals to tools, systems, and structures, the graveyard of obsolescence will beckon. (Smith and Pickett, 2011, p. 43)

REFERENCES

Academic Business Library Directors. 2012. At: http://www.abld.org (accessed 19 February 2013).

Applegate, R., 2009. The Library is for Studying: Student Preferences for Study Space. *Journal of Academic Librarianship*, 35(4), 341–6.

Beagle, D.R., 2006. *The Information Commons Handbook*. New York: Neal-Shuman Publishers.

Bennett, S., 2011. Learning Behaviors and Learning Spaces. *Libraries & the Academy*, 11(3), 765–89.

Christensen, C.M. and Radnor, M.E., 2003. *The Innovator's Solution: Creating and Sustaining Successful Growth*. Boston, MA: Harvard Business School Press.

Gayton, J.T., 2008. Academic Libraries: "Social" or "Communal"? The Nature and Future of Academic Libraries. *Journal of Academic Librarianship*, 43(1), 60–6.

Hartman, C.W., 2000. Memory Palace Place of Refuge, Coney Island of the Mind. *Research Strategy*, 17(2–3), 107–21.

Hawawini, G., 2005. Future of Business Schools. *Journal of Management Development*, 24(9), 770–82.

Jackson, H.L. and Hahn, T.B., 2011. Serving Higher Education's Highest Goals: Assessment of the Academic Library as Place. *College & Research Libraries*, 72(5), 428–42.

Library as Place: Rethinking Roles, Rethinking Space, 2005. Washington DC: Council on Library and Information Resources.

Lippincott, J.K., 2004. New Library Facilities: Opportunities for Collaboration. *Resource Sharing and Information Networks*, 17, 147–57.

Nitecki, D.A., 2011. Space Assessment as a Venue for Defining the Academic Library. *Library Quarterly*, 81(1), 27–59.

Oliver, K.B., 2005. The Johns Hopkins Welch Medical Library as Base: Information Professionals Working in Library User Environments. In: *Library as Place: Rethinking Roles, Rethinking Space*. Washington, DC: Council on Library and Information Resources, 66–75.

Parchuck, J., Director, Center for Science and Social Science Information, Yale University. Personal communication, 2013.

Schonfeld, R.C. and Housewright, R., 2010. US Faculty Survey 2009: Key Insights for Libraries, Publishers, and Societies. Ithaka S+R. At: http://www.sr.ithaka.org/research-publications/us-faculty-survey-2009 (accessed 27 April 2013).

Silkotch, C., School of Management Librarian, Yale University. Personal communication, 2013.
Smith. R.A., Associate Professor, Business Information Services, University of Illinois. Personal communication, 2013.
Smith, S. and Pickett, C., 2011. Avoiding the Path to Obsolescence. *American Libraries*, 42(9–10), 40–3.
Stuart, C., 2009. Learning and Research Spaces in ARL Libraries: Snapshots of Installations and Experiments. *Research Library Issues: A Bimonthly Report from ARL, CNI, and SPARC*, no. 264, 7–18. At: http://publications.arl.org/rli264/8 (accessed 27 April 2013).
Welch Medical Library, 2013. The Welch Library Embedded-Informationist Program. At: http://welch.jhmi.edu/welchone/Informationist-Program (accessed 31 January 2013).

FURTHER READING

Christensen. C.M., 1997. *The Innovator's Dilemma: When New Technologies Cause Great Firms to Fail.* Boston, MA: Harvard Business School Press.
Christensen, C.M and Eyring, H.J., 2011. *The Innovative University: Changing the DNA of Higher Education from the Inside Out.* San Francisco, CA: Jossey-Bass.
Demas, S. (ed.) 2005. From the Ashes of Alexandria: What's Happening in the College Library? In: *Library as Place: Rethinking Roles, Rethinking Space.* Washington, DC: Council on Library and Information Resources, 25–40.
Freeman, G.T., 2005. The Library as Place: Changes in Learning Patterns, Collections, Technology, and Use. In: *Library as Place: Rethinking Roles, Rethinking Space.* Washington, DC: Council on Library and Information Resources, 1–9.
MacWhinnie, L.A., 2003. The Information Commons: The Academic Library of the Future. *Libraries and the Academy*, 3(2), 241–57.
Paulus, M.J. Jr, 2011. Reconceptualizing Academic Libraries and Archives in the Digital Age. *Libraries and the Academy,* 11(4), 939–52.
Staley, D.J. and Malenfant, K.J., 2010. Futures Thinking for Academic Librarians: Higher Education in 2025. *Information Services & Use*, 30, 57–90.
Welch Medical Library, 2012. Creation of the Committee for the 21st Century Library. At: http://welch.jhmi.edu/welchone/Welch-Library-Transition/#section1 (accessed 27 April 2013).
What Future for Business Schools? 2005. *Management Today*, November, 42–9.

CHAPTER 11

CONCEPTUALIZING THE FUTURE OF THE BUSINESS SCHOOL LIBRARY

CHRIS FLEGG

INTRODUCTION

The library as a physical or architectural space developed hand-in-glove with the development of an organizational structure that evolved specifically to deliver the functionality of that space to the user. Although not the only driver, the *contents* of that space were the dominant driver shaping that organizational structure: that in turn defined the roles and the optimal skills required of the people associated with the library entity, along with the reporting lines and the financial and administrative controls they exercised.

Within that arrangement, the traditional business school library carved its own niche by amassing the specialized business, management and finance collections needed to support the research interests of its members and by aligning its services to the overall success of the business school, most typically expressed by the upward or downward movement of the school in the global business school rankings.

Conversely, with business school rankings playing out as the ubiquitous and high-profile indicators of success, the pressure to outperform competitors has played well in the acceptance of the distinct business school library as a necessary and dedicated service provider, charged with playing its part in the delivery of high-touch tailored services, in keeping with the high-touch and 'champagne' customer service that business schools regard as a critical component of the business school brand.

However, with information becoming increasingly digital, mobile and disaggregated from single and exclusive points of creation, location, distribution and access, and with information becoming increasingly liberated from traditional library collections, the very notion of a library, along with its organizational paraphernalia, has come under increasing scrutiny and pressure.

How business school librarians will fare in this future will depend largely on where they might best find a fit in an information world in which roles and value are no longer defined predominantly by their collections.

INFORMATION OWNERSHIP AND INFORMATION ACCESS

In 1086 William the Conqueror sent some 20–30 royal commissioners to record everything that belonged to him by having them travel across England to list, in meticulous detail, everything in his domain, thus creating the remarkable *Doomsday Book*. In 2005 a global technology company had a fleet of specially equipped cars trawl the world to map the entire globe to further a mission to 'organize all the world's information' (McClendon, 2012). One effort was born of a desire to create a record by which to protect ownership of assets and raise taxes, the other to craft a commercial empire by creating and controlling access to information.

Of course, the move from ownership to access has not been the purview of solely the technology giants. For decades, libraries have been leaders in the delivery of electronic content – particularly of journal content – which they did not so much own as manage in gatekeeper fashion on behalf of the content aggregators or publishers, for those users designated as entitled to access. In this way, libraries were able not only to offer impressively augmented journal collections which far outstripped in number and depth what they could individually purchase or store in print form, but also to provide access – anywhere and at any time – without the massive inconveniences inherent in the use of print collections. In a relative instant, users were saved the constants of physically dispersed journal runs, missing or borrowed issues, poor or no indexing, torn or incorrect references, articles having to be photocopied with varying success and so on.

But while libraries enthusiastically embraced the provision of some content through the access, rather than the ownership, model and justifiably garnered the avid appreciation of their users, the positive value of the library as the provider of this electronic bounty was experienced largely as an *augmentation* of the value of the library as space, of the library as a dispenser of information guidance and instruction, and of the library as the stereotypically most cost-effective distribution model for all the additional materials for which print remained the favoured norm. Put another way, while libraries had useful collections of teaching texts, reference books and duplicate runs of journals in print, which their users could borrow and scan rather than needing to purchase, and while libraries offered good study spaces, approachable and skilled information professionals and banks of PCs or wireless access for mobile devices, all was well and good.

However, there is now a sense in the broader ranks, as there has been in the information community generally, that a tipping-point has been reached in the public perception of where libraries sit in the hierarchy of information providers, and it is this view of the tipping-point that sits at the heart of the urgency being felt by many librarians to find alternative roles or shore up those roles which they have hitherto seen as exclusively theirs (Research Information Network, 2010).

LIBRARIES IN THE INFORMATION PROVIDER HIERARCHY

It would be tempting to think that in the information world the natural law of the market would apply, so that whoever owns or manages the information is seen to occupy the information space. Yet, to the modern user, it is the major search engines such as Google or Yahoo, along with the high-profile players, such as Wikipedia and HathiTrust, that are viewed as the giant cogs in the supply chain linking content to user, even though these players, by and large, achieve their prominence on the back of content created and owned by others or – in the case of the high-quality academic content – made accessible through library-acquired and library-managed collections.

Indeed, most librarians would accept that in the search-engine-dominated environment their libraries have lost their place as the dominant information providers in the public psyche. Nevertheless, they can rightly take a good deal of comfort in the fact that most of the quality scholarly content has reached the user from *their* collections and subscriptions, irrespective of whether it has done so via the Internet and trawled for by the search engines, or accessed down the chain via library discovery systems.

However, with the juggernaut of the open access movement starting to reshape where and how scholarly output is located and distributed, the question that should be uppermost is: where, in the provider supply chain, will libraries sit when true open access to scholarly content reaches critical mass – a mass that is gaining considerable momentum with the increasing numbers of governments, grant bodies, university administrators and departmental heads issuing their researchers with 'open access mandates' or face the risk of losing financial support for their research (University Leadership Council, 2011, p. 43)?

For the individuals who are hungry for this content, there are real positive gains with the relocation of journal articles away from library journal subscriptions that are locked behind pay walls to open access institutional repositories that sit outside the library collections of subscribed journals, or into the free open access sections of the publisher distribution sites.

Add to this scenario the very real possibility that in the foreseeable future academic e-book publishers will switch from selling their e-books through third-party suppliers and via the purchasing arm of libraries, to selling directly to the end user, and the critical mass suddenly looks plainly in sight, with libraries substantially vanishing from the resource delivery chain.

More alarmingly, libraries could vanish not just from the delivery chain, but simultaneously from the resource *discovery* picture. This is because, at the end of the day, in a digital information world in which the bulk of both the book and journal markets are 'born digital', libraries won't own the books and journals any more than the search engines currently do, but whereas libraries are ever strapped to what most users experience as clunky, over-complex catalogues or discovery tools based on archaic subject headings and rigid taxonomies, the likes of Google and Yahoo have evolved mega-capacities in their discoverability and access technologies that, through their sheer simplicity and usability, have become, for most users, the finding aid of first choice: discovery tools that surpass anything that even the world-class and national libraries are able to emulate.

Some libraries may still seek to act as the backstop recipients and long-term curators of the digital content, but to the user, the visibility of the library within the information provider hierarchy will be even more opaque, if at all visible, and may ultimately be reduced in the public mind to repository status.

So how will this play out for the future of libraries and for the value propositions by which librarians might seek to establish their place within the broader educational enterprise?

LIBRARY COLLECTIONS AND THE VALUE PROPOSITION

Notwithstanding the major impacts that open access will have on the future of our industry, today's librarian has already had to face the inescapable need to reassess, reprioritize, restructure and reframe the value propositions by which the financial outlays required to maintain or develop library services have had to be articulated, demonstrated and defended. This is not only because of the simplistic but populist view that 'it's all on the Internet', but because of the not unreasonable premise that all educational institutions faced by shrinking budgets occurring alongside increases in costs need to be fiscally more responsible and accountable.

In this more challenging environment many have looked to the use of quantifiable rather than qualitative measures as offering the more persuasive sort of vehicles by which to prove the library's impact on, and value to, the organization. Regrettably, some of these quantitative measures of library value, while well intentioned, may have inadvertently installed ticking bombs in the organization–library value dialogue when they have been based, as many have, on linking the value of the library and its services directly to library collections and their use – collections for and to which librarians may not be able to claim exclusive ownership or access in the future.

This is particularly the case with many of the ROI (return on investment) value-seeking exercises that have used an array of quantitative measurements to connect the supposed value of the library to a cost equivalent, such as that embodied in the user cost avoidance argument: an argument which seeks to establish the savings that users can be argued to have made by accessing library collections which they would otherwise have had to purchase or obtain for a fee from an alternative, commercial outlet. This would involve, for example, taking the commercial cost of a video purchase or hire from a commercial outlet, and deducing from that the total savings made by library users who chose to borrow videos from their libraries as opposed to purchasing or renting those videos from those commercial outlets.

This is an argument that works well where (a) relative costs remain fairly static so that the cost parity remains significant and (b) the assumption holds true that the people investing in the libraries share the view that it is a legitimate role of libraries to spend money so that library users can save theirs, an argument that even if held today may not be held tomorrow. More fundamentally, it relies on the library collection retaining a static overall value despite any changes in societal developments such as video on demand, or home movie streaming at reduced costs relative, say, to the total cost of travel to a library site.

In similar ROI vein is the linking of the number of funding grants awarded to a business school or university department to the number of library journals cited in the grant applications (Kaufman, 2010). This may indeed establish a direct link between grant funding success and the use of scholarly research, but from the moment the library's journal collections are made redundant by freely accessible articles obtained within open access regimes, it will no longer establish a correlation between the relevance of the library to the school's or university's research mission.

Similarly, we can see an inherent difficulty in attaching library value to article citation counts in peer-reviewed library journals when the very use of citation counts as the measure of choice by which to measure impact value is starting to be seriously questioned, as it increasingly is: some, like Jason Priem of the University of North Carolina (UNC) at Chapel Hill, for example, are strong advocates of the use of different metrics (most commonly referred to as *altmetrics*) or web-driven scholarly interactions on blogs, tweets and bookmarks as a preferred methodology by which to measure impact (Priem, 2012). Again, while others are advocating caution in attaching too great a value to alternative measures that circumvent the peer-review publishing track, some have found tweet-based social impact measures as highly predictive of which articles will be highly cited, and thus able to complement the traditional citation metrics (Eysenbach, 2011).

Whatever the outcome of this sturdy debate, we should be cautious about assuming a long-term and sustainable correlation between the number of article citations located in library journals and the value of the library to scholarly output.

It should be no surprise, then, that with library collections being at risk of diminishing from the bag of tricks by which we might define our fit and value within the broader educational enterprise, there is a drive to create new roles or raise in profile some old ones. Just look at the flurry of the current job titles by which we are now seeking to be known, and the search for broader identities becomes very transparent – knowledge manager, information adviser, academic support librarian, development officer, customer services manager, support services manager, research assistant in data mining and so on – with the overwhelming emphasis in language shifting from the collection procurement and management end to the customer and information servicing end of the library's activities.

FROM COLLECTIONS TO SERVICES

In its somewhat alarmist but sobering report, *Redefining the Academic Library* (2011), the University Leadership Council points out that – notwithstanding the common assumption that threats to the academic library emanate from outside the profession – criticism of the traditional library model is now coming from within our industry, with library professionals predicting that: by 2015 patrons will go elsewhere for information; there will be no need for traditional librarians; and the library will be a space for more than just books. It adds that 'successful libraries will be those that have managed to turn over the majority of their staff or reassigned staff to different roles within the library' (University Leadership Council, p. 7).

This mirrors the sense throughout the profession that librarians need to extend their skills and be constructive and flexible in adopting new roles, and that they be seen to be more actively service-oriented as opposed to more passively collection-focused. Responses to that pressure have been taken up and woven through a variety of narratives, including: the broadening of the teacher and instructor role; the partnering of library staff with research staff in collaborative projects; the overseeing of copyright and intellectual property risk management; the management of metadata and research repositories; and the curation of research data. Some have been shaped around the articulation of real skills rising up to fit latent needs, while others have not risen much above marketing and public relations exercises designed to ward off perceptions of irrelevance.

Of all the varying roles, the teaching and research support roles have tended to take a prominent place, and while librarians have delivered base-level library sessions for as long as libraries have existed within educational institutions, many are now pushing to be seen to be more seriously and deeply engaged in the teaching and research support functions, and to have their contribution championed more aggressively as critical to successful educational outcomes.

According to the general evidence across the literature, in many instances recognition and acceptance of librarians in a teaching role is well established in business school libraries, and the 2012 Sage-commissioned study of libraries in the UK, the USA and Scandinavia found, that '[e]mbedded teaching and co-teaching are extremely valued by teaching staff, who can observe the benefits in the quality of the assignments they receive from students' (Creaser and Spezi, 2012).

However, as noted in that same report, the degree to which librarians have been successful has varied depending on the in-depth knowledge, maturity, personality, teaching skill and experience of the individual librarians who are being called on to take these roles, noting a recurrent view from teaching staff that 'not all librarians had appropriate teaching skills to make this collaboration successful' (Creaser and Spezi, 2012, p. 14).

This confirms the findings of the 2010 study by the Association of College and Research Libraries (ACRL) which makes the telling point that 'most of the published evidence of the impact of libraries on student learning is sporadic, disconnected, and focused on limited case studies' and that the profession is still in need of an evidence-based store of coherent and systematic evidence of the academic library's contributions to student learning (Oakleaf, 2010, p. 14).

It may be that, as a community of professionals, we have yet to evolve a shared understanding of exactly what the librarian is there to teach. Anecdotal evidence suggests that what we collectively do ranges wildly from teaching the basic mechanics of library and database usage, along with the basics of plagiarism and referencing rules – all to a great degree able to be conveyed by non-specialist staff and deliverable outside the classroom – to, at the higher end, the imparting of more in-depth knowledge of the publishing world, where and how good research starts, how it is executed, completed and carried down through the publishing and data curation chain, and how it may be rendered more impactful through the skilled exploitation of the communication opportunities offered by the publishing and social media channels.

The problem of disparity in skill levels is further exacerbated by the more general discomfort some librarians feel in moving from a support provider role to one of upfront teaching and research partner – roles that require vastly different skill-sets. This discomfort will no doubt be heightened by increasingly high-fee educational environments in which the consumers may feel entitled to be less forgiving of bad teachers and irrelevant facts – a concern even more tangible within business schools in which competition is fought to a greater extent through the quality of the teaching and pedagogical content on offer.

Nevertheless, librarians everywhere are making strong and concerted efforts to fill this space, and the effort, when executed by skilled, knowledgeable and mature professionals, is able to reap real rewards not just for the library, but also for the reputation of the institution, if and when the teaching is informed by a deep understanding of how students and staff consume and use information, and how information can be translated into knowledge that ultimately allows each individual to meet or exceed their educational, professional, scholarly and personal aspirations.

However, to fully capitalize on their instructional role, business school librarians should redraw the business school stakeholder map to ensure that it is fully inclusive of all the groups that are critical to the school's success and use that map as a basis for the range and type of services they should develop and grow. By enhancing and enriching the use of information by all those stakeholders, librarians in business schools, perhaps more than those in any other discipline, have an unprecedented opportunity to realize the library's potential as a critical and indispensable service in the realization of the business school's overall mission.

THE BUSINESS SCHOOL, THE BUSINESS SCHOOL LIBRARY AND THE OPEN ACCESS MOVEMENT

Though not immune from the impact of the open access movement, the dependence of business school libraries on academic journals – while still acute – is mitigated by equal, if not greater, reliance on economic, financial and industry data, most of which, because of their third-party provenance, are unlikely to ever be free and open, since, unlike the case for scholarly journals articles, there is no supportive argument for this proprietary content to be available for anything other than what the market will pay.

In that sense, then, business school libraries will continue to retain as one of their critical and important roles the assessment, selection, sourcing and servicing of these unique business-critical data collections.

Nevertheless, in business school libraries, as elsewhere, the shift of focus from collection acquisition and collection management to service support will continue: the critical question for the business school library will be to identify which services to develop, and how to align this service development with the business school's changing and developing priorities to deliver tangible, visible and cost-effective outcomes for the communities with which the school has strong allegiances, or desires for closer ties.

SO WHO MIGHT THE BUSINESS SCHOOL LIBRARY SERVE?

To a great extent, the open access movement – which would render journal content more freely accessible without the need for the intermediation of libraries – has been fuelled by a tide of irritation being expressed in senior administrative and academic circles against the lock-down of scholarly output by publishers holding tight rein on the copyright of the articles they publish, despite this very output having originated from the academics' own labours and their own publicly funded educational institutions. This irritation is made all the more cancerous by the pressure on these institutions to provide greater levels of financial support to their libraries to cover rising serial prices or risk loss of access to critical journal content, while they are themselves experiencing reductions in their overall budgets.

Nevertheless it would be short-sighted for business school librarians to suppose that this open access movement has had as its only driver the desire by the internal members of academic institutions to reap greater benefits from the scholarly output at a cheaper (or no-cost) rate.

The recent UK government-led Finch Report, *Accessibility, Sustainability, Excellence: How to Expand Access to Research Publications* (Finch, 2012) which advocates a form of free open access (the so-called gold open access model) – whereby the cost of publishing is pushed to the authors and, by domino effect, thereon to the libraries, academic institutions and funders of education – was born of the conviction that scientific research output produced through taxpayer-funded universities should benefit all researchers and produce 'closer linkages between research and innovation, with benefits for public policy and services and for economic growth' (Finch, 2012, p. 5), and that publicly funded research should be available to anyone who wants to use it, for whatever purpose. As Professor Adam Tickell, who served on the group, is quoted as saying, UK universities "'recognise and embrace the strong moral case that the public who fund our research should have unimpeded access to the results of that research'" (Jha, 2012).

The UK government's support for taking publishing down this route to open access for one and all is as significant a single step as it is a compact and direct reference to a fundamental and highly significant shift from an acceptance of scholarly output for scholarly purpose, to a view that the educational sector, to the extent that it is publicly funded, must be clearly and directly supportive of the broader social and economic agenda.

This is despite the not unpredictable push-back against the Finch recommendations by a number of academics and research institutions who rely heavily on their own journal revenues, and by a growing number of authors who are counting the monetary losses and gains inherent in such freeing up of research output. As Alice Meadows, writing in the *Scholarly Kitchen* asks:

> *Are UK authors, their institutions, and the UK government really happy to give up all claims to any monetary gain made from the results of their published work? To allow commercial companies to text-mine their articles, extract anything of commercial value, and increase their own profits? (Meadows 2013)*

It could be argued, however, that the quite reasonable concern being expressed about the flow of commercial gain from scholarly effort only serves to bring to greater clarity the fact that the obstacles to the broad concept of open access have been largely to do with managing a fair allocation of commercial rights rather than any principled attachment to the internal academic-use versus external commercial-use divide enshrined in copyright law and commercial contracts.

And, like the scrambled egg that cannot be remade whole, the idea of releasing for broader access the fruits of research, whether through the UK's contentious gold open access, or the more palatable green open access option – whereby authors can satisfy the open access mandates by depositing author versions of their papers in institutional repositories – is well and truly in the popular public domain from where it is unlikely to be retracted. And should these initiatives ripple through the research output landscape elsewhere, the breath-taking implications of this new rationale for open access provision – by which the broader community of users, commercial or otherwise, are being championed in their right to feed freely off research output (as long as authors, institutions and departments are allocated their fair share of any commercial gain) – cannot be ignored by librarians.

More tantalizingly and promisingly for the business school librarian, this welcoming in out of the cold of the non-academic, commercial world into the community of research consumers should resonate loudly with business schools, which, ahead of most other players in the educational sector, have long maintained a strategy of close engagement with two groups who have sat on the fringe of the academic information bounty, but who are pivotal to the success of the business school itself. These are the legion of business men and women hungry for continuous learning opportunities, who make up the lucrative and highly prestigious executive education market, and the business school alumni who are in positions to support the business school in a myriad powerful ways.

Additionally, in the highly competitive environment in which business schools operate, business school deans know that performance standards have to be at their highest in every department and unit of the enterprise – from the marketing, enrolment, careers, IT, HR and finance departments though to the cleaning and catering units – to ensure that the business school customer has a high-quality experience, and that the school has a high level of organizational support for delivery of its strategy.

OPEN ACCESS AND THE IMPACT FACTOR: A MARRIAGE MADE IN HEAVEN

Further, for those working in the business school sector, the open access movement, quite coincidentally, meshes in magically with the equally powerful driver of research activity currently working its way through the educational sector – that of research impact.

As today's universities and business schools are being increasingly challenged to show the value of investments by funders and the public purse, the ground has shifted from an expectation that our institutions will be about good research to an expectation that they will be about research that is both relevant and high-impact: a theme that has been irrevocably picked up in the UK through the establishment of the various incarnations of the Research Excellence Framework (REF) as the preferred methodology for assessing the value of research. In the interconnected global education market, it is likely that impacts or outcomes of research, as the criteria influencing funding and support, will most likely gain currency to become the norm elsewhere (REF2014).

This should, of course, resonate very strongly with what business schools have always been about. One could indeed make the case that, in hindsight, business school deans have been ahead of the societal game in promoting and chasing high-impact activity. Take a sweeping look at the mission statements of the top business schools – 'London experience, world impact' (London Business School), 'Knowledge for action' (The Wharton School), 'Transforming knowledge into action' (Cranfield School of Management), 'The business school for the world' (INSEAD), 'We educate leaders who make a difference in the world' (Harvard Business School), 'Educating leaders for 800 years' (Oxford's Saïd Business School), 'Change lives, change organizations, change the world' (Stanford Graduate School of Business) – and it is immediately obvious that, at their heart, business schools have had external focus and transformative intent as an overarching goal.

For that reason, business schools have long seen themselves as located not just within the educational sector, but also within business communities, and have long nurtured solid connections with business and industry leaders, governments, the public sector and heads of NGOs, and the professions generally. This has been persuasively articulated and driven through both the executive education programmes that thrive within this sector and efforts by business schools to engage with their alumni.

To date, business school librarians have walked less confidently in the delivery of services to these groups than to their more traditional MBA, doctorate and other accredited business programme students. However, the convergence of three factors creates an ideal environment in which modern business school librarians can escalate their attention to meeting head-on the unique needs of these very distinctive groups with services designed specifically for them: (1) the growing importance of internal business support personnel to the business school's success in an increasingly competitive business school market; (2) the push to free up content for use by society at large through the open access initiatives; and (3) the call by government bodies, university administrators and funders to show the relevance and impact of educational programmes.

For business school librarians, then, there is an opportunity to radically recalibrate the focus from serving predominantly course-based award programme students to, instead, extending equal support service importance to each and every member of each unit and department that constitute the entire school community. To date, making access to information accessible to those who have existed on the periphery of the institutionally registered educational programmes has been fraught with difficulties. This has been particularly the case with the provision of information access to people working in the finance departments or business development units, and the business school alumni who, paradoxically, recognize and value – probably more than any other group in society – the long-term benefits of being recipients of verifiable and quality-assured business information (Flegg, 2012).

THE SERVICE CHALLENGE FOR THE BUSINESS SCHOOL LIBRARY

In many of the top-ranked business schools, executive education programmes and alumni services have posed both challenges and obstacles to seamless delivery of library services.

In the case of alumni, both the graduates and the business school deans want to develop more substantive levels of co-engagement and support. But, for many of the information stakeholders, the opening up of information resources to this community is fraught with obstacles that, as indicated earlier, are less to do with questions of copyright and contract compliance as they are to do with the safeguarding of lucrative markets for publishers – a situation that, as I have argued, will need to be recalibrated with the shifting of pay-walls via the open access initiatives.

In the case of the executive education market, powerful reservations about the provision of resources and services are often experienced and acted on, even while not always precisely articulated. This is because, in the case of executive and continuing education course participants, not all librarians have felt sufficiently emboldened to champion and defend their entitlements to full access to information resources regardless and irrespective of where and how the fruits of that access will be applied.

But slaying and putting to rest the old bogey of scholarly or educational licence products being used by these course participants to garner new knowledge and insights that will drift back as value to their organizations (which, after all, is precisely what business schools and universities promote in their branded marketing material) will need fortitude if the educational sector is to truly show how scholarly research is translating into real-world benefits not only for public policy and services, but also for economic growth.

There may also be at play a deeper underlying anxiety among some librarians about delivering instructional sessions to these groups, or fronting classrooms generally, due to the seniority and level of experience and expertise that the individuals who make up these groups typically possess – a fear sometimes assuaged by a variety of convenient assumptions made about this group: that they do not *want* to personally do research (leaving that to their minions or paid consultants); that they don't *need* to do any research because they are highly knowledgeable; and that they *can't do* research because they aren't familiar with this type of activity.

In fact, however, the truth is more likely to be the exact opposite: that people who return to take up executive education programmes – if appropriately coached and assisted – are singularly motivated to be stimulated by the research process; that they are extraordinarily able to appreciate information that 'wows' them by its currency, breadth and relevance; and that they are highly appreciative of the way in which their experience is enriched by the new skills they have acquired – skills which they can use to independently explore the breadth of information that business school and university libraries are uniquely able to provide them and which, more often than not, will challenge many of their fundamental preconceptions and assumptions.

For these information consumers – as for the business school graduates, and the finance, HR, business development staff and all the other staff that are often regarded as fringe to learning – tailored approaches, although time- and resource-intensive, will reap immeasurable benefits for both the reputation of the library and that of the business school.

CUSTOMIZATION: BOUTIQUE SERVICES VERSUS BOUTIQUE LIBRARIES

The massive changes that have occurred through mergers of distinct separate libraries into larger administrative or physical units by the consolidation of services or departments, and in some cases by the rationalizing away of whole collections and staff units, have been painful experiences for many librarians struck down by budget cuts and service rationalizations.

It is therefore not surprising that, in response, we see the championing of boutique libraries as offering specialized services that cannot – it is argued – be offered by the larger administrative units or libraries by which the smaller libraries might be subsumed or entirely eliminated. This position rests on the supposition that the consolidation of discrete independent libraries into bigger organizational units, championed for their greater efficiencies and economies of scale, carry the risk of a loss of customization and a depersonalization of customer service, resulting in a loss in *quality* of the services to the point where they will no longer be valued enough to garner institutional support.

There is indeed a strong argument that can be made for the fact that just as differentiation from the pack and distinction from the norm are key to business schools excelling in the competitive business school market, the ability of the business school librarian to be close to, and intimately *au fait* with their users is a necessary precondition for the design and delivery of services that can have a real impact and deliver real value.

However, to the extent that they have it in their power to steer their libraries into new or amended organizational structures, librarians wishing to occupy the niche library service space should take care to avoid slipping from niche services to niche libraries if and where there is a danger of them becoming trapped in isolated silos, while their counterparts in larger organizational units are able to leverage off the multidisciplinary networks and large collaborative ventures that can deliver the technology- and resource-rich environments that will be needed to support emerging activities.

This is particularly the case as faculty and researchers become increasingly global in their research orientation and in their membership of professional communities that cross traditional fields, and where course design specialists within business schools are capitalizing on the benefits of cross-subject fertilizations to broaden and enrich their curricula. Specialist library staff will need to find ways of becoming active members of broad subject-based networks if they are to bridge the pathways to resources in fields as diverse as public policy, geography, philosophy, music, ethics, engineering and demography, to name just a few.

They will also need to work with the fact that information is becoming not only increasingly digital but, for many, increasingly data-based, with new research opportunities offered by the world of 'big data'. Many researchers will see 'the new data they create as their most significant research outcome' (Williford and Henry, 2012, p. 3) for which data access, data analysis and extraction, data storage, data curation and data dissemination will arise as key concerns.

In that emerging world of computationally massive datasets, business school librarians will need to work cooperatively and creatively with others across campuses and beyond those departments with which they have traditionally worked. They will need to actively engage with staff in research and grant offices, academic computing departments, programming and data analysis centres, as well as deal with network security, data privacy, copyright, intellectual property and legal matters, or be able to triage these issues as part of their support services.

Notwithstanding the value of 'niche' in the design and delivery of services, in the world of global scholarly outreach, massive datasets and data stores, massive support systems and ever more complex data manipulation and analysis techniques and tools – whether in the skill-sets or networks we are able to bring into play – size will increasingly matter.

CONCLUSION

This chapter started with a reference to the library as an organizational structure designed to serve the largely print holdings by which much of the library purpose, and the role of those who deliver that purpose, were defined.

While most libraries have made spectacularly successful transitions from being managers of print to managers of print and digital content, it is likely that 'content' – whether print or digital – will feature far less as something to collect and manage as something to steer our customers to use effectively and productively.

In this new paradigm, the value of the librarian will have to rest more squarely and more transparently on the skills they singularly own and can bring into play to provide broader and more adaptive support services. Success will entail, on the one hand, building strong relationships with the individual members of the school community to understand intimately how they need, seek, consume, process and use information, while, on the other hand, being strongly outward-looking and collaborative with external communities in order to bring back the broadest knowledge and understanding of the external environment needed to act as informed and skilled information champion and research enabler.

The 21st-century business school librarian will require not only a highly adaptive and flexible mindset, but also a library team whose breadth and depth of skills is constantly refreshed and broadened to include expertise in whatever areas emerge as critical to the business school's success. To name just a few these currently include such areas as: data management and curation; management of collaborative and interdisciplinary projects; use of analytical tools for data processing; and navigation across the publishing and research dissemination options. The business school librarian, as always, will need to keep ever watchful for change and the continuing need for adaptation to remain relevant.

Despite the proliferation of information in the digital world – or perhaps because of it – the challenge faced by many of our library users will not lie in finding information, or discerning where information is located or who owns it, but in being sufficiently skilled to find and process the appropriate bits of information to produce the knowledge and understanding that will satisfy their needs and aspirations.

For the 21st-century business school librarian – freed from the confines of collection management and equipped with a singular and powerful set of skills – the future has the potential to be infinitely liberating.

ADDENDUM: WHAT OF THE LIBRARY AS SPACE?

It might be tempting to read into this chapter a trivialization of the future value of the library as space. This is not my intention. Just as civic communities evolve whatever architectural and community spaces best serve the needs of those communities, libraries will evolve appropriate spaces for each campus: the group study space, the contemplative quiet space, the social meeting space and the serendipitous 'stuff of life' space that libraries, in their various physical permutations, have always provided. What will be distinctive is that the 'librarian' – by whatever name he or she will be known – will be able to define his or her value beyond and irrespective of the confines of the space and its accoutrements – the 'library' and the 'librarian' coexisting in complementary worlds, but in an unfettered symbiotic independence with all the potential freedom that independence can deliver.

REFERENCES

Creaser, C. and Spezi, V., 2012. *Working Together: Evolving Value for Academic Libraries* [online]. A report commissioned by Sage. At: http://libraryvalue.wordpress.com/report/ (accessed 15 December 2012).

Eysenbach, G., 2011. Can Tweets Predict Citations? Metrics of Social Impact Based on Twitter and Correlation with Traditional Metrics of Scientific Impact [online]. *Journal of Medical Internet Research*, 13(4). At: http://www.jmir.org/2011/4/e123/ (accessed 4 January 2012).

Finch, J., 2012. *Accessibility, Sustainability, Excellence: How to Expand Access to Research Publications: Report of the Working Group on Expanding Access to Published Research Findings* [online]. At: http://www.researchinfonet.org/wp-content/uploads/2012/06/Finch-Group-report-FINAL-VERSION.pdf (accessed 1 January 2013).

Flegg, C., 2012. Alumni, Libraries and Universities: Whereto the Relationship? *Journal of Academic Librarianship*, 38(1): 60–2.

Jha, A., 2012. Open Access is the Future of Academic Publishing, Says Finch Report [online]. *Guardian,* 19 June. At: http://www.guardian.co.uk/science/2012/jun/19/open-access-academic-publishing-finch-report (accessed 19 June 2012).

Kaufman, P., 2010. Library as Strategic Investment. Results of the University of Illinois 'Return on Investment' Study, June 26 2010 [online]. University of Illinois at Urbana-Champaign. At: http://hdl.handle.net/2142/12031 (accessed 10 January 2012).

McClendon, B., 2012. Google's Mr Maps Sets his Sights on World Delineation [online]. *Guardian*, 7 December. At: http://www.guardian.co.uk/technology/2012/dec/07/google-maps-street-view-world (accessed 7 December 2012).

Meadows, A., 2013. The Historians Are Revolting — Leading History Journal Editors Take on the Research Councils UK [online]. *The Scholarly Kitchen*, 9 January.

At: http://scholarlykitchen.sspnet.org/author/alicejmeadows/ (accessed 20 January 2013).

Oakleaf, M., 2010. *Value of Academic Libraries: A Comprehensive Research Review and Report* [online]. Association of College and Research Libraries. At: http://www.ala.org/acrl/sites/ala.org.acrl/files/content/issues/value/val_report.pdf (accessed 10 November 2012).

Priem, J., 2012. Scholars Seek Better Ways to Track Impact Online [online]. *Chronicle of Higher Education*, 29 January. At: http://chronicle.com/article/As-Scholarship-Goes-Digital/130482/ (accessed 4 March 2012).

REF2014. Research Excellence Framework [online]. At: http://www.ref.ac.uk/ (accessed 16 January 2013).

Research Information Network, 2010. Challenges for Academic Libraries in Difficult Economic Times: A Guide for Institutional Managers and Policy Makers [online]. At: http://www.rin.ac.uk/challenges-for-libraries (accessed 10 January 2012).

University Leadership Council, 2011. *Redefining the Academic Library: Managing the Migration to Digital Information Services* [online]. At: http://www.theconferencecircuit.com/wp-content/uploads/Provosts-Report-on-Academic-Libraries2.pdf (accessed 15 January 2012).

Williford, C. and Henry, C., 2012. *One Culture: Computationally Intensive Research in the Humanities and Social Sciences: A Report on the Experiences of First Respondents to the Digging into Data Challenge* [online]. At: http://www.clir.org/pubs/reports/pub151 (accessed 10 December 2012).

CHAPTER 12

BUSINESS SCHOOL LIBRARIES' FUTURES?

TIM WALES

I would like to conclude this book by examining the future (or possible futures) for business school libraries as viewed by the people with the most at stake – the heads of service themselves. Using the joint ABLD/EBSLG/APBSLG mailing list as my sampling frame[1] for international business school library heads of service, I invited members in August 2012 to complete a short (10-question) 'Delphi survey' to determine whether there was any consensus around the shape of things to come.

SURVEY RESULTS

Twenty-three responses were received, of which 11 (48 per cent) were from the USA, nine (39 per cent) from Europe and the remaining three (13 per cent) were from the Asia-Pacific region.

Acknowledging again from Chapter 1 the importance of determining institutional structure when studying the business school library sector, the majority of respondents (52 per cent) classified themselves as a 'business and management library site within a university library service' (therefore 'federated' or 'satellite' using my classification scheme), 22 per cent as 'the sole library for an institution' ('autonomous') and 17 per cent as a 'business and management collection within a library' ('collections-based'). The rest were specialist categories ('national' or 'specialist').

Future Challenges

Respondents were asked to rank eight suggested future challenges in order of importance, and the results are shown in Table 12.1.

---

1 Unfortunately, I was unable to include librarians from the South American Business Schools Association, CLADEA, in the survey on this occasion.

Table 12.1 Key challenges affecting business school libraries in the next five years (1= most important)

Challenge	1	2	3	4	5	6	7	8	Ranking average
Reduced budgets	21.70%	8.70%	26.10%	8.70%	17.40%	8.70%	4.30%	4.30%	3.57
Loss of physical space	4.30%	8.70%	4.30%	0.00%	13.00%	21.70%	13.00%	34.80%	6
Loss of identity/purpose	13.00%	4.30%	13.00%	21.70%	13.00%	13.00%	21.70%	0.00%	4.43
Institutional issues/politics	13.00%	17.40%	8.70%	17.40%	17.40%	8.70%	8.70%	8.70%	4.13
Disintermediation of libraries in delivering content	13.00%	21.70%	21.70%	21.70%	4.30%	0.00%	17.40%	0.00%	3.52
User expectations	21.70%	0.00%	17.40%	17.40%	8.70%	26.10%	8.70%	0.00%	4.04
Technological change	8.70%	39.10%	8.70%	13.00%	8.70%	8.70%	13.00%	0.00%	3.52
International campuses/partners	4.30%	0.00%	0.00%	0.00%	17.40%	13.00%	13.00%	52.20%	6.78

Note: Shaded cells = highest ranking for each individual challenge.

Depending on your interpretation, any one of 'disintermediation of libraries in delivering content', 'technological change' or 'reduced budgets' could be considered the main challenge highlighted by business school library heads. But there is no doubt that neither 'international campuses/partners' nor 'loss of physical space' were considered to be representing any difficulty. The latter is certainly supported by the authors writing on space in this book.

Respondents were also given the opportunity to list in a free-text box any other significant challenges facing them. Such unprompted responses are always fascinating for the additional insight they offer into individual institutional circumstances and whether or not there are any commonalities. Sure enough, the following five main themes for other challenges emerged:

1. *The relationship between the library and teaching*
   Comments related to the rapid changes to curriculum and the disconnect between library and teaching staff.
2. *Vendor issues*
   Most of the comments in this theme referred to vendors targeting the end-user and bypassing the library. Another comment related to vendor mergers.
3. *Free Internet information*
   Students' perception that information is freely available online without the need to use library resources was another theme that emerged from the responses.
4. *The disconnected library*
   Comments for this theme related to ensuring the library aligned with the school's mission and that the business library may not exist if institutional mergers were to occur.
5. *Library staff*
   These comments related to ensuring that library staff had access to the appropriate training to ensure the supply of the right kind of business specialists (and leaders) for the future.

Other interesting challenges that were identified related to: changes in government policy; a growing number of users; changes to user behaviour, distance education; and the 'inability to quantify service outcomes'.

Future opportunities

Table 12.2 flips the coin and looks at the potential opportunities identified for business school libraries in the next five years. Once again, respondents were asked to rank an overall list.

Table 12.2 Opportunities for business school libraries in the next five years

Overall rank	Opportunity Specified
1	Specialist resource/research support
2	Flexible study space
3	Discovery support
4	Information literacy
5	Learning technologies
6	Research data management
7	Careers & entrepreneurship support
8	Open access
9	Digitization
10	Knowledge management
11	Social media
12	iTunes U content/Library apps

As before, an open-ended question was also inserted to capture any other opportunities not already included. The responses were more varied than for the challenges question and so have been listed in full below:

- Working more closely with faculty, particularly in delivering learning and research
- Embedded librarians; highly tailored services
- Support research and academia
- Getting to know your users really well
- Partnerships with interdisciplinary programmes
- Teaching/integrating IL within the curriculum
- Advising on course content
- Realization that libraries will play a key role in developing human resources
- Instruction, reference, training
- Finding ways to capitalize on business knowledge requirements in non-traditional areas, including the humanities
- Support of research and activities that are undertaken by faculty and research centre staff
- Curriculum review and development
- Dissolving the library and integrating its services in the university (obviously also a threat)
- Increased focus on user experience
- Resource-sharing.

Future expectations

The most intriguing question of all was centred on perceptions of the anticipated longevity of business school libraries: In response to the question 'How confident are you that business school libraries will exist in 20 years' time?', 52 per cent of respondents were either very confident or confident that business school libraries will exist in 20 years' time with 22 per cent undecided and 22 per cent not confident. Only one respondent (Scandinavian) checked the 'zero confidence' box. It would be interesting to ask the same question every five years to see if these confidence levels increase or decrease.

The final question in the survey gave respondents a chance to share any free-text thoughts on the overall theme and yielded five interesting responses:

1. 'As long as there are [*sic*] business research and students there will be a need for a business library.'
2. 'The future of business school libraries will also depend on the collective delivery of services through consortia and professional groups.'
3. 'I'm confident that business school librarians will exist but [business school] libraries maybe not.'
4. 'We are busier than ever in our library. There are so many databases with such complex, difficult-to-use interfaces and so many students studying Business that our job security seems assured to me (unless standards are lowered greatly and no one cares about the quality of the information they are using).'
5. 'Aligning library services, facilities, and collections with the institutional mission of the business school is essential to the future of business libraries.'
6. Discussion.

It is worth reflecting on how many of the above are uniquely in the gift of business school librarianship. Certainly specialist resources are for as long as they exist in their current commercial client-based form, which may not be much longer than another five years as tablet devices and associated apps become ever more powerful. Of the rest, one could argue that only entrepreneurship support is distinct as everything else is being addressed in other subject disciplines, often on a greater scale (research data management and open access in STM librarianship, for example). The reorganization of the UK University of Manchester Library in 2012 away from traditional discipline-based structures to a centrist, four-core themes approach with their own senior librarians in charge of a site (including Manchester Business School) perhaps reflects this critical view (echoed in point 3 above) and could be read as an early warning for business school libraries who have 'satellite' or even 'federal' structures. Indeed, in the UK academic library sector currently there is a trend towards broadening senior library director roles to assume responsibility for other student-facing services such as careers, English-language courses for foreign students and cultural services (acknowledged with the addition of senior university titles such as Associate Dean or Pro-Vice Chancellor to the business card). This has an inevitable knock-on effect on middle-manager roles beneath, challenging the existence of perceived narrow subject- or site-focused roles such as 'Head of Business School Library'.

CASE STUDY: LONDON BUSINESS SCHOOL LIBRARY

In an amazing quirk of fate, as I was writing this conclusion in March 2013 about the future for business school libraries, I was also asked to prepare and write, at short notice, a document articulating my vision for the London Business School Library beyond 2017. This was to inform final senior management decisions around whether or not the library should move into the school's new teaching campus, the Sammy Ofer Centre, planned for 2016 (a to be refurbished, Grade II-listed, town hall building, 10 minutes' walk from our main campus near Regent's Park in London). Suddenly, it felt like I had the future of my service and my staff in my hands with one chance to get it right, knowing how supposedly long-term plans can have short-term implications. I was deliberately instructed to avoid cost and staff resource implications so that my creativity would not be inadvertently compromised.

In typical academic fashion, I decided to answer the question indirectly without offering a single straight answer or recommendation, but rather a choice of four different visions or futures (although some elements of each vision were interchangeable) akin to a scenario-planning exercise. I was careful to build on my existing five-year Library Strategy 2012–2017 (which had advocated a transitional 'move to e-only' strategy for the library), and so I included a 'direction of travel' section to estimate how many years (and the steps needed) needed for the library to be operating completely e-only. I was also encouraged to draw on as much usage data as I could lay my hands on to identify trends (including the library's balanced scorecard KPIs, circulation, dataset accesses and enquiry data). My existing strategy had also included external trends gleaned from analysis of topics from recent ABLD, EBSLG and APBSLG conferences which I was able to update and include as further justification for my set of visions. These I named as follows:

- Embedded library research team
- Library hub
- Heritage library
- Virtual library.

I also included two other rejected visions at the end ('Contracted-out' and 'Termination') so that I could be seen to have considered all possible avenues, however difficult they would be for me or the library service. I will now summarize the visions in turn.

Embedded library research team

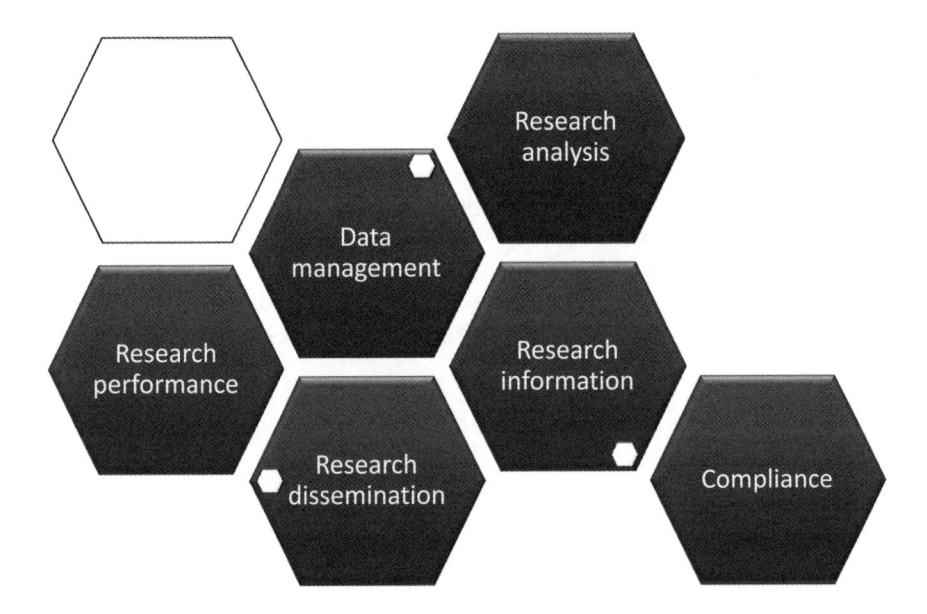

Figure 12.1 Embedded library research team model

The vision
The library team's activity is now entirely geared to supporting the research of faculty. Freed from the operational obligations of managing a physical collection and associated space, the team is free to act as research para-professionals, filling the gap between research assistant and faculty providing hands-on services and consultancy relating to:

- data management
- research and statistical analysis
- research output dissemination (including london.edu. SSRN and so on)
- research performance
- research information access, literature reviews and reference management
- copyright compliance.

The skills required go beyond librarianship, so the team is recomposed with a mixture of different skills and responsibilities brought in from within existing parts of the Research Faculty Office (RFO) or bought in externally – for example, as research fellowships.

Physically, the team are embedded in the faculty areas of the school, whether in the RFO or allocated to each subject area wing to work alongside the subject area managers (SAMs).

Key assumptions

- The REF 2014[2] outcome is favourable for the school and its research reputation is preserved.
- The faculty growth strategy continues.
- Demand from faculty and researchers for e-journals and datasets remains high and commercial sources remain the sole source of data.
- There is no demand for what would have been considered library resources in teaching, and any demand for dataset training is provided by commercial information providers.

Key features

- Librarians are now part of an integrated and expanded research support team in the RFO.
- The team handles management of faculty research outputs and dissemination.
- The team is multiskilled.
- Library support for alumni and executive education and external users is withdrawn.
- The internal market system operates with team time bought and charged back to subject areas.
- Traditional 'library' study space is now maintained by Operations Delivery equivalent.

School departments impacted

- RFO and subject areas (directly).
- Degree Progammes Office (DPO), Executive Education and Advancement (indirectly).

Advantages

- Matches approach already being taken by 'best of breed' – for example, Harvard Baker Library Research Services team.
- Reflects the reality that the majority of the library's budget and resource activity is geared to servicing faculty needs.
- Helps release researcher time.

---

[2] The UK's national research assessment exercise, conducted every four to five years.

- Extends skills base of traditional library staff.
- Concentrates research support in one section of the school.

Disadvantages

- No explicit 'library' support for other school user groups in this model, so their existing lower-level needs may not be addressed adequately or support will have to be decentralized into other departments (especially the DPO) leading to longer-term duplication of effort and resource.
- Doesn't address support for the teaching side of faculty work which would have to be picked up by the DPO and SAMs in this model.
- Tension between expectations for PhD students and what the research support team would be expected to provide – that is, danger of doing PhD work for them?

Library hub

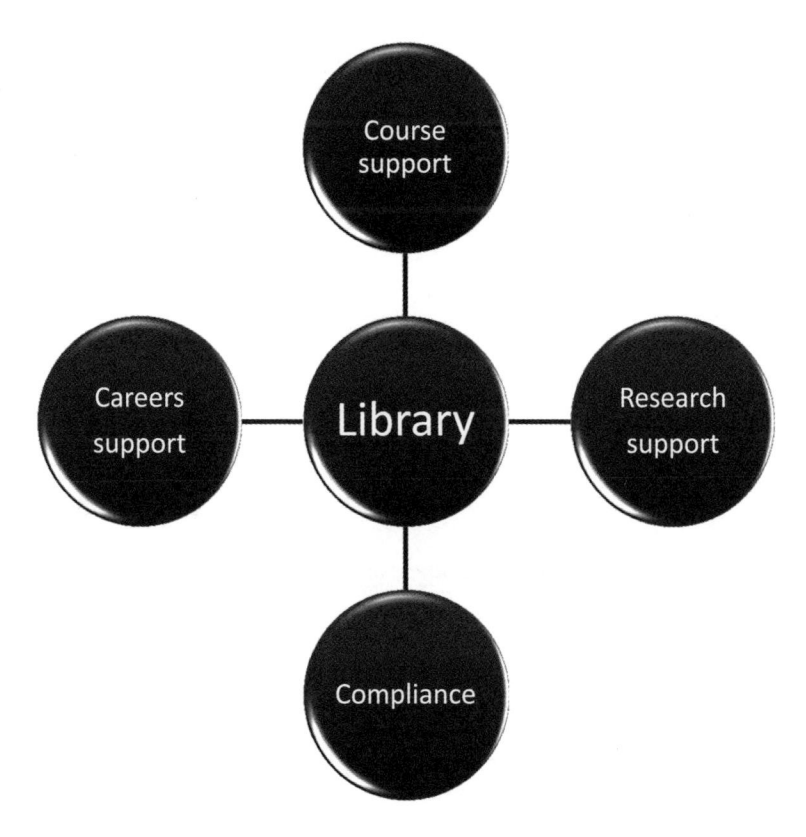

Figure 12.2   Library hub model

The vision
The library becomes an e-only service at the hub of school's activities. Freed from the daily operation of supporting a physical library and space and harnessing the power of a new content management system, school virtual learning environment (VLE), Portal and communications infrastructure delivered by the five-year IT strategy, the library's services are redefined and reorganized as:

1. *Course support.* This encompasses on-course resource acquisition and discovery for the VLE (or MOOC), harnessing the team's licensing and copyright expertise to buy the information in the right format via the right distributor at the best price for the school and deliver it flexibly to meet lecturer needs. Activity undertaken by the DPO in this area is effectively centralized into one new team.
2. *Careers support.* This includes provision of specialist training and resources to enhance employability and tailored content provision for careers services.
3. *Research support.* This encompasses some or all of the activities in the embedded library research team vision above, but also includes support for student project research (especially around prospective employers). Some merging of RFO functions would be required.
4. *Knowledge hub and consultancy.* As at Harvard, the library team offers metadata expertise for internal content in Portal and new london.edu and document/records management services on behalf of the school. Consultancy time can also be bought for special one-off projects – for example, for the benefit of school partners. Copyright and licensing compliance advisory work is retained.

Key assumptions

- The move to e-only course materials happens, and associated complexity of rights management and access methods continues.
- An appetite exists for making changes in responsibilities across the school in tandem with any library changes.
- There is support for increasing the remit of the library team (and resourcing) in a wider context.
- Faculty buy in to a more centralized approach.

Key features

- Librarians are now part of integrated and expanded course and research support teams at the hub of school activity.
- The team handles management of faculty research outputs and dissemination
- The team is multiskilled.
- Support for external library users is withdrawn, which may help precipitate the school withdrawing from the University of London.

- An internal market system operates for research support with team time bought and charged back.
- Traditional 'library' study space is now maintained by Operations Delivery as part of wider Estates Strategy.

School departments impacted

- Dean's Office
- DPO and Careers
- Marketing and Communications
- Operations Delivery
- RFO

Advantages

- Centralizes course support activity, which addresses the duplication of content procurement across the school and operational knowledge in areas like licensing and copyright compliance.
- Offers dedicated support for faculty in line with peer groups.
- Offers a progression from current activities.

Disadvantages

- Potentially disruptive to set up as it impacts on multiple stakeholder groups and would need careful planning and timing to fit in with the course production cycle.
- Matrix line management models required in some areas may be challenging.
- New team does not fit easily into school organizational structure.
- Will increase demand for specialist and possibly dedicated IT support – for example, for VLE/MOOC.
- Not clear whether model could support alumni and executive education service provision as well.

Heritage library

The vision
Recognizing that other peer group libraries retain a physical and identifiable physical library space as a symbolic feature of a university (something that prospective students would expect to find) and that the student body has been by far the largest user of the physical library in the past, the school relocates the library to the Sammy Ofer Centre Annexe and revitalizes a former public library space in the process.

The Rotunda Reading Room in the Annexe proves very popular with students due to its high-quality solid furniture with discrete in-built technology and studious feel.

Figure 12.3 Heritage library model

A small-print postgraduate collection is deliberately retained both as a heritage feature and as a practical noise and sight barrier to divide up the study space. The library continues to maintain a finance zone of commercial financial datasets but with wider access, thanks to sponsorship by a major company.

However, just as importantly, the library helps maximize the customer experience of the Sammy Ofer Centre (and other campus space) by piping its content dynamically round the buildings on wonderwalls, projectors, touchscreens and mobile devices, both to serve courses and presentations in lecture theatres and seminar rooms, but also to showcase school intellectual property rights (IPR) in public areas.

Librarians become, in effect, adjunct teaching faculty, contributing optional sessions to the various programmes. The new school VLE facilitates this role further by allowing the powerful manipulation of multimedia and print course assets.

The additional storage space in the Annexe basement is used by the library to undertake document management functions for the school as the amount of paperwork reduces and offsite storage is no longer required.

The library continues to support all sections of the school community, hosting events for alumni and prospective donors, and revitalizes an external membership scheme for corporate school partners so that they can benefit from walk-in access to the e-library. Access for non-school students is stopped to coincide with the school's withdrawal from the University of London in 2017.

Key assumptions

- Students of the future will still expect to see a physical library space even if print collections have almost disappeared.
- A need for a defined finance datasets zone may still exist due to commercial providers' licensing models.
- The library team is retained as a separate operational entity.

Key features

- Librarians are accepted as learning technologists and can help champion new teaching spaces.
- The library continues to provide services to all members of the school community.
- The library becomes a selling point and feature in school communications and events, attracting prospective donors.
- Copyright and licensing compliance work is returned.

School departments impacted

- None impacted directly, but closer work with Dean's Office, Marketing and Communications and Advancement required.

Advantages

- More student experience-friendly than previous two visions.
- All members of the school continue to benefit from library services.
- Easier to brand and communicate library services on the back of library space?
- Harnesses library heritage of Sammy Ofer Centre building.

Disadvantages

- Library team potentially more organizationally isolated.
- Doesn't ensure that library services are embedded into school activity.
- Unless aspects from other visions are added, does not meet faculty's future research support needs.

Virtual library

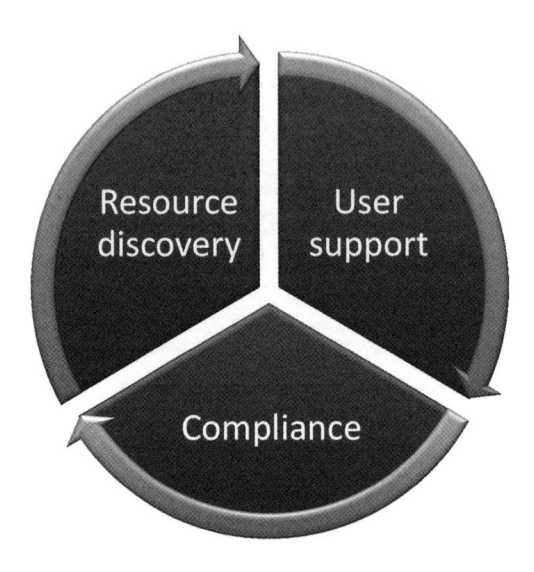

Figure 12.4 Virtual library model

The vision
The school decides it does not need a 'heritage' physical library in the Sammy Ofer Centre and nor does it want to create a load of disruption to other school departments during a period of growth and expansion by creating new units around research and teaching support activities/processes. The Taunton Centre Library has been gradually reduced in size over the past five years, with collection space turned into offices and the gym expanded.

Acknowledging that demand for research resources remains high and that students are struggling with zetabytes of digital information when preparing their projects or researching prospective job opportunities, the school decides that it still needs some kind of specialist library expertise centred on:

- resource discovery: specialist resource acquisition and associated e-library support
- user support: research, careers and project enquiries support and specialist training
- copyright and licensing compliance.

A new IT infrastructure is now in place, including a new Moodle VLE and MOOC with an MBA and Executive Education distance learning programme now offered, harnessing the new virtual communications and collaboration technology. Library-sourced content is integrated into all learning environments.

The library presence is now completely virtual, with both real-time, ad hoc videoconference information consultations via Microsoft Lync now taken for granted and a librarian avatar popping up on mobile devices (including special vision spectacles) across the school.

Nevertheless, flexible touchdown physical librarian 'pods' can be deployed anywhere across the school estate as required to support specific events or teaching.

Any legacy demand for print items is met via a direct ordering service from the British Library or print-on-demand units pulling formatted book data directly from cloud providers.

Key assumptions

- The demand from faculty and researchers for e-journals and datasets remains high, and commercial sources remain the sole source of data.
- The demand from the student body for project support continues.
- The IT and learning technology infrastructure is in place.
- Some form of e-learning strategy is agreed in the school.
- The library team is retained as a separate operational entity.

Key features

- There is an interactive responsive virtual library presence across all school interfaces and devices.
- The library has a small physical footprint with a focus on e-content.

School departments impacted

- None impacted directly.

Advantages

- Flexible library provisioning model.
- Little disruption to other school units.

Disadvantages

- The library can still be a virtual isolated team in the organizational structure in this vision.

- The library's mission is still relatively indistinct unless it is part of new teaching and learning or e-learning strategies.
- Doesn't address overlap of resources and/or activities across the school or fragmentation of knowledge.

Other (rejected) possibilities

Contracted-out
Although not sufficiently advanced to be a vision, there is also a future scenario in which some kind of 'outsourced' version of the library could exist, delivering some variation of the scenarios outlined above (especially the virtual library scenario).

This could take the form of, for example, a group of public-sector institutions developing the appropriate legal entity to deliver a cloud-based e-library service at scale to different higher-education institutions with staff and resource costs outsourced in return for a membership or subscription fee. This model is currently being explored for a shared library management system project with selected University of London libraries (Bloomsbury Library Management Consortium, 2012). A successful variation of this model has been up and running for several years with the NorMAN out-of-hours university IT support in the UK.

Although no university library service is currently being run on an outsourced basis, three companies (Wipro, BT Global Services and Capita) were shortlisted in 2012 for the since abandoned London Metropolitan University estates, IT and library outsourcing contract (Savvas, 2012). It is highly likely that another teaching university will explore this option with these companies, although whether a purely library-focused service could be commercially viable is open to question (as past experience with the library's own corporate information brokerage in the 1990s has shown).

Termination
The 'elephant in the room' of the complete cessation of library services should also be addressed. Although it is possible for every individual in the future to identify, acquire, manage and manipulate the information they need, I still believe that it is most cost-effective and time-efficient (especially from a faculty and school point of view) for there to be a dedicated body of expertise, however structured, to take on that task. The alternative organizational chaos of hundreds of cottage industries replicating the content and organizational systems with thousands of individual agreements, payments and contacts with suppliers surely does not bear thinking about. The usage trends show that there is strong demand for a dedicated e-library.

REFLECTION

It is salutary to the spirit of 'action learning' to consider the extent to which I have been influenced or not by the contributions to this book as I have edited them. All four of my visions to some extent reflect Chris Flegg's emphasis on divorcing the library from collection-building as my prognosis is that my library could become functionally e-only by 2020 if all goes to plan. Two visions pick up on the theme of the 'embedded librarian' articulated by Kathy Long in her chapter on physical space: one very much centred on research support integration with other departments in the school; the other adding in course and careers support integration (as espoused by Marcella and Cathy) as well. Of the remaining two, one retains control of the physical study space as a kind of heritage library feature as part of the content provision role of the library in the new campus. The final vision (and the least satisfying of all) sees the library live on in some kind of virtual, ghost-in-the-machine-like role, trying to communicate with the school as best it can through different media, devices and channels – requiring the full arsenal of Andy Priestner's communication techniques to survive. What has struck me is how unique this selection is to my institution; if my structure was more 'federated' or 'satellite' (cf. Chapter 1), then slightly different permutations would apply. Alternatively, if my library had extensive print collections, then additional options involving internal or external storage solutions would come into play.

OUTCOME

So which vision did my senior team opt for in the end? I was first asked to work up the library hub and virtual team models further to include the following:

- a customer impact analysis for each of the two visions against the current 2013 provision
- a gap analysis explaining how any services impacted negatively in by the customer impact analysis could be delivered
- a five-year trend analysis of available internal usage data
- a benchmark analysis of each vision against external trends (for which I used the survey results revealed earlier in this chapter).

My interpretation of the final decision made by senior management on the basis of my work above was as follows. Given that:

1. the library was not likely to be e-only until 2020 given the current state of the e-book market and library e-book infrastructure,
2. the so-called Stanford 'bookless' engineering library still had 25,000 books (the same size as the school's collection),

3. there was still a demand (albeit gradually in decline) for the print collection,
4. there were no major customer service gaps in future,
5. the library had already begun reducing its print collections (for example, by digitizing its 30,000 print corporate annual reports collection in the 2012–13 financial year),

then it was feasible for the library to move into the new Sammy Ofer Centre Annexe space in 2016–17 with a smaller, reducing print collection (along the lines of the heritage library vision). This would be on the understanding that it would probably become a 'virtual library' around 2020 with the possibility of further reorganization along the lines of the 'library hub' model if deemed appropriate for delivering the school's mission. In my mind, this was the right outcome even if in the short time available there was no opportunity for (or expectation of) stakeholder consultation.

CONCLUSION

So, in many ways, as my case study above illustrates, the future is already here for business school libraries as we are now forced to take important fundamental decisions about ourselves as we seek to fit around a wider school mission and strategy. But, then again, our future was already here in 2002:

> *As the predictions ... regarding the transformation of traditional business libraries to 'virtual libraries' continue to materialize, one can expect that changes in the collections and services affected by business libraries, as well as the skills required of business information specialists will continue to be dramatic . The ability to deliver business information in an effective, reliable, customised, and user-friendly manner has always been a goal of business libraries; the changes brought about by twenty-first century technology have made this goal more attainable, at the same time as the array of choices has become more complex. (Moore McGinn 2002, p. 121)*

The uncertainty articulated above is nothing new, of course. Oort was commenting on it in his thesis on business school libraries in 1986 in the context of innovation and the uncertainties arising from new technologies. It may be that to survive into this kind of uncertain future, the business school librarian will have to become a data manipulator with programming skills, a negotiator/licensor, facilities manager or an online tutor/facilitator – all job titles without the 'L' word.

To conclude, I believe we are now in a transitional phase for the next five or so years and our medium- to longer-term futures are now surely predicated on the skills that librarians bring, the specialist knowledge of content (and associated tools), the internal/external networks and understanding of what those networks need and offer. If we can continue to make a difference in these areas then we will survive, in the words of Dean Nohria from this book's Foreword, as 'important players in the lives of our communities'. If not, business school libraries will follow their commercial or special library 'cousins' along the path to extinction.

REFERENCES AND FURTHER READING

Bloomsbury Library Management System Consortium, 2012. At: http://www.blms.ac.uk/ (accessed 28 April 2013).

Moore McGinn, J., 2002. In: R. Karp (ed.), *The Basic Business Library: Core Resources*, 4th edn. Westport, CT: Greenwood Press, 109–26.

Oort, B.B., 1986. An Evaluation of the Organisation of Some European Business School Libraries, and the Services They Supply. PhD thesis, Loughborough University.

REF 2014. At: http://www.ref.ac.uk/ (accessed 28 April 2013).

Savvas, A., 2012. London Met University Axes IT Outsourcing Plans [online]. *CIO*, 23 October 2012. At: http://www.cio.co.uk/news/supplier-management/london-met-university-axes-it-outsourcing-plans/ (accessed 28 April 2013).

Soules, A., 1996. Forecasting the Future. In: C.A. Sheehy (ed.), *Managing Business Collections in Libraries*. Westport, CT: Greenwood Press, 1996, 217–57.

WEBSITES

Microsoft Lync, 2013. At: http://lync.microsoft.com/ (accessed 28 April 2013).

NorMAN, 2013. At: http://www.outofhourshelp.ac.uk/ (accessed 28 April 2013).

INDEX

360 Counter 96

Abel, C. 122
Abels, E.G. 126
ABI Inform 66
Academic Business Library Directors of North America (ABLD) 57, 124, 161–2, 193, 198
academic visitors 78
academics *see* faculty
access, user 92–5
account management 92–3
accountability 15, 17, 19, 25, 51
accumulator role of libraries 161, 162, 166
Administrative Science Quarterly (ASQ) 96
administrative staff 55
Africa 3
Ahmedabad Library Network 80
Alemano, Alberto 115
alumni 79, 184, 185, 186, 200
Amabile, Teresa 23
Amazon 86, 98, 100
American Library Association 124
Americans for Libraries Council (ALC) 68
Anderson, B. 122
Anderson, Rick 49
Android 86, 100, 153
Apple 86, 98, 100
application programming interfaces (APIs) 88, 89–90
apps 12, 57, 197
archives 105–19
Arns, J.W. 69
ArXiv 105, 107, 117
Ashridge 4
Asia 3, 125
Asia-Pacific Business School Librarians' Group (APBSLG) 57, 124, 193, 198

Association des Directeurs et Personnels de Direction des Bibliothèques Universitaires et de la Documentation (ADBU) 108
Association des responsables des Centres d'Information des Ecoles de Gestion (ACIEGE) 111
Association of College and Research Libraries (ACRL) 49, 70, 181
Association of Research Libraries (ARL) 21
Association to Advance Collegiate Schools of Business (AACSB) 146
Au, K. 139
autonomous libraries 4, 5, 193
Azure 86

Baker Library (Harvard KLS) 13–26, 28, 200
balanced scorecard 14, 69, 97, 101
Baldwin, Leslie 4
Bangor University 62
Barnhart, Marcella 8–9, 121–41
Barr, Stephen 62
'barriers' 170
Base Institutionalle de Recherche de l'Université Dauphine (BIRD) 113
Bass Center 168–9
Batt, S.J. 122
Beckhard, R. 38
Bell, Suzanne 131, 133
Bemis, Dorothy 135
Bennett, Scott 143, 144
Berlin School of Library and Information Science 70–71
Berthaud, C. 107
Bieraugel, Mark 133–4
'big data' 98–100, 101, 188
BIRD 113
blended learning 171

'blended librarians' 154
blogs 6, 55, 58, 59, 179
Bloomberg 87, 88, 89, 91, 97, 169
BookShelf 98
boutique libraries 1, 187–9
brand-building 78
BRASS-L 124
bring your own device (BYOD) 60, 100, 151
British Business School Librarians' Group 4
    see also Business Librarians Association (BLA)
British Library 117, 207
Brown, J. 72
browsing 80
Budapest Open Access Initiative 106
budgets 3, 56, 61
    constraints 29, 65
    cuts in 187
    future challenges 194, 195
    Harvard KLS 23, 25
    India 72, 74, 75, 77
    new courses 50
    see also funding
buildings see library spaces
business and economics library (BEL) 165
business ecosystems 85–7, 102
Business Librarians Association (BLA) 5, 6
BUSLIB-L 124

cafes 151
Cain, D. 66
Cal Poly 133–4
Cambridge University 52
Camp Library 166
Campbell, Diane 133
Canada 66, 124, 125
Capital IQ 91, 92
career services 2, 8–9, 121–41
    careers support integration 209
    future opportunities 196
    library hub model 202
CareerWiki 122
case studies 2, 11, 12
catalogs 14, 177–8
Centre for Learning Enhancement and Research (CLEAR) 146, 153
Centre National de la Recherche Scientifique (CNRS) 106
Centre pour la Communication Scientifique Directe (CCSD) 106, 117

Chadwell, F.A. 72
champions 54
change 7, 11–12, 14, 27
    change impact diagram 38
    change management 29–30, 33–47
    embedding 45–6
    Harvard KLS 16, 17, 18–19
    implementing 44–5
    preparing for 33–44
    resistance to 37–8, 40, 42
Chartered Management Institute 5
Chinese University of Hong Kong (CUHK) 143, 144–5, 146–55
Christensen, Clay 159
Chung, H. 123
citation counts 179
Citrix 88
CLADEA library directors' group 124
classroom teaching 61
cloud-based services 8, 12, 86, 90, 208
co-location 9, 172
collaboration 60, 172, 180
    career services and entrepreneurship 121–41
    Chinese University of Hong Kong 152, 155
    collaborative learning zone 151
    Harvard KLS 17–18, 25
    Information Commons 162
    ZBW 37
collection-based libraries 4, 5, 9, 193
collection development 50
collections, reduction in onsite 161, 162, 166, 167, 210
College and Research Libraries News 49
Collins, Jim 42
Colorado 68
commercial rights 183–4
communication 6, 7, 49–63
    career services and entrepreneurship 129
    change management at ZBW 41, 46, 47
    Chinese University of Hong Kong 149
    Harvard KLS 15, 18–19, 26
    open archives 110
community libraries 65
compact shelving 154, 169, 170
content delivery 8
contingent valuation 69
contracting out 208
convergence 85, 101

copyright
   embedded library research team 199
   heritage library 205
   librarian's role 180, 188
   library hub model 202, 203
   open access 182, 184
   open archives 113, 114
   virtual library model 206
   see also licences
core collections 14
Cornell University 72
cost-benefit analysis 69, 77
costs
   career services and entrepreneurship 131
   database subscriptions 51
   e-books 98
   e-journals 96
   financial desktop software 89
   gold open access model 183
   journal subscriptions 105
   open archives 109
   quantitative measures 178
   return on investment 67, 68, 71, 77, 82, 178–9
   sharing 131
Counting Online Usage of Networked Electronic Resources (COUNTER) 95, 96, 97, 99
Couperin Consortium 105, 106
course support 202
Cranfield School of Management 185
Creaser, C. 180–81
critical success factors 26
curriculum
   contribution of library staff 80
   Harvard KLS 17, 20, 21
customer relationship management 20, 21, 22
customization 187

Darden School 166, 172
data collection 51–2, 68
Data Link Express (DLX) 87
data manipulation and analysis 188–9
databases 2, 57, 61, 143
   access to 6, 50
   Chinese University of Hong Kong 146
   cost of subscriptions 51
   Economists Online 112, 113
   expenditure on 6
   open archives 113
   sharing costs 131
   SHERPA RoMEO 112, 113
   Thomson Quantitative Analytics 91
   usage statistics 51
   see also repositories; software
DataFeed Toolbox 89
Datastream 87, 88–9, 152
Dawson 6
decision making
   Harvard KLS 22
   ZBW 32, 35, 36, 37
Degree Programmes Office (DPO) 200, 201, 202, 203
DeHart, B. 122, 128
Dewey classification 113
Dewland, Jason 129
'digital natives' 143–4
digital object identifiers (DOIs) 95, 96, 100
Digital Repository Infrastructure Vision for European Research (DRIVER) 106
digital scholarship 17
digitization 196
direct benefits 67, 69
direct costs 68, 77
disaggregation 9
discovery tools 14, 57, 86, 101, 177–8
   e-resource management 95, 96
   Harvard KLS 24
disintermediation 194, 195
distance learning 170, 206–7
DRIVER project 106
DSpace 106, 109, 113
Dugan, M. 122, 123

e-books 6, 53, 97–8, 143, 209
   direct sales of 177
   e-resource management 95
   reader software 80
   usage statistics 52
E-Financial News 92
e-journals 99, 143, 167, 176
   e-resource management 95
   embedded library research team 200
   subscription costs 96
   virtual library model 207
e-resource management (ERM) 86, 87, 92, 95–7, 102
e-resources
   expenditure on 56
   Harvard KLS 14
   impact on library space 161
   India 66
   Information Commons 162

information literacy 144
shared services 100
usage statistics 89, 101
see also databases; e-journals
Eaton, Jonathan 8, 85–104
EBSCO 66, 94
'echo chamber' 7, 56–7
Economists Online database 112, 113
EIKON 87
elevator pitches 53–4
Elsevier ScienceDirect 99
email 6, 52, 58–9, 129, 130
embedded librarians 9, 123, 137, 163–5, 172, 196, 199–201, 209
employment 135, 138
enquiries 52, 57
enrolments 70
'entrepreneurial university' 121
entrepreneurship support 8–9, 121–41, 196, 197
EPrints 106, 109
EQUIS 113
Europe
　career services and entrepreneurship 125
　history of management education in 1–2
　number of business school libraries 3
　self-archiving 106
European Business School Librarians' Group (EBSLG) 2, 57, 124, 193, 198
European Quality Improvement System (EQUIS) 113
Excel 88, 89
executive education 184, 185, 186–7, 200, 206–7
ExLibris 96

face-to-face communication 6, 110
Facebook 6, 65, 101
facilitator role of libraries 161, 163–6, 170
FactSet 87, 88, 89, 152
faculty
　benefits of libraries for 78, 81
　career services and entrepreneurship 127–8, 130, 133, 134
　Chinese University of Hong Kong 152
　communicating with 50, 53, 54–5, 58, 62–3
　embedded library research team 199, 200
　future opportunities 196

global research orientation 188
grants 70, 71
Harvard KLS 16, 17
library hub model 202, 203
library spaces 172
research productivity 70
Stanford Graduate School of Business 167
Twitter used by 59
University of Illinois 165
federated access management 6, 86, 92, 93–5
federated libraries 4, 193, 197, 209
Feedly 55
financial crisis 65, 66, 72, 74, 101
financial data and software 2, 87–91, 97, 169, 182, 204, 205
Finch Report (2012) 183
Firoaso, Geneviève 116
Flegg, Chris 9, 175–91, 209
flexibility 151, 154, 160, 171
Florida 68
Fonseca, T. 71–2
footfall 51, 53, 57
Forcadell, Sophie 8, 105–19
Forrester 92
France 8, 106–17
FT.com 92
funding 6, 49
　cuts in 51, 53, 65
　Harvard KLS 14, 23
　Hong Kong 145
　India 65–6
　return on investment 179
　ZBW 33
　see also budgets
furniture 147, 148, 151, 153, 203
future scenarios 198–210
　embedded library research team model 199–201, 209
　heritage library model 203–5, 209
　library hub model 201–3, 209, 210
　virtual library model 206–8, 209, 210

Gates, Bill 100
Gayton, J.T. 171
German National Library of Economics – Leibniz Information Centre for Economics (ZBW) 4, 5, 7, 30–47
Ginsparg, P. 105
Glasgow Caledonian University 149
Glasser, William 26
Global Open Knowledgebase (GOKb) 100

globalization 171
goals 39, 62
Google 12, 29, 65, 86, 177, 178
  BIRD 113
  Google Scholar 57, 113, 114
  shared services 101
government regulation 66
graduate employment 66, 135, 138
graduation rates 70
Grandes Ecoles 108–12
grants 70, 71, 179
Gray, Gwen 134
group work
  change management at ZBW 44
  Harvard KLS 16, 19
  library spaces 144, 147, 151, 152–3, 162, 168
  Stanford Graduate School of Business 167
Grzeschik, K. 70–71

Hahn, T.B. 72
HAL 106–7, 108–9, 110–11, 113, 117
Hamburg World Economic Archives (HWWA) 30, 40
Harnard, Stevan 105
Harris, R.T. 38
Hartman, C.W. 159
Harvard Business School (HBS) 4, 5, 7, 11, 12–26, 28, 185, 200
Harvard case-study teaching method 2
Harvard University 24
HathiTrust 177
Haver Analytics 87, 89
HEC Library, Paris 8, 114–15
Henry, C. 188
heritage library 203–5, 209
Hollister, C. 122
Hong Kong 9, 143, 145–55
Hong Kong University of Science and Technology (HKUST) 145
Housewright, R. 161
Humboldt University 70–71
Hyper Articles en Ligne (HAL) 106–7, 108–9, 110–11, 113, 117

i-schools 12
'idea exchange' 153
identity 9, 179
  future challenges 194
  organizational 108–9
  physical building equated with 163, 172

IESE 5
Imholz, S. 69
incentives 36, 46
India 8, 65–6, 72–6, 77, 79, 80–81
indirect benefits 67, 69
indirect costs 68, 77
information
  access to 176, 186
  information provider hierarchy 177–8
  proliferation of 189
  sharing 22
  translation into knowledge 181
Information Commons 144, 162–3, 172
information literacy (IL) 67, 81, 144, 196
information management services 13, 20, 21, 26
information technology (IT)
  Harvard KLS 14, 24–5
  Information Commons 162
  IT departments 59, 60, 87
  Learning Garden 151–2
  virtual library model 207
  see also databases; Internet; technology
'informationists' 163, 164
infrastructure
  Harvard KLS 21, 22, 24–5
  India 65
  ZBW 33
innovation
  disruptive 159
  Harvard KLS 17
  speed of 29
INSEAD 5, 114, 185
instant chat 52, 53
Institut National de la Recherche Agronomique (INRA) 108
Institut National de Recherche en Informatique et en Automatique (INRIA) 108
institutional reputation 70
intangible benefits 67, 68, 79, 82
integrating mechanisms 16, 20–22
Intellectual Commons 168
intellectual property rights (IPR) 180, 188, 204
interactivity 144
interlibrary loans 24, 71, 72, 153, 165
international campuses 194, 195
International Federation of Library Associations and Institutions (IFLA) 106

Internet 80, 105, 143, 144, 177, 195
  see also cloud-based services; social media; web-based services
Internet Protocol (IP) authentication 6, 94, 95
interns 78, 80
intranets 41, 114
iPad 100, 153
iPhone 100
ISBNs 95, 96
ISIDORE 113
ISSNs 95, 96
iTunes 86, 196

Jackson, H.L. 72
JEL codes 113
job designs 16, 19–20
John Hopkins University 163–4
Johnson, Emory 135
Joint Information Systems Committee (JISC) 94
Joint Science Conference (GWK) 32
Joint University Research Archive (JURA) 154
Joranson, K. 122–3, 128
Journal of Academic Librarianship 49
Journal of Business and Finance Librarianship 123
journals 6, 177, 182–3
  citation counts 179
  contribution of library staff 80
  dissemination of post-prints 116
  open archives 107, 111
  subscription costs 105
  see also e-journals
Judge Business School 7, 53, 56, 57, 58

Karp, R. 1
Kaufman, P.T. 71
Kaufmann FastTrace TechVenture 134
Kindle 100
Kirkwood, Hal 127, 133
Knight Management Center 168
Knowledge and Library Services (KLS) 13–26, 28
knowledge bases (KBs) 95, 96
knowledge bases and related tools (KBART) 95
knowledge management 196
KnowledgeBase Plus (KB+) 100
Kotter, J. 39
Kumar, H. Anil 8, 65–84

laptop computers 72, 147, 148, 151–2, 167
leadership
  Harvard KLS 17, 21–2, 25, 26
  India 74
  ZBW 36–7
learning
  blended 171
  collaborative learning zone 151
  learning activities 147
  measuring library value 70
  new ways of 143–4
  from others 149
  self-directed 161, 163
  student preferences 147
Learning Commons 143, 144–5, 146, 149, 150, 154–5, 162
Learning Garden 150–52
'learning resource centres' 55–6
lectures 6, 80
legal issues 112
Leibniz Association 30, 32–3
Li, Lai Fong 9, 143–57
Liberty Alliance 94
LibQUAL 148
librarians
  anxiety of 187
  'blended' 154
  career services and entrepreneurship 121, 122, 127–8, 130–31, 133–4, 137, 139
  Chinese University of Hong Kong 152
  communication by 49–63
  disaggregation of 9
  embedded 9, 123, 137, 163–5, 172, 196, 199–201, 209
  full time equivalent 6, 125
  future for 175, 189
  Harvard KLS 16
  heritage library 204, 205
  identity 9
  Indian business school libraries 72–6
  job titles 179–80, 210
  library hub model 202
  niche services 188
  one-to-one consultations 153
  open archives 109–10, 112
  Research Commons 153
  roles of 176
  service delivery 185
  service-orientation 180–82
  teaching by 61, 180–81

University of Illinois 165
value of 189
Yale University 165
see also staff
The Librarians (TV show) 56
library and information science (LIS) 80
Library and Information Statistics Unit (LISU) 62
library hub model 201–3, 209, 210
library management systems (LMSs) 24, 86
library spaces 9, 143, 159–74, 175
   communication with users 149
   facilitator role of libraries 163–6
   future challenges 194, 195
   Information Commons 162–3
   Learning Commons 144–5, 149, 150, 154–5, 162
   Learning Garden 150–52
   new ways of learning 143–4
   Research Commons 152–3
   Stanford Graduate School of Business 166–71
   trends in academic libraries 160–62
   user needs 146–8
Library User Group (LUG) 149
licences 88, 131
   see also copyright
Liebetruth, Claudia 3, 7, 29–48
Lippincott Library 135–8
loans 51
login systems 93–4
London Business School 2, 4, 5, 8
   COUNTER data 99
   future visions for 198–208
   job cuts 62
   mission statement 185
London Metropolitan University 208
Long, Kathleen 9, 159–74, 209
Lorenzen, E.A. 122
Loughborough University 62
Luther, J. 70–71
Lyons, C. 127

Macintosh 88, 89, 100
Magi, T.J. 126
management
   Harvard KLS 17–18
   management development 80
   ZBW 36–7, 43, 46
Management Library Network 80, 124
Manchester Business School 5, 197
market and industry information 2

marketing 54, 135, 180
   branded material 186
   career services and entrepreneurship 129–30
   communication of benefits to users 80–81
   HBS Marketing and Communications 24
   Lippincott Library 135
   marketing departments 59, 60
   use of quantitative data 52
   see also communication
massive open online course (MOOC) 202, 203, 206
Master of Business Administration (MBA) programs 5, 6, 160, 162, 185
   career services and entrepreneurship 122–3, 125–6, 128–9, 133, 136–7
   case-based learning 172
   Chinese University of Hong Kong 146
   distance learning 206–7
   graduate employment 135
   Harvard Business School 12, 13, 17
   Stanford Graduate School of Business 165–6, 167
   Yale University 165
MATLAB 88, 89, 91
Mays, R. 71
Meadows, Alice 183
media convergence 85
Melot, Agnès 8, 105–19
metadata 106, 109, 118, 180, 202
MetriDoc 99
Meyer, Thorsten 3, 7, 29–48
Microsoft 86, 89, 91, 100
   Lync 207
   Systems Center Configuration Manager 88
Middle East 125
milestones 15, 16, 45, 46
mission statements 185
mobile technologies 12, 86, 90, 100, 143
Moore McGinn, J. 210
multidisciplinary teams 164
multifunction printers (MFPs) 151
MyiLibrary 6

National Center for Education Statistics (NCES) 68
national libraries 4
Neal, J. 72
NetLibrary 6

Network of European Regions Using Space Technologies (Nereus) 112, 113
networks 188–9, 210
niche services 188–9
Nitecki, Danuta 9, 161
Nohria, Nitin 12, 211
NorMAN 208
North America
　career services and entrepreneurship 124, 125
　number of business school libraries 3
　see also United States
North Carolina State University (NCSU) 123

Ogur, Cathy 8–9, 121–41
Oliver, Kathleen 163
one-to-one consultations 153
online information exchange (ONIX) 95
Oort, B.B. 1–2
open access 50, 177, 179, 182–4
　future opportunities 196
　Harvard KLS 24
　open archives 8, 105–19
　STM librarianship 197
　see also repositories
Open Access Infrastructure Research for Europe (OpenAIRE) 106
Open Archive Initiative Protocol for Metadata Harvesting (OAI-PMH) 105
open archives 8, 105–19
Open Directory of Open Access Repositories (OpenDOAR) 113
open forum 151, 155
open-source software 80, 97, 106, 113
OpenURL 86, 95, 96, 100
operating systems (OS) 88, 89, 90–91
Oracle 91
organizational culture 15, 24, 25
organizational design 15–18, 19–23, 25–6, 27, 36
organizational identity 108–9
organizational review 43
organizational structure 4–5, 12, 175, 188
　embedded library research team model 199–201, 209
　Harvard KLS 15, 19
　heritage library model 203–5, 209
　library hub model 201–3, 209, 210
　virtual library model 206–8, 209, 210
　ZBW 30–32, 35–6, 43, 44–5, 46

ORI-OAI 109
outreach 135, 137, 138, 139
outsourcing 208
Ovid 94
Oxford University 52
Ozzie, Ray 85

Paris Dauphine University 112–14
passwords 93, 95
Penn Career Services 136
Pennsylvania State University 99
performance measures 16, 23, 61
personalization 92–5
PhD students 6, 126, 160, 162, 167, 201
Pickett, C. 160, 172–3
portals 97, 114–15, 202
postgraduates 152–3
　see also PhD students
Potter, Ned 56–7, 58
Powis, Chris 54
Prezi 59, 60
Priem, Jason 179
Priestner, Andy 1, 6, 7–8, 49–63, 209
print-on-demand 207
printers 147, 151
professional associations 3
Project NEEO 112
promotion 129–30
　see also marketing
ProQuest 94
proxy servers 6, 52, 86, 97
public libraries 65, 68–70
PubMed Central 105, 107, 117
Purdue University 123, 133

qualitative data 52
quantitative data 52, 178
quiet zones 148, 150, 151, 153, 162

Radnor, Michael 159
rankings 2, 5, 78, 79, 175
RAPTOR 97
reading rooms 13, 152, 169, 203
Real Deals 96
recession 51
　see also financial crisis
Redefining the Academic Library (2012) 180
refreshment zone 151
registration issues 92
Registry of Open Access Repositories (ROAR) 113
regulation 66

RePEc 107, 117
reporting 16, 28, 97
repositories 8, 180, 184
    DRIVER project 106
    Harvard KLS 24
    open archives 111, 113
    organizational identity 108
    speed of deposit 116
    see also databases
repurposing of library space 161, 162, 165
reputation 70, 181, 187
research
    career 122, 123, 126–7, 132, 138
    co-location of research centers 172
    curation of research data 180
    data repositories 24
    embedded library research team 199–201
    executive education 187
    future opportunities 196
    global research orientation 188
    Harvard KLS 14, 17
    impact 184–5
    India 66
    INSEAD portal 114
    library hub model 202
    library spaces 168
    open access 183–4
    open archives 106, 116
    productivity 70
    requests 123
    research data management 13, 196, 197, 199
    research support integration 209
    ZBW 33
research assistants 78
Research Commons 152–3
Research Excellence Framework (REF) 185
Research Faculty Office (RFO) 199, 200, 202, 203
researchers
    Darden School 166
    global research orientation 188
    HEC Paris portal 115
    INSEAD portal 114
    open archives 106, 110, 111, 116, 117
resources
    career services and entrepreneurship 131, 133, 139
    costs 77
    expenditure on 3, 6, 56
    Harvard KLS 14, 18, 23

    market and industry information 2
    value of libraries 80
    see also e-resources
restructuring processes 30–47
retention 70, 78
return on investment (ROI) 8, 67–76, 101, 121, 123, 178–9
    academic libraries 69–72, 77
    definition of 67
    e-resource management systems 87
    Indian business school libraries 72–6
    public libraries 68–70
    tangible and intangible benefits 67–8
Reuters MarketData System 89
rewards 36, 46
Reynolds, G.L. 66
Rider University 133
Rigeade, M. 105–6, 107
Roubini 92
roving service 61, 153–4
RSS feeds 6

Sage 62
SAGE Publications 117
Saïd Business School 52, 185
salaries
    graduates 2, 66
    staff 67, 68, 77
Sammy Ofer Centre 203–4, 205, 210
SAS 88, 91
satellite libraries 5, 193, 197, 209
scenario planning 198–210
    embedded library research team model 199–201, 209
    heritage library model 203–5, 209
    library hub model 201–3, 209, 210
    virtual library model 206–8, 209, 210
Schonfeld, R.C. 161
School of Management (SOM), Yale University 164–5
screen-capture software 6
SDC Platinum 87
search engines 65, 177
    see also Google
secondary economic impact analysis 69
self-archiving 106, 107
self-service options 6
self-study 80
Serial Solutions 96
service delivery 102, 185, 186
    budget constraints 29
    Harvard KLS 20
    niche services 188

service desks 169, 171
service-orientation 180–82
service provider role of libraries 161, 162, 166, 175
shared services 4, 100, 101, 118
Sheehy, C.A. 1
shelving 154, 169, 170
SHERPA RoMEO database 112, 113
Sidorko, P.E. 71
silos 32
six-boxes model of change 35
skills
 cross-domain 101
 development of new 29–30
 embedded library research team 201
 executive education 187
 programming 210
 support services 189
 teaching 181
SLA-BF 124
small business development centers (SBDCs) 127, 133, 137
smartphones 86, 144
Smith, S. 160, 172–3
social bookmarking 6
social media 6, 59, 60, 61–2, 65, 138, 196
Social Return on Investment (SROI) 69
Social Sciences Research Network 8
 see also SSRN portals
software
 financial 2, 87–91, 97, 169
 open-source 80, 97, 106, 113
 see also databases
Sokoloff, J. 121, 138
Song, X. 33
Soules, A. 1
South America
 career services and entrepreneurship 124, 125
 number of business school libraries 3
special collections 20, 21
Special Libraries Association Business and Finance Division (SLA-BF) 124
specialist libraries 5, 193
Spesi, V. 180–81
SSRN portals 114–15, 116
staff
 access to training 195
 administrative 55
 benefits of libraries 78–9
 career services and entrepreneurship 123, 127–8, 131
 contribution of 80–81

cross-domain skills 101
cuts in 62
full time equivalent 6, 125
Harvard KLS 13–14, 16, 17, 18–19, 25–6
open archives 109–10
Paris Dauphine University 112
restructuring processes 30
roving 61, 153–4
salaries 67, 68, 77
staff development 154
ZBW 36, 37, 40, 41–2, 43, 44–5, 46–7
 see also librarians
standardization 92, 97
Standardized Usage Statistics Harvesting Initiative (SUSHI) 95
Stanford Graduate School of Business 4, 5, 9, 165–71, 185
statistics 51–2, 92, 95, 97, 101
 activity data 99–100
 COUNTER 96, 97, 99
 Harvard KLS 21
 INSEAD portal 114
 Paris Dauphine University archive 113
Stirling University 4
strategy
 change management 41
 Harvard KLS 12, 13, 14–15, 21–2, 25, 26
 ZBW 32, 33
Strouse, R. 71
Structured Query Language (SQL) 91
student helpers 155
subject area managers (SAMs) 200, 201
support services 2, 61, 188–9
supporting mechanisms 37
surveys 9, 193–8
 career services and entrepreneurship 124, 125, 126–7, 134–5
 contingent valuation 69
 graduate employment 138
 ROI in India 72–6, 81
 student 66, 147–8
 value of libraries 68
Systems Center Configuration Manager (SCCM) 88

table spaces 148, 151, 171
tangible benefits 67, 82
Taunton Centre Library 206
teaching 5, 6, 50, 54, 180–81
 career services and entrepreneurship 128–9

classroom 61
contribution of library staff 80
future challenges 195
Harvard Business School 11
measuring library value 70
technology 6, 8, 85–104
   'big data' 98–100, 101
   business ecosystems 85–7
   disruptive 159
   e-resource management 86, 87, 92, 95–7, 102
   financial software 2, 87–91, 97, 169
   future challenges 194, 195
   future opportunities 196
   Harvard KLS 14, 17, 24–5
   heritage library 204
   Learning Garden 151–2
   library spaces 147, 148
   open archives 109
   speed of innovation 29
   standardization issues 92
   user access 92–5
   WRDS 90–91
   see also databases; e-resources; social media
telephone communication 6
Templeton College 52
Tenopir, C. 71
theses 109
'thin-client' applications 88, 89
Thomson Quantitative Analytics (TQA) 91
Thomson Reuters 87, 88–9, 91, 97
Tickell, Adam 183
Tilley, Elizabeth 1
touchdown suites 164
training
   career services and entrepreneurship 131–2
   embedded library research team 200
   future challenges 195
   roving staff 153–4
   student helpers 155
triple bottom line 69
tutorials 6, 155
tweets 179
Twitter 6, 59, 60

unique selling point (USP) 9
United Kingdom
   number of business school libraries 3
   open access 183, 184
   Research Excellence Framework 185
   self-archiving 106

types of library 5
typical libraries 6–7
United States
   career services and entrepreneurship 125
   entrepreneurship 121
   i-schools 12
   private institutions 5
   Public Library Peer Comparison Tool 68
   reduction in onsite collections 161
   student surveys 66
University Grants Committee (UGC) 145
University Leadership Council 180
University of Arizona 128–9
University of British Columbia 149
University of Cambridge 1
University of Hong Kong (HKU) 145
University of Illinois Urbana-Champaign (UIUC) 70–71, 165
University of London 202, 205, 208
University of Manchester 197
University of Missouri 134
University of North Carolina (UNC) 179
University of Northampton 54
University of Pennsylvania 90, 135, 137
University of Rochester 131, 133
University of Sheffield 149
University of Virginia 166
University of Warwick 149
University of York 56
Urban Libraries Council (ULC) 68
usage statistics 51–2, 89, 92, 95, 97, 99–100, 101, 113
user access 92–5
usernames 93, 95
users
   benefits of libraries 77–81, 82
   communication with 149
   expectations of 194
   Harvard KLS 20
   needs of 76, 146–8
   reaching 57
   showing value of library to 55
   Stanford Graduate School of Business 170–71
   support for specialist user groups 2
   websites 58
UStat 96

value of libraries 68–72, 75, 76–7, 178
   see also return on investment
value proposition 13, 25, 26, 27, 178

vendor issues 195
Vernon, K.D.C. 2
Vieille, Nicolas 115–16
virtual learning environments (VLEs) 87, 143, 202, 203, 204, 206
virtual library model 206–8, 209, 210
vision 39, 42
visioning *see* scenario planning
VitalSource 98
vocational education 65

Wales, Tim 1–10, 160, 193–211
Wallace, Deb 7, 11–28
Web 2.0 101, 164
web-based services
   access management 92
   archiving 24
   open access 105
   WRDS 90–91
   see also cloud-based services; Internet
webinars 129
websites 57, 58
   career services and entrepreneurship 126, 129, 130
   visitor numbers 51, 53
   Welch Medical Library 163, 164
Weisbord, Marvin 35
Welch Medical Library 163–4
Wharton Business Plan Competition (WBPC) 137

Wharton Business School 5, 129, 135–8, 185
Wharton Research Data Services (WRDS) 90–91, 92, 93
Wharton Small Business Development Center (WSBDC) 137
White, L.N. 67
Wi-Fi access 147, 148
Wider, E. 122–3, 128
Wikipedia 177
Williford, C. 188
Wilson, Lizabeth 143–4
Windows 89–90, 91, 97, 100–101
   financial desktop software 87, 88, 89
   Windows 8 86
workflows
   e-resource management 92, 96
   ZBW 32, 33, 35–6, 43
workshops 6
   career services and entrepreneurship 127, 128, 132, 135–6
   change management at ZBW 41, 44–5, 47
writing 58

Yahoo! 177, 178
Yahoo! Finance 89
Yale University 164–5

zoning 150, 151